Postcard History Series

Summers County in Vintage Postcards

POSTCARD HISTORY SERIES

Summers County

IN VINTAGE POSTCARDS

The Summers County Historical Society

ARCADIA
PUBLISHING

ISBN 978-0-7385-4151-8

Published by Arcadia Publishing
Charleston, South Carolina

Printed in the United States of America

Library of Congress Control Number: 2005924865

For all general information contact Arcadia Publishing at:
Telephone 843-853-2070
Fax 843-853-0044
E-mail sales@arcadiapublishing.com
For customer service and orders:
Toll-Free 1-888-313-2665

Visit us on the Internet at www.arcadiapublishing.com

Contents

Acknowledgments

The Summers County Historical Society would like to thank these people for all their help: Those who first formed the project committee and those who contributed postcards from their collections—Betty Cooper from Hinton; Bob Evans from Elkton, Maryland; Thomas N. Clark from North Carolina; Mrs. Julia Cox from Farmville, Virginia; John and Pat DiStefano from Hinton; Conrad Graham; Barbara Flinchum; and David Bair. David Bair is a nature photographer who graciously allowed us to use his cards. Reprints and enlargements can be ordered from him at Bair Studios, P.O. Box 877, Shady Springs, WV 25918. We thank Margaret ("Chick") and Jim Martin, who shared their time, albums, postcards, and other materials with us. Margaret's patience knew no bounds. Thanks also to John Kesler, director of the Memorabilia Room at Dillon's Superette in Talcott, West Virginia, who simply opened the door and let us borrow postcards. Others who contributed were Wayne Harvey, president of the historical society, who approved the project; Dolores and Larry Moorman; Bonnie Duncan; Amy Parker; Dot Turman; Everett Crawford; and Jack Pack, who furnished information on Jumping Branch. Thanks go to Billy Joe Edwards for the cover; to Fred Long and Steve Trail, for permission to use material from their book, *Historic Pence Springs Resort* (*c.* 1983); to Virginia Gadd and Ben Vest, for research; and Curt Messer, for allowing us to use his material. All of the individuals listed here were reluctant to accept thanks, responding with a gracious, "Don't mention it; I was happy to help."

Introduction

Summers County, West Virginia, located in the Appalachian Highlands, was at one time very isolated. When the Chesapeake & Ohio Railroad (C&O) came to Hinton in 1871, Summers County was founded and began to flourish. The New and Bluestone Rivers, which encouraged that growth, were once a means of transportation for both the Native Americans and the pioneers. They are now a means of recreation. Millions of people visit the Pipestem and Bluestone State Parks to enjoy fishing, boating, swimming, and golf, and to visit the Canyon Rim Visitor's Center. Tourists can stand on a balcony and watch the aerial tramway soar out over the Bluestone Gorge while the turkeys feed at their feet.

There are many natural resources in the county, such as coal, gas, oil, gravel, sandstone, and limestone. When the Washington Monument was being constructed, a request was made for stone from each state. West Virginia's contribution was taken from Summers County's sandstone quarry. This is just one of the many contributions the county has made to the nation's progress.

One

Hinton

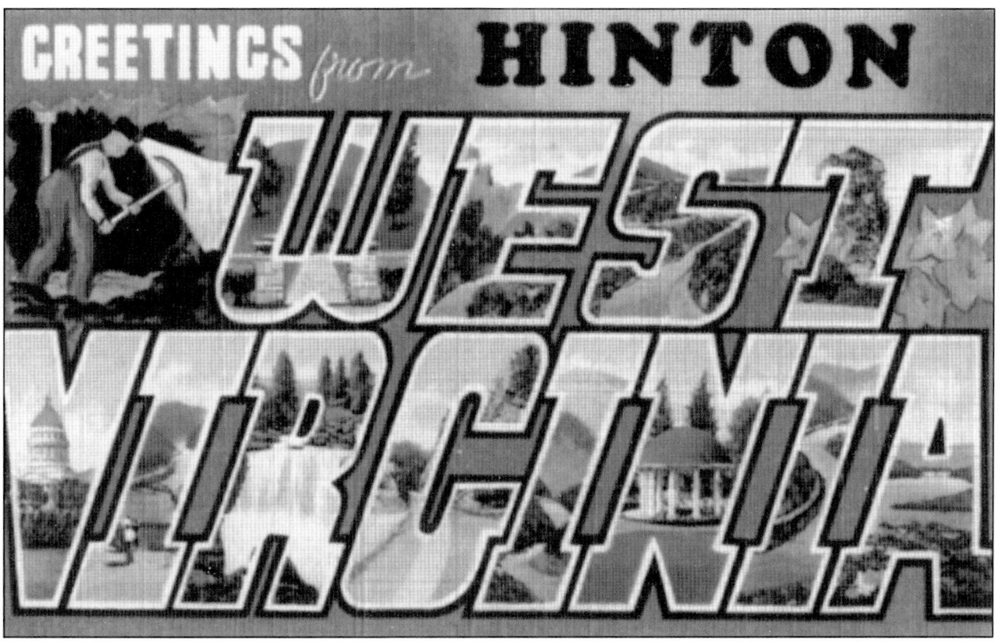

Greetings from Hinton, West Virginia. Hinton, the seat of Summers County, was named for the founder, Capt. John Hinton. The first permanent settlements in the area were those of James Graham at Lowell and Robert Lilly at Little Bluestone from 1770 to 1772. (Courtesy of Thomas N. Clark.)

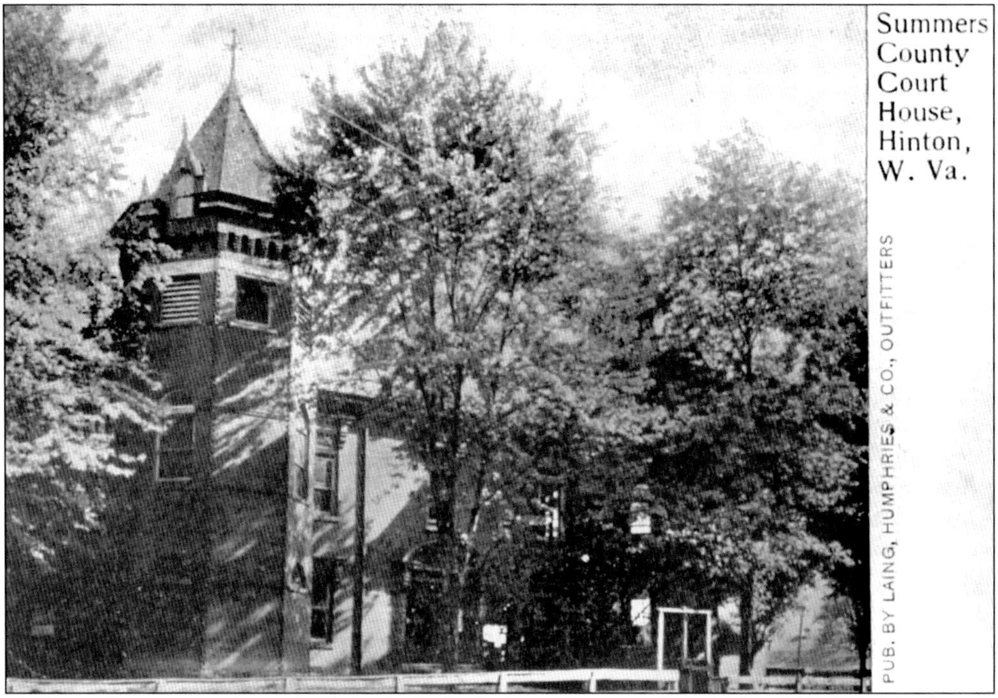

SUMMERS COUNTY COURTHOUSE. The county of Summers was formed in 1871. The government was made up of five supervisors. In 1873, the law establishing the county commissioners took effect. Frank Milburn was hired to draw up plans for a courthouse. The octahedral towers were omitted at this time because money was scarce. (Courtesy of Laing, Humphries, and Company, Outfitters.)

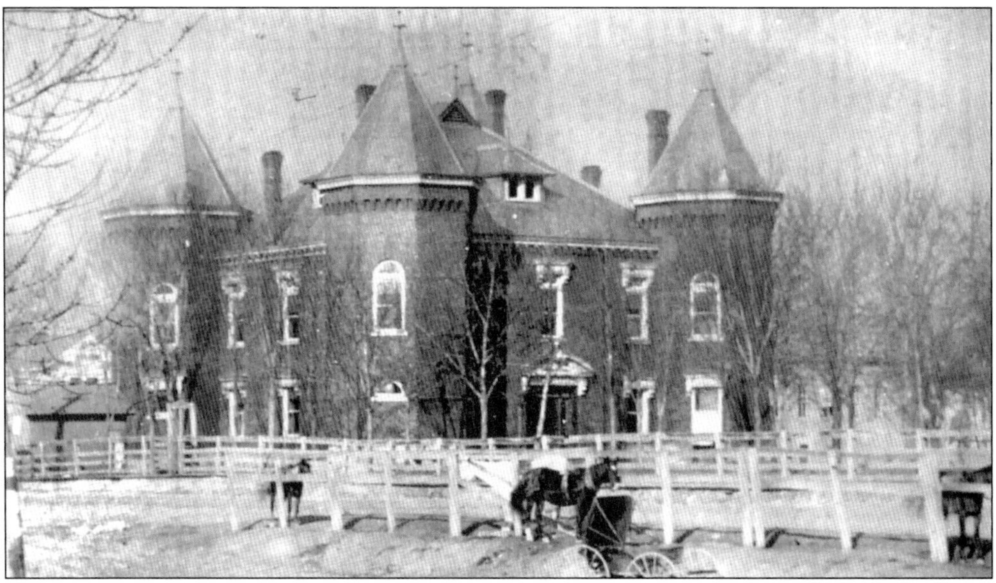

SUMMERS COUNTY COURTHOUSE. In 1874, the C&O Railroad signed a deed giving three acres of land for public use. At this time, the land was open and being used for pasture for cows and horses. There was a "curfew" saying that the livestock had to be home and in the barns at sunset. (Courtesy of Laing, Humphries, and Company, Outfitters.)

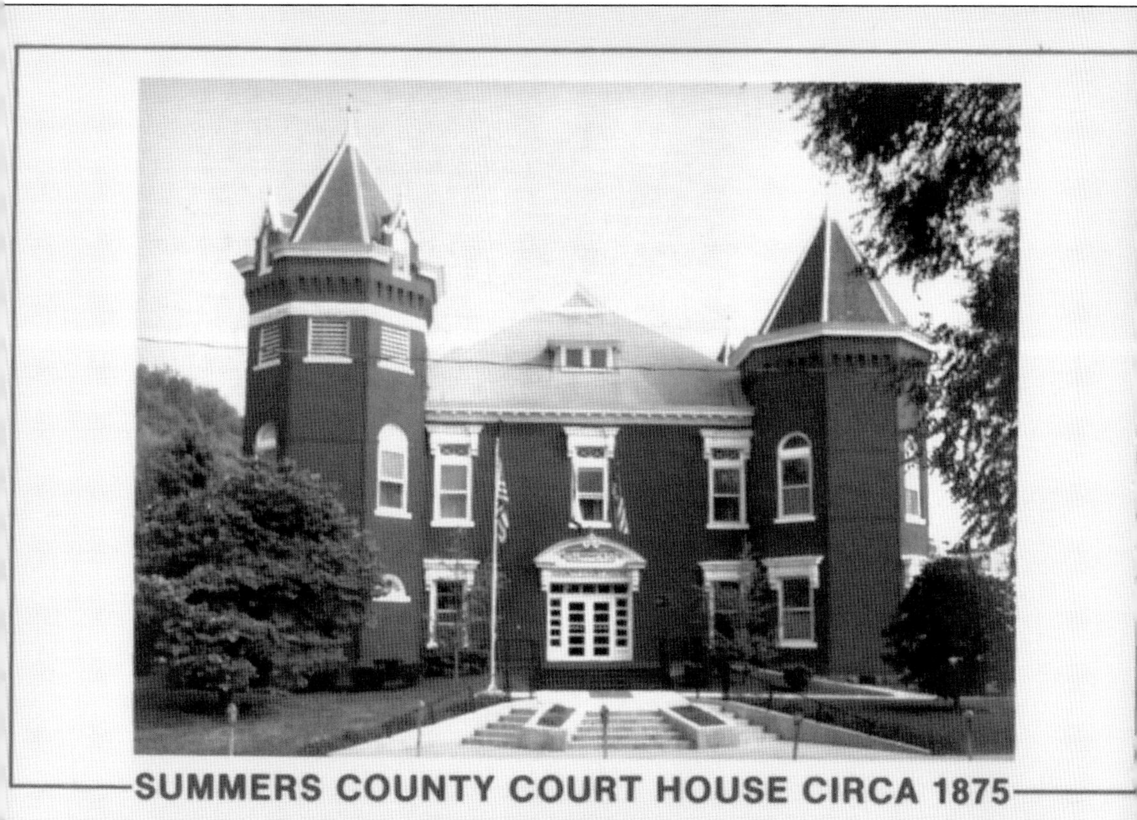

SUMMERS COUNTY COURTHOUSE. Completed in 1875, the Summers County Courthouse is listed on the National Register of Historic Places. This image is from the collection of the late John Gilbert, charter member of the Summers County Historical Society. (Photograph by Curt Messer.)

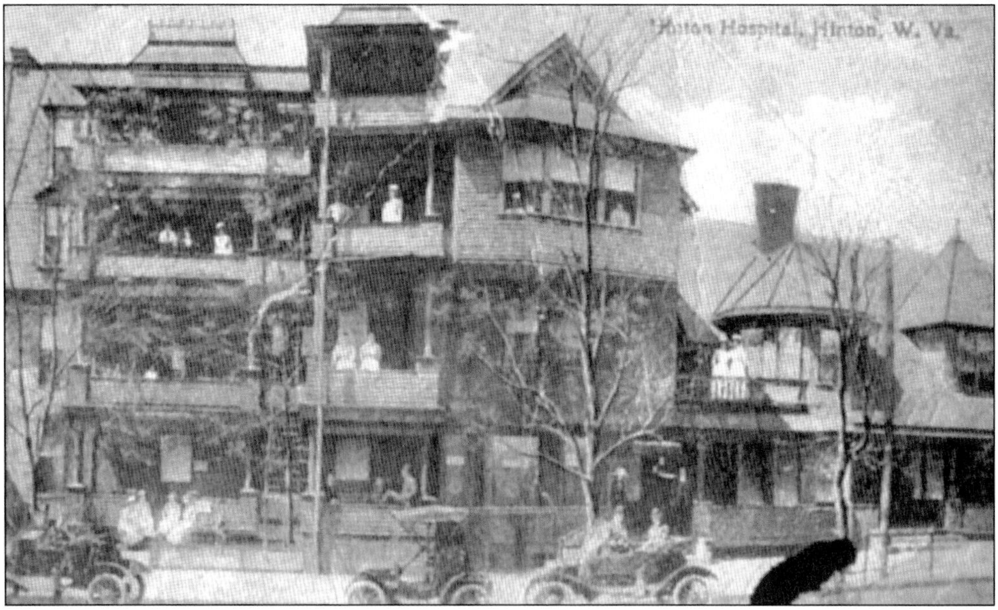

OLD HINTON HOSPITAL. A two-story brick building next door, which was purchased from Andy Flanagan and connected by a passageway, enlarged the capacity to 20 beds. (Courtesy of Betty Cooper.)

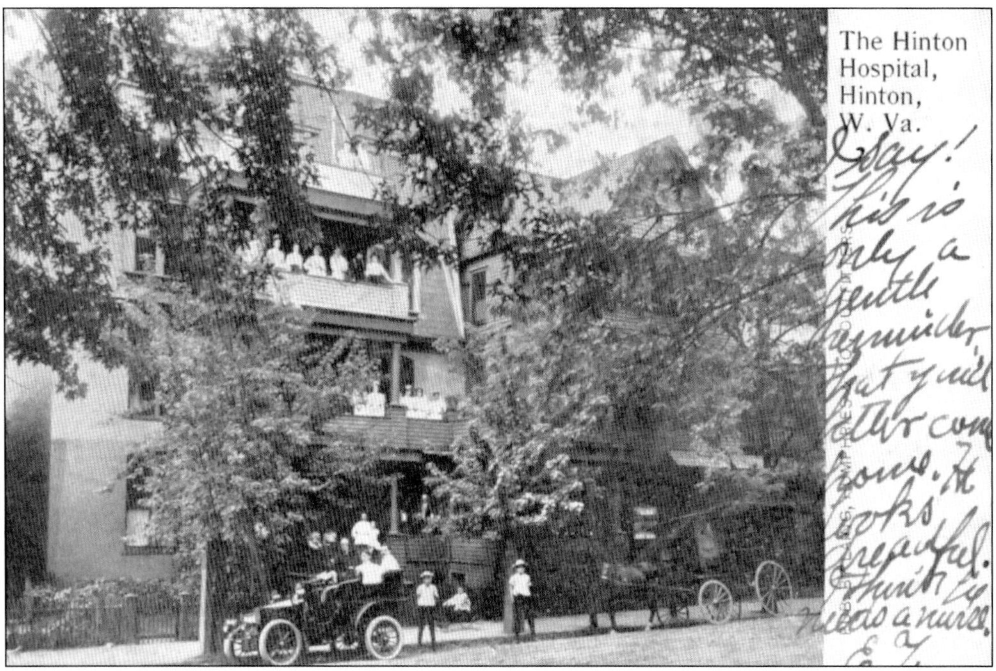

HINTON HOSPITAL. The message on this postcard reads, "This is only a gentle reminder that you'd better come home. He looks dreadful. I think he needs a nurse." It is signed, "E. T." (Courtesy of James Pettry.)

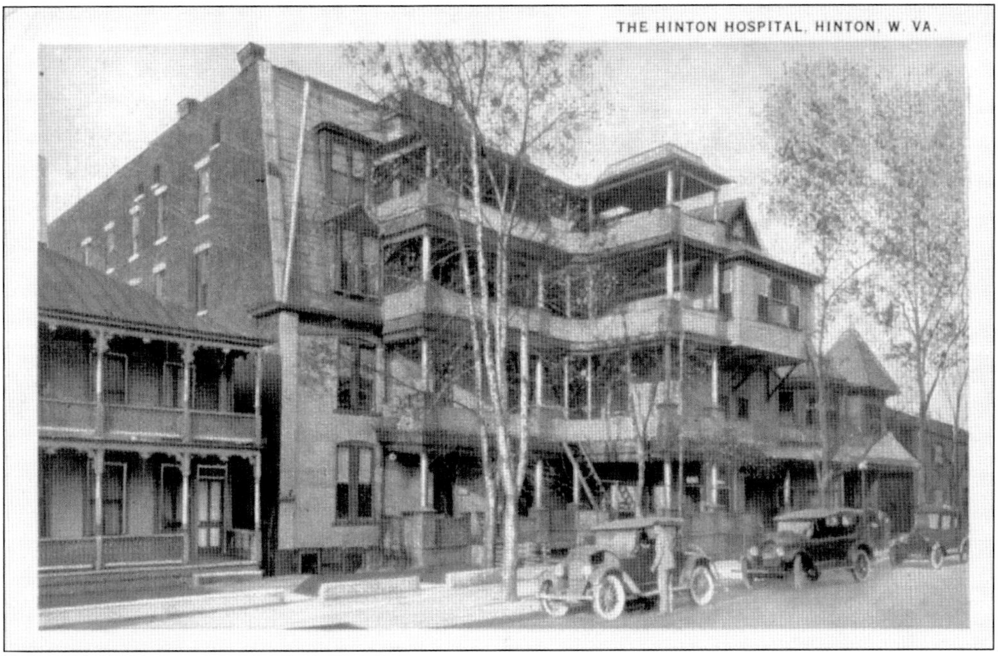

HINTON HOSPITAL. Hinton Hospital opened in 1899. The hospital's founder, Dr. O. O. Cooper, specialized in appendectomies. (Courtesy of Bonnie Duncan, James Pettry, and Margaret Martin.)

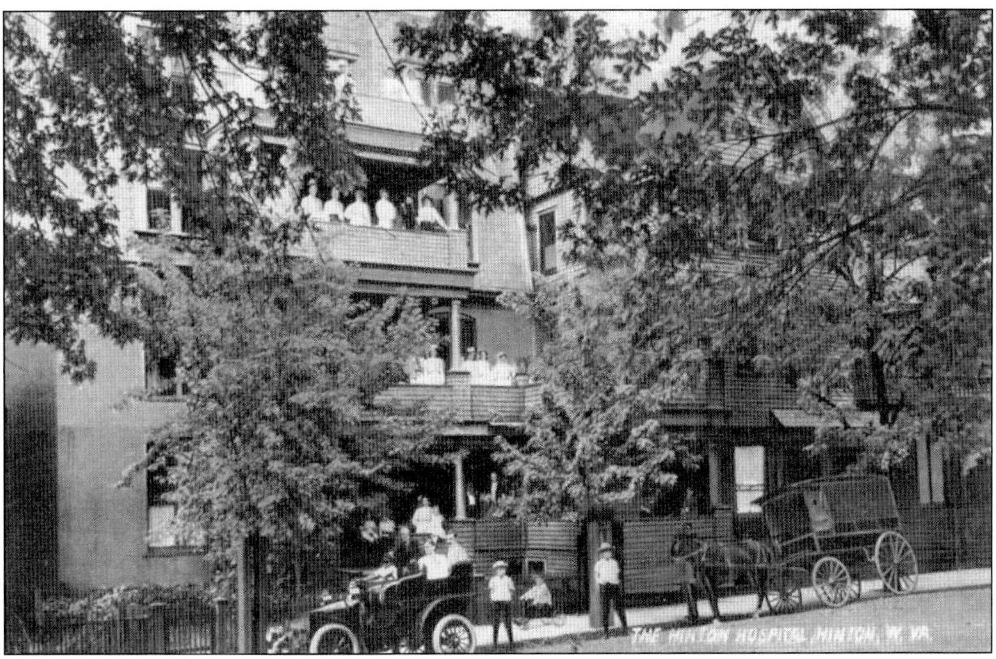

HINTON HOSPITAL. Note the nurses and hospital staff standing on the balconies. People in the cars and buggies could be family members or just people passing by. (Courtesy of Margaret Martin.)

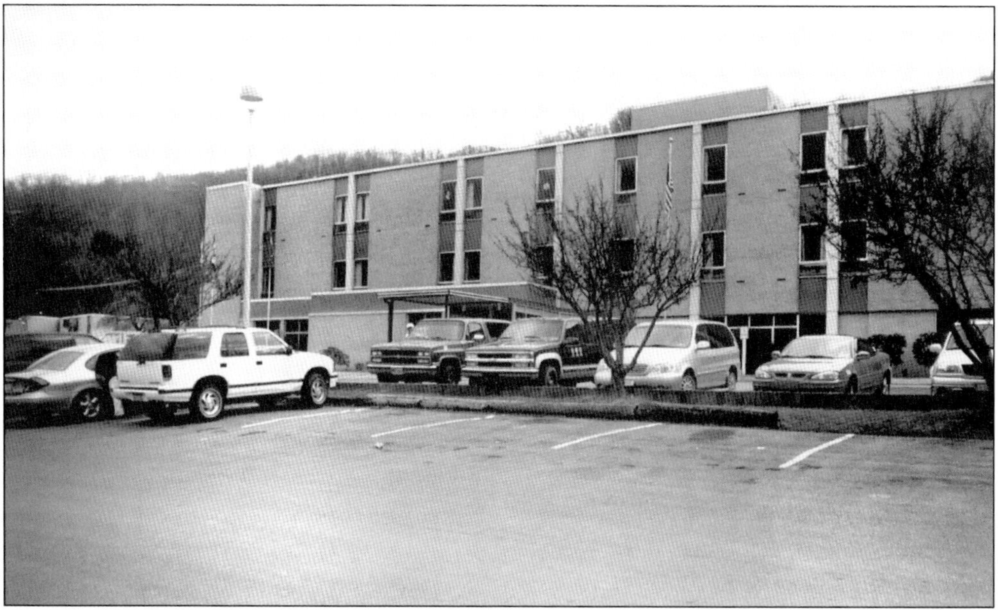

SUMMERS COUNTY APPALACHIAN REGIONAL HOSPITAL. In 1962, the Jaycees decided Summers County needed a hospital. The club adopted the project to get a federal grant under the Public Works Acceleration Act. Groundbreaking ceremonies were held May 30, 1967, at the National Guard Armory. The hospital was completed and dedicated in 1969. (Courtesy of Dot Turman.)

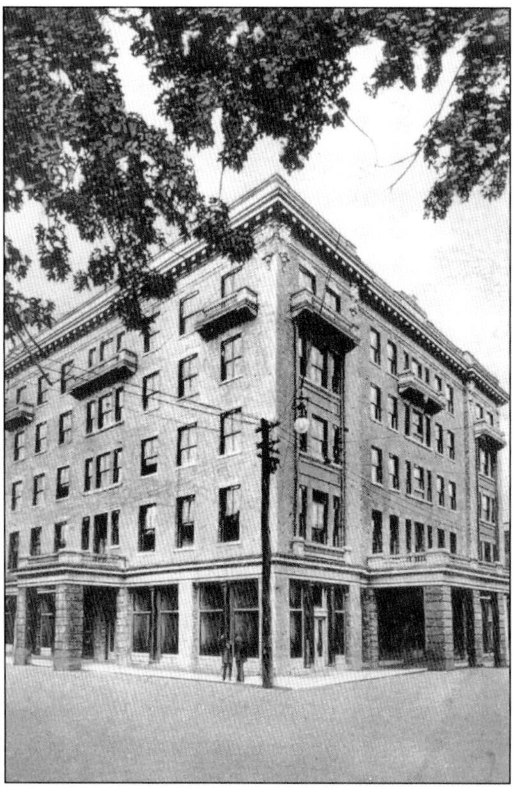

HOTEL MCCREERY. Built in 1907, Hotel McCreery had the reputation of being one of the finer hotels on the C&O line. This image comes from a brochure produced by the Summers County Convention and Visitors Bureau. (Courtesy of Bonnie Duncan, Margaret Martin, and Thomas N. Clark.)

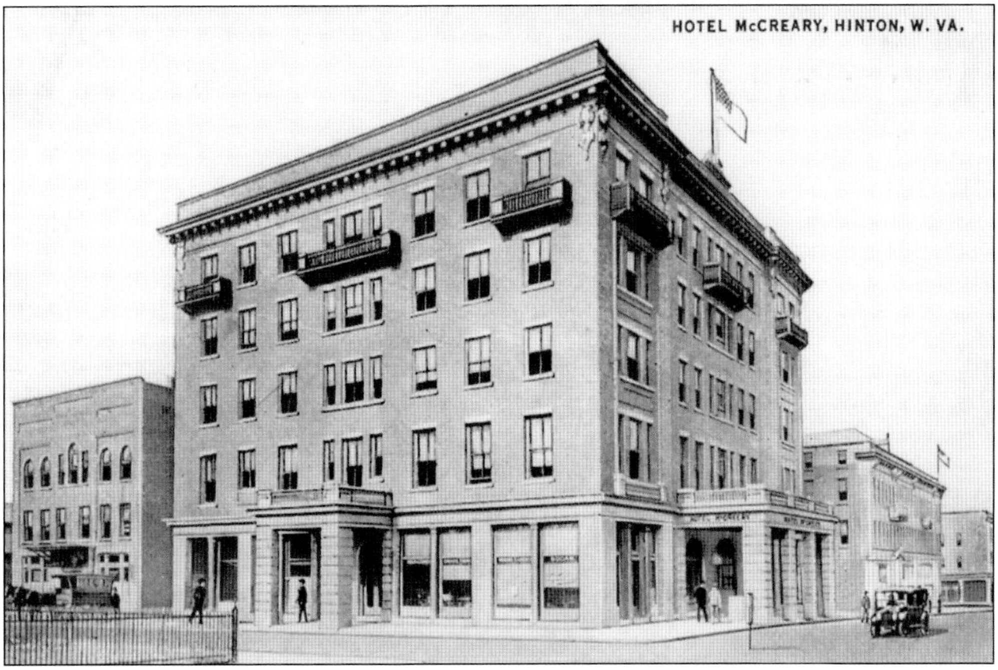

HOTEL MCCREERY. The hotel is shown here flanked by the Ewart-Miller Building on the left and the Elks Building on the right. (Courtesy of Thomas N. Clark.)

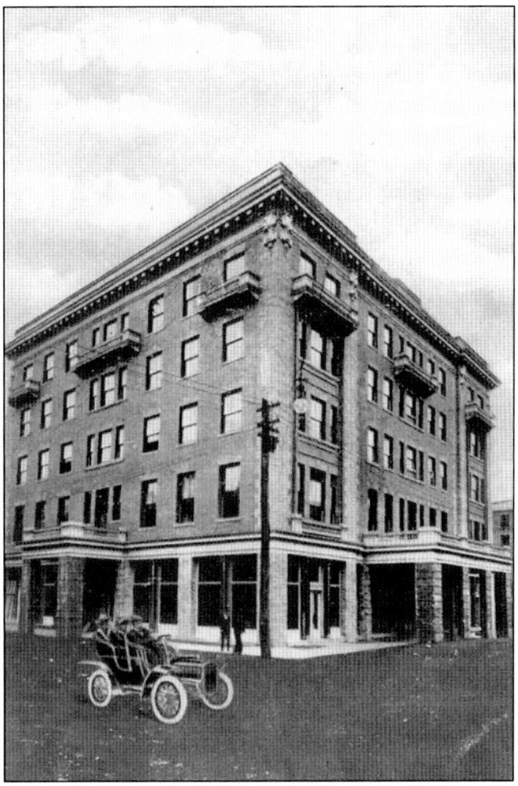

HOTEL MCCREERY. Containing 80 rooms, a restaurant and dining room, lounge, and ballroom, the hotel closed in the 1950s. It is now occupied by business enterprises. (Courtesy of Thomas N. Clark.)

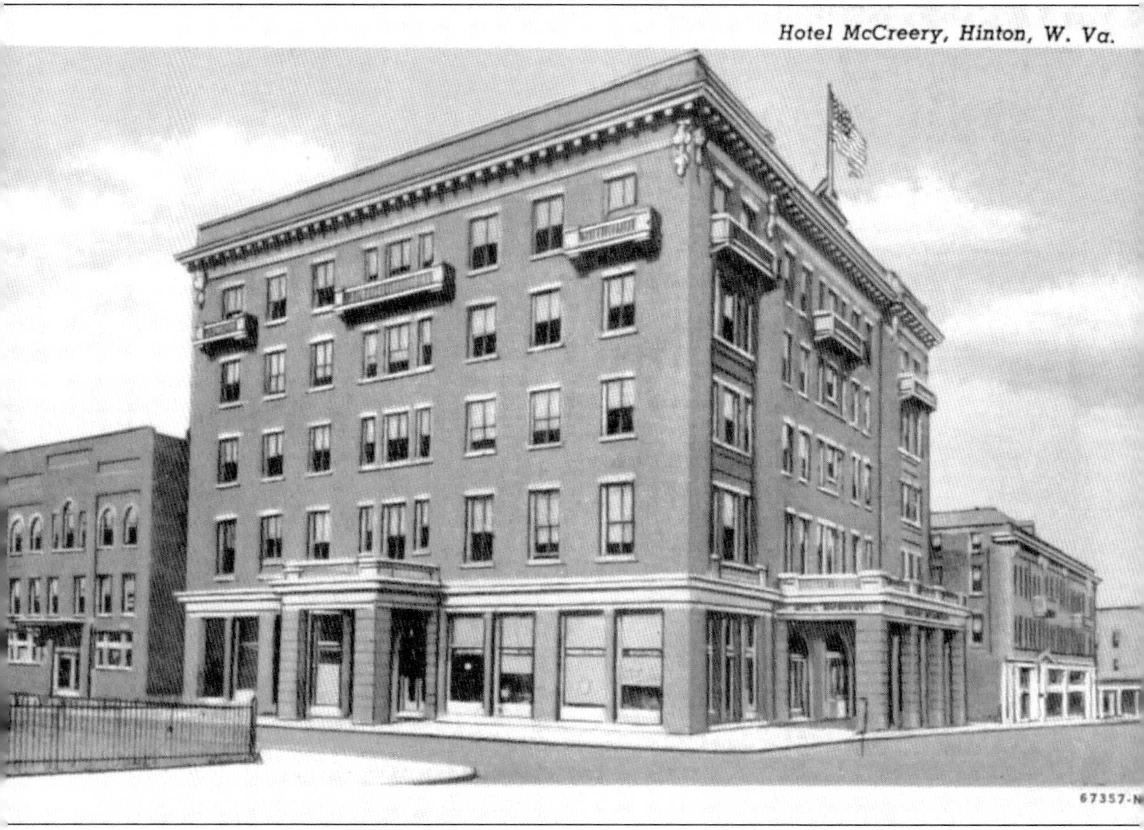

HOTEL MCCREERY. Please note the wrought-iron fence across the street. This is now part of the Hinton Historic District. (Courtesy of Bonnie Duncan.)

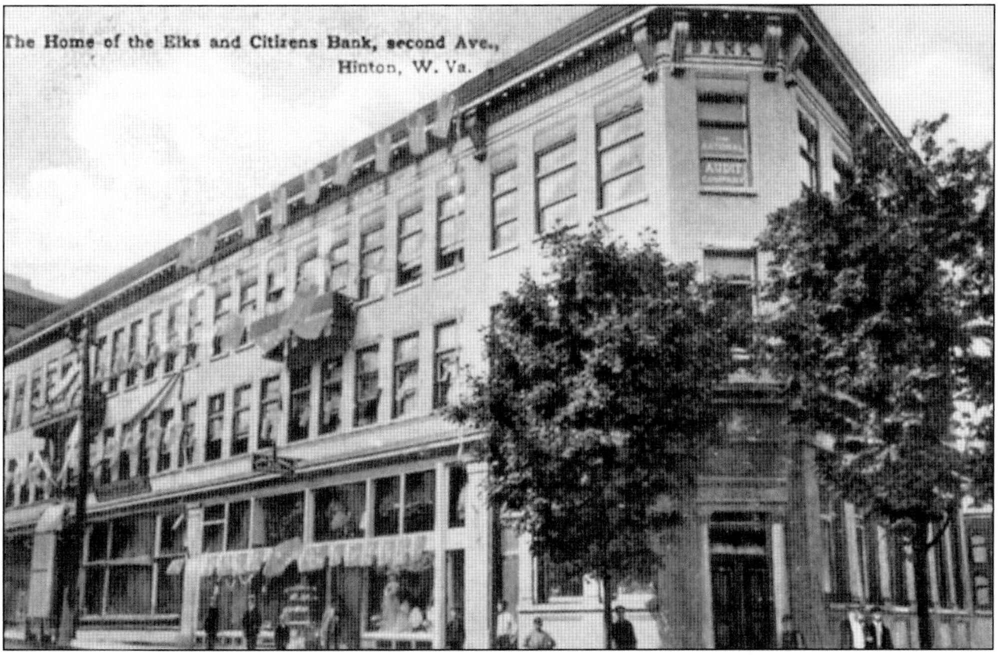

The Elks and Citizens Bank Building on Second Avenue, Hinton. The building pictured here was constructed in 1907. In 1945, the Elks Lodge, which was organized in 1903, bought a controlling interest in the Willow Wood Country Club. (Courtesy of Thomas N. Clark and Margaret Martin.)

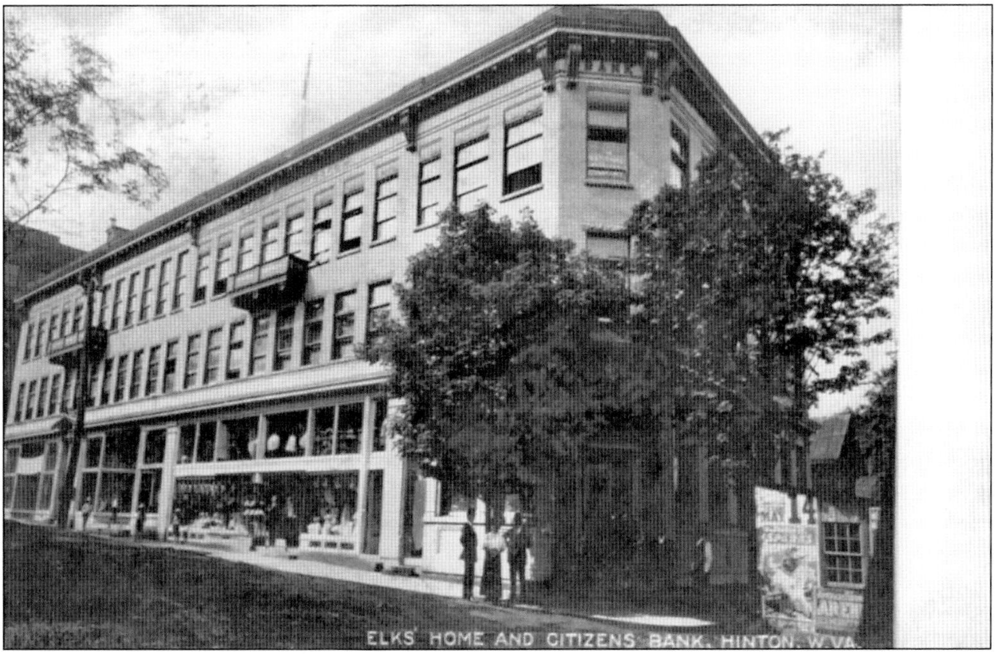

The Elks and Citizens Bank Building. The Elks Lodge has answered many calls for help from the underprivileged. (Courtesy of Margaret Martin.)

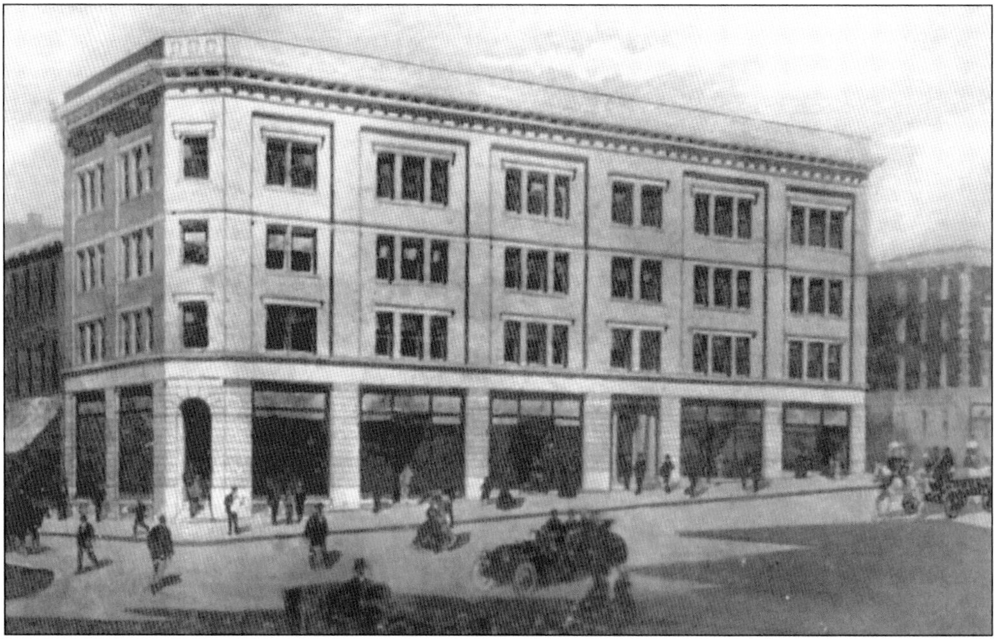

BIG FOUR BROTHERHOOD BUILDING. This building was constructed by the four railroad brotherhoods as a lodge building in 1907. The brotherhoods consisted of the Order of Railway Conductors, Brotherhood of Railway Trainmen, Locomotive Engineers, and Locomotive Firemen. In 1929, the building was converted to the Hinton Hospital. It closed in 1977. (Courtesy of Margaret Martin and Thomas N. Clark.)

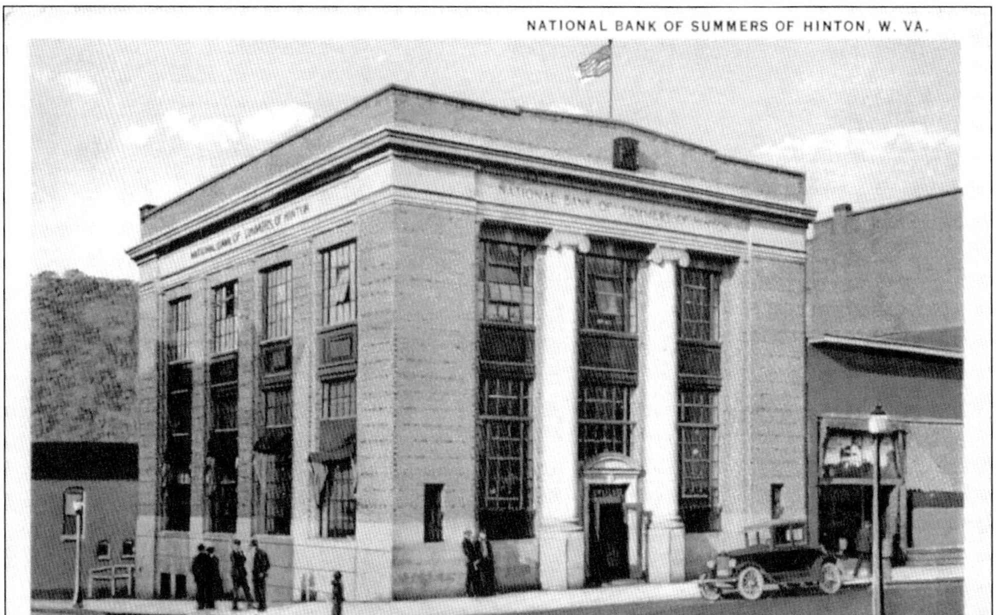

NATIONAL BANK OF SUMMERS. This white-columned building on Temple Street is now the Summers County Library. It was donated for library use in 1982 by Hume K. Nowlin, in memory of his wife, Pearl. (Courtesy of Virginia Gadd, Bonnie Duncan, and Thomas N. Clark.)

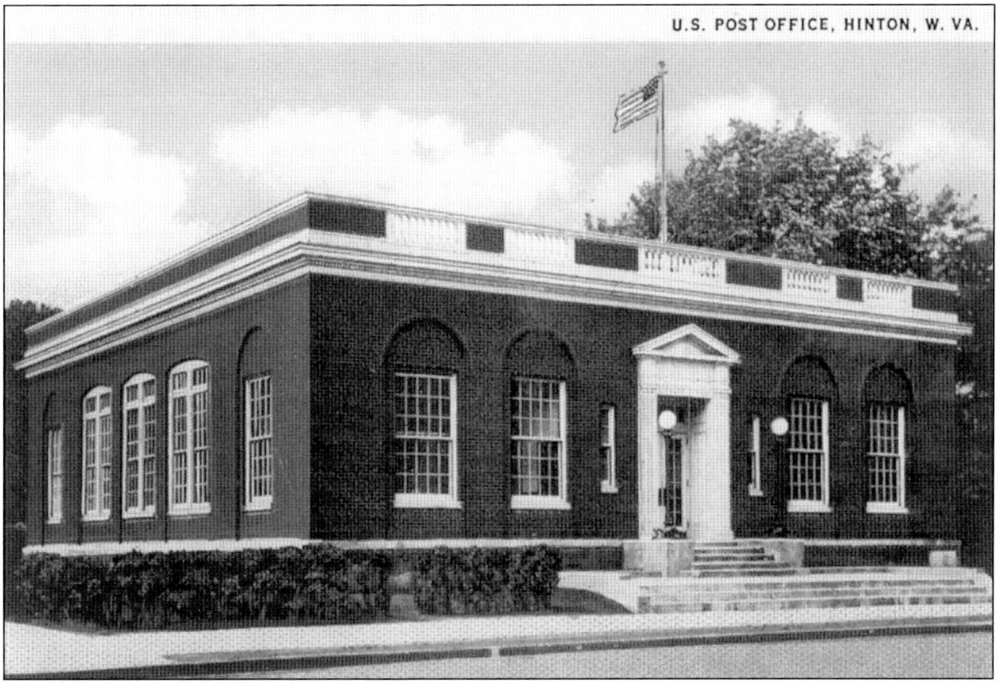

POST OFFICE. This Hinton building was dedicated in 1926 and was later added onto. (Courtesy of Thomas N. Clark.)

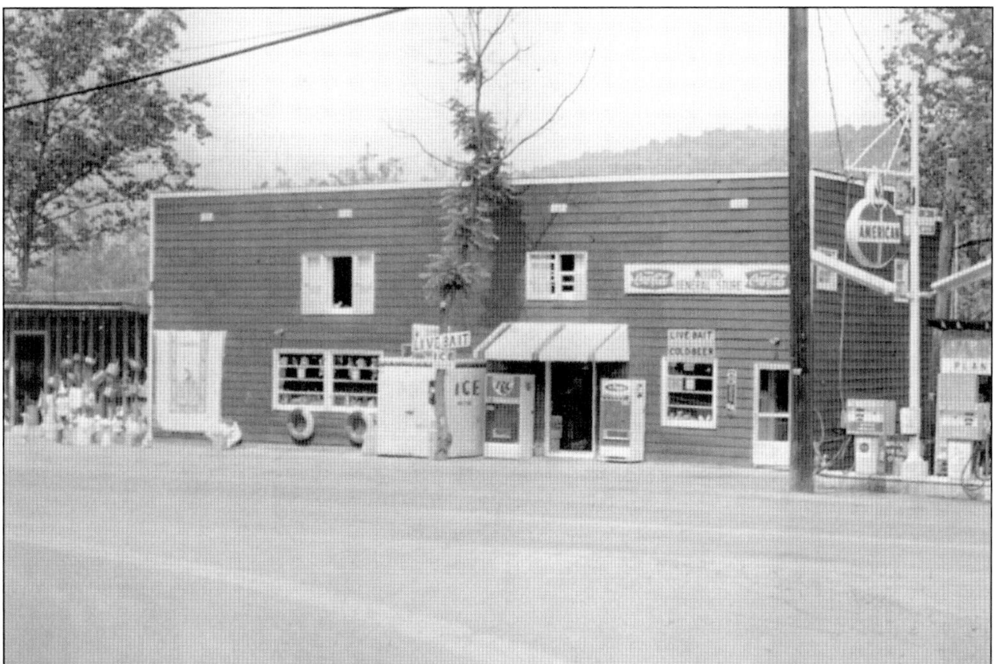

WOOD'S GENERAL STORE, HINTON. This establishment sold groceries, bait, Amoco gas, souvenirs, baskets, pottery, and West Virginia glass. Now, in 2005, it is known as Three Rivers Store. (Courtesy of Curt Messer.)

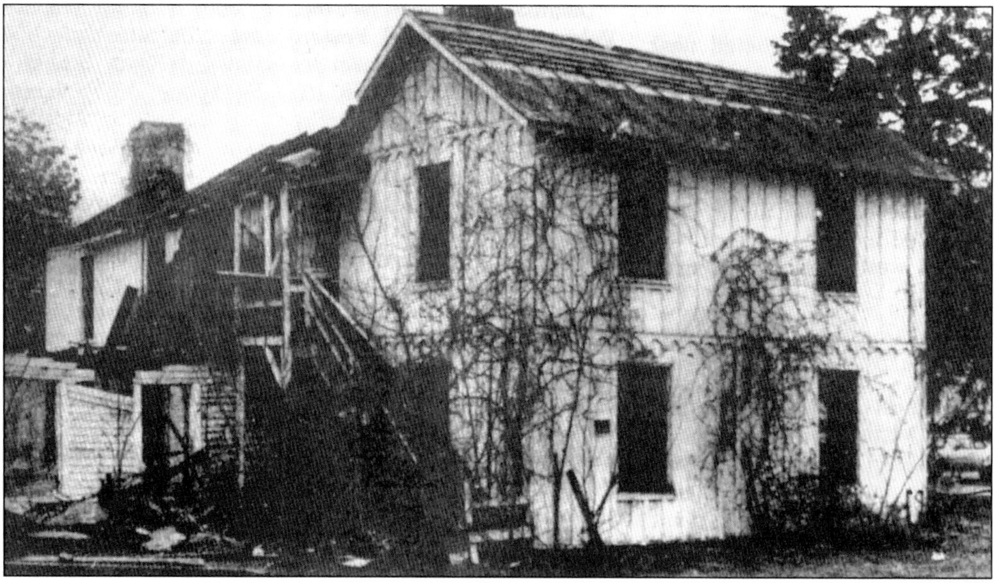

OBITUARY. An early-1980s newspaper printed this "obituary": "The Hinton Home died Monday, Feb. 22, 1982 after a short illness. Many were shocked by its sudden death. It died by dismemberment and consumption by fire from Feb. 22 to Feb. 25, 1982. Born 1872, it was erected under the hands of the late Avis Hinton. The deceased was the oldest building in Hinton. Friends may call forever, but the Hinton Home will not answer. Survivors include not only the residents of Hinton, but those of the county. Pallbearers include those who lacked either the foresight or the resources to preserve the structure. The forces of time will serve as flower bearers." (Photograph by Fred Long.)

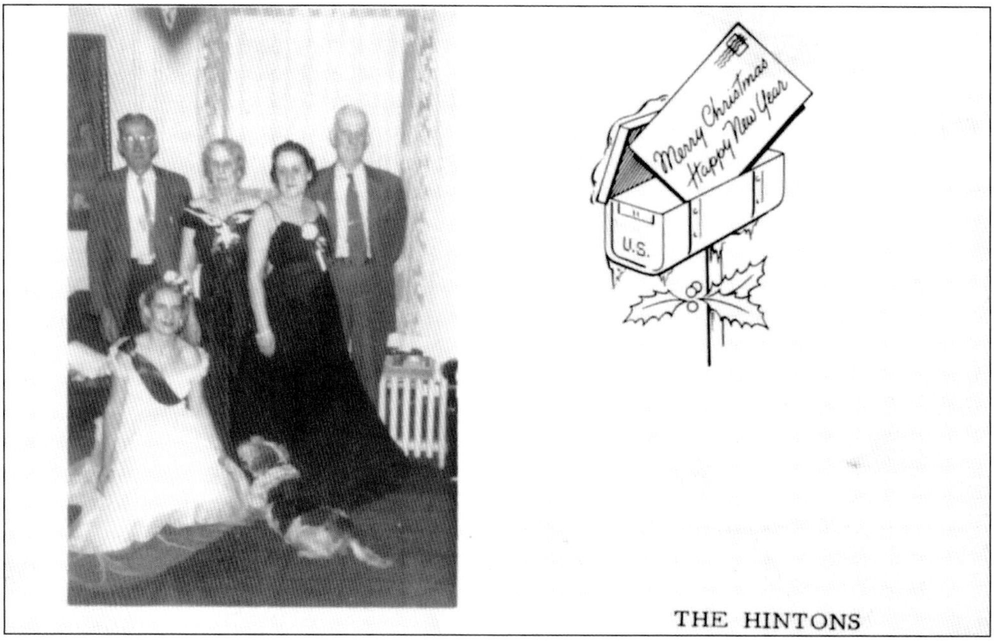

HINTON FAMILY. Descendants of the founders pictured here, from left to right, are (standing) Carl Hinton, postmaster; Ethel Hinton, art teacher; Louise Hinton; and Howard Hinton. The child (seated) is Mary Avis Hinton. (Courtesy of Margaret Martin.)

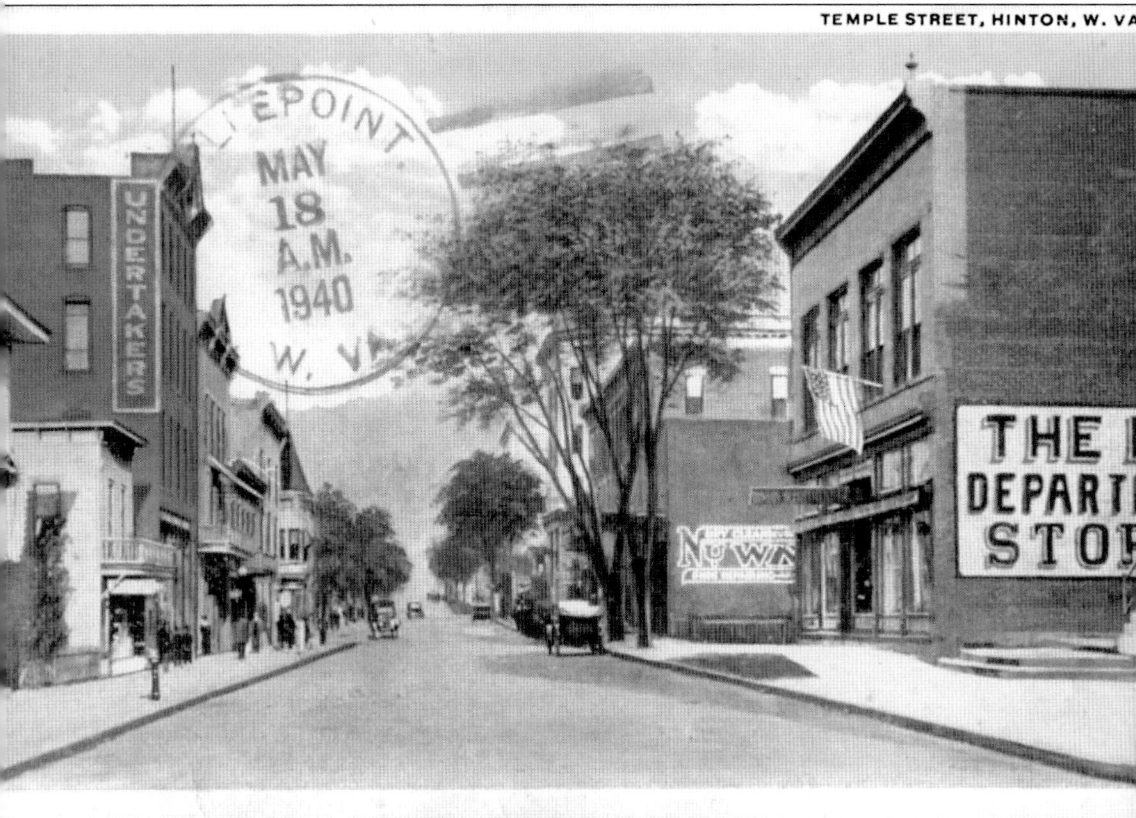

Temple Street, Hinton. This card, postmarked 1940, shows Temple Street as it looked then. Note the "undertaker" sign. Today, the vacant lot is a parking lot. (Courtesy of Bonnie Duncan.)

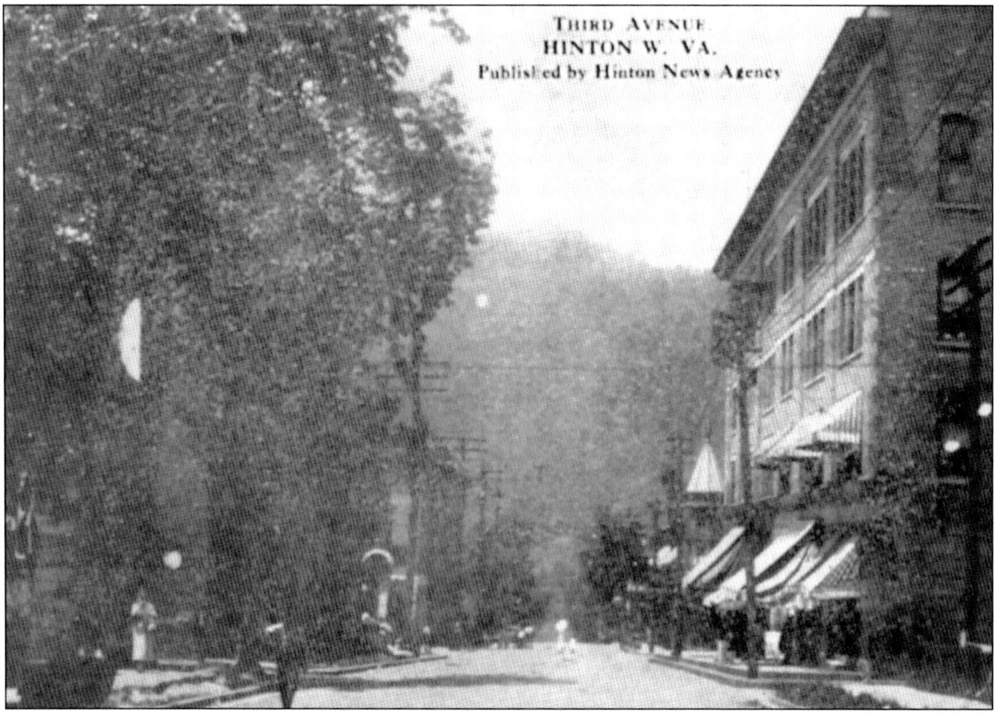

THIRD AVENUE, HINTON. Note the gaily-striped awnings at the windows. This card was published by the Hinton News Agency. (Courtesy of Thomas N. Clark.)

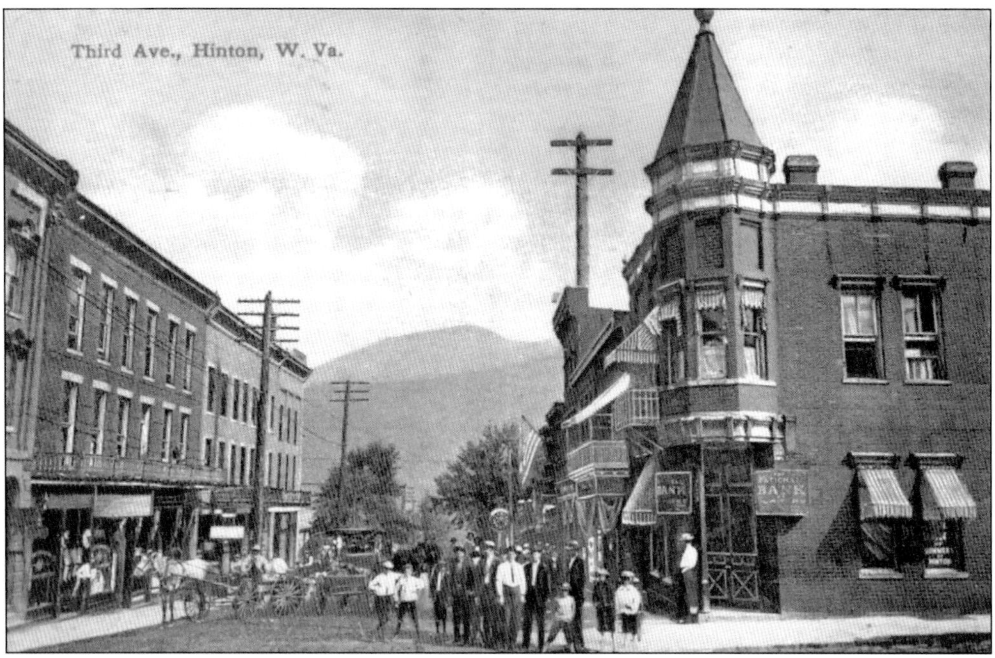

THIRD AVENUE. It seems to be a busy day in Hinton. Note all the shoppers in the streets. Sometimes, photographers would ask whoever was standing around to be in the picture. (Courtesy of Bonnie Duncan.)

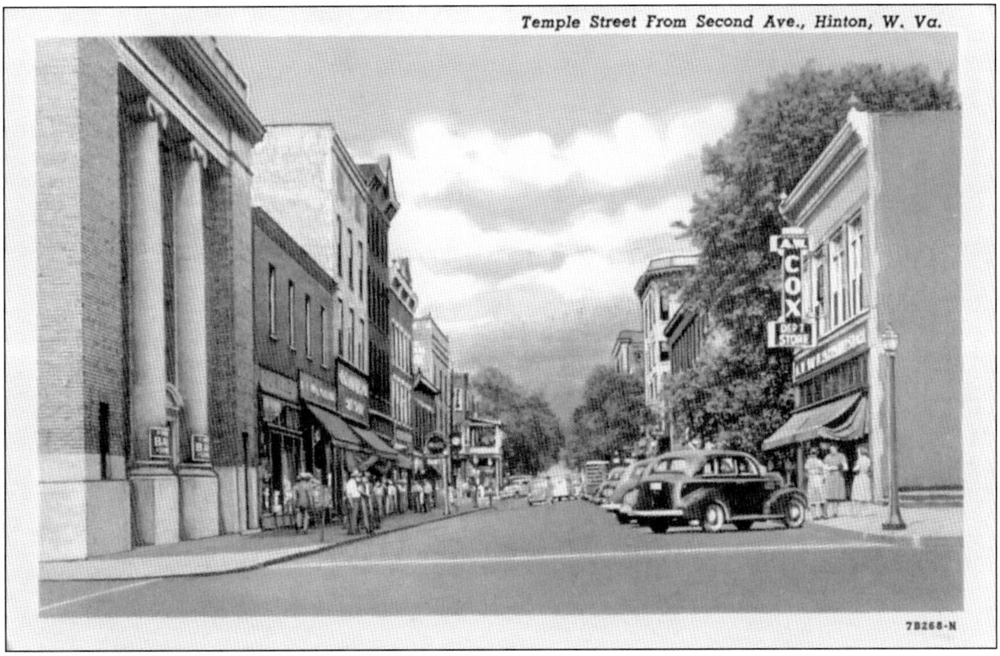

TEMPLE STREET AND SECOND AVENUE, HINTON. The Cox Department Store is pictured on the right and the National Bank of Summers is on the left. (Courtesy of Virginia Gadd, Bonnie Duncan, Bob Evans, and Margaret Martin.)

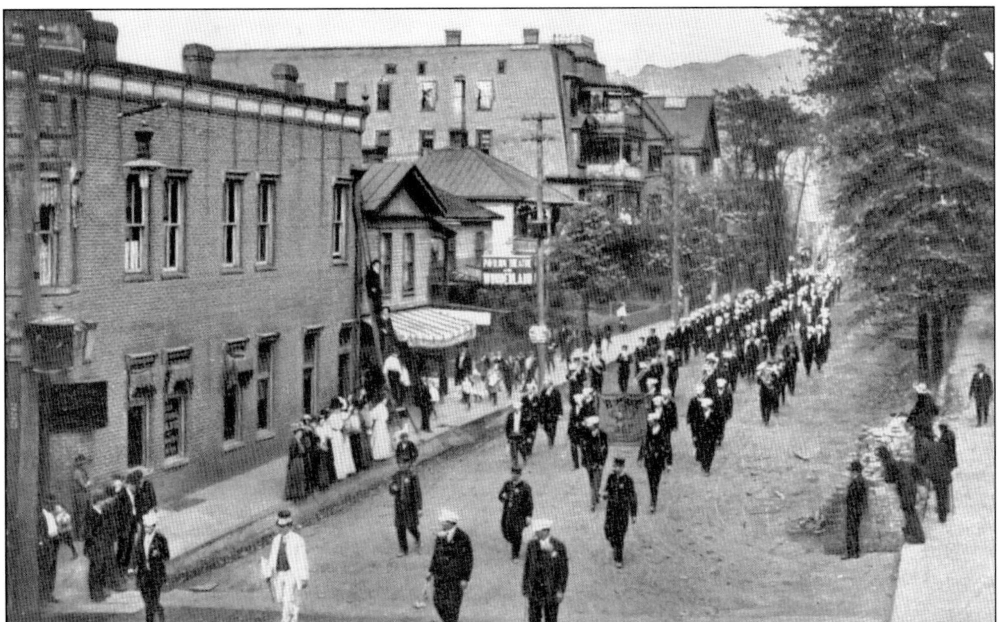

TEMPLE STREET SCENE. This Elks Parade took place on October 23, 1907. (Courtesy of Margaret Martin.)

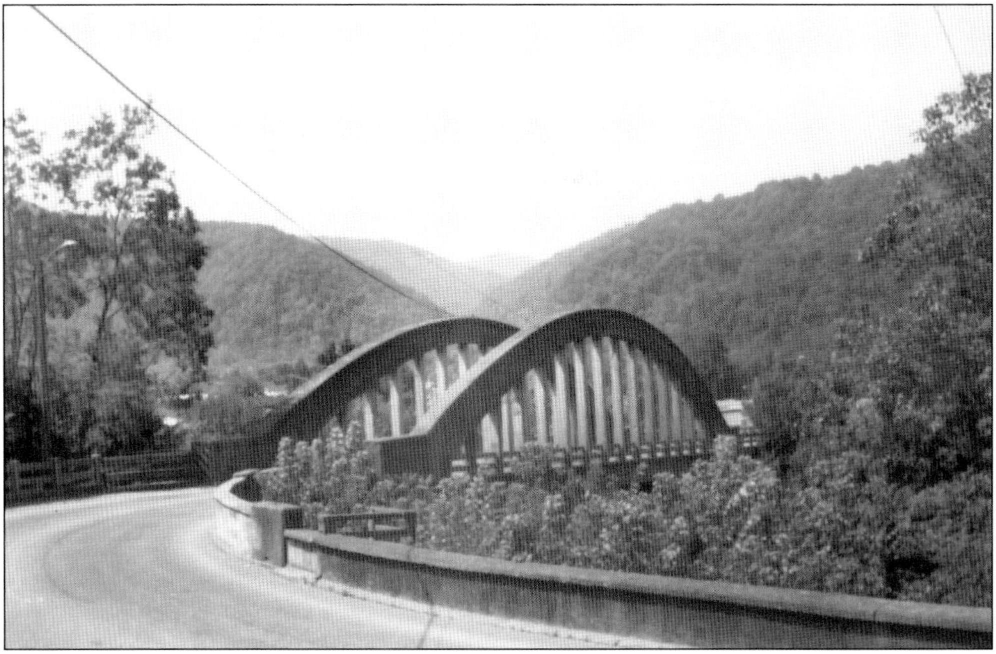

AVIS OVERHEAD BRIDGE, HINTON. This bridge was constructed in 1928 by the City of Hinton and the C&O Railroad. E. M. Meadows was mayor at the time. Luten Bridge Company, designers and builders of reinforced concrete bridges, were the contractors. The bridge was named for Avis Hinton. The formal opening was held on June 28, 1929. (Courtesy of John Kesler.)

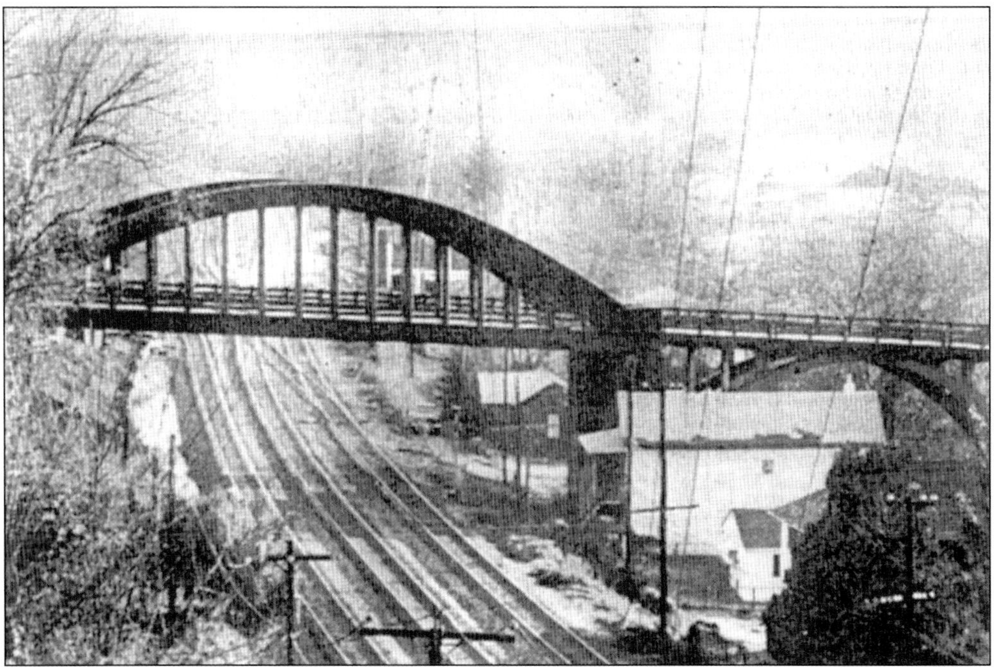

AVIS OVERHEAD BRIDGE. The bridge has been slated to be converted into a walking bridge and tourist attraction. (Courtesy of Everett Crawford.)

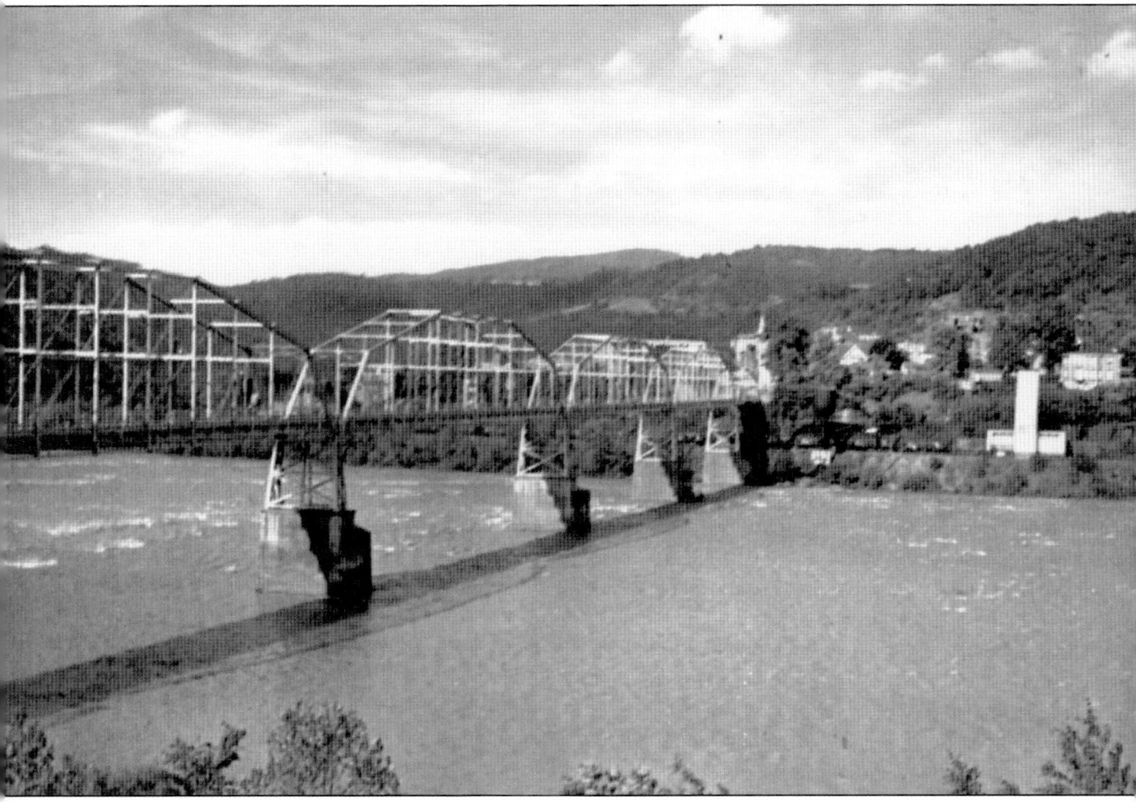

SUMMERS COUNTY FROM ACROSS THE NEW RIVER. This card was published by Beckley News Company of Beckley, West Virginia. (Courtesy of John Kesler.)

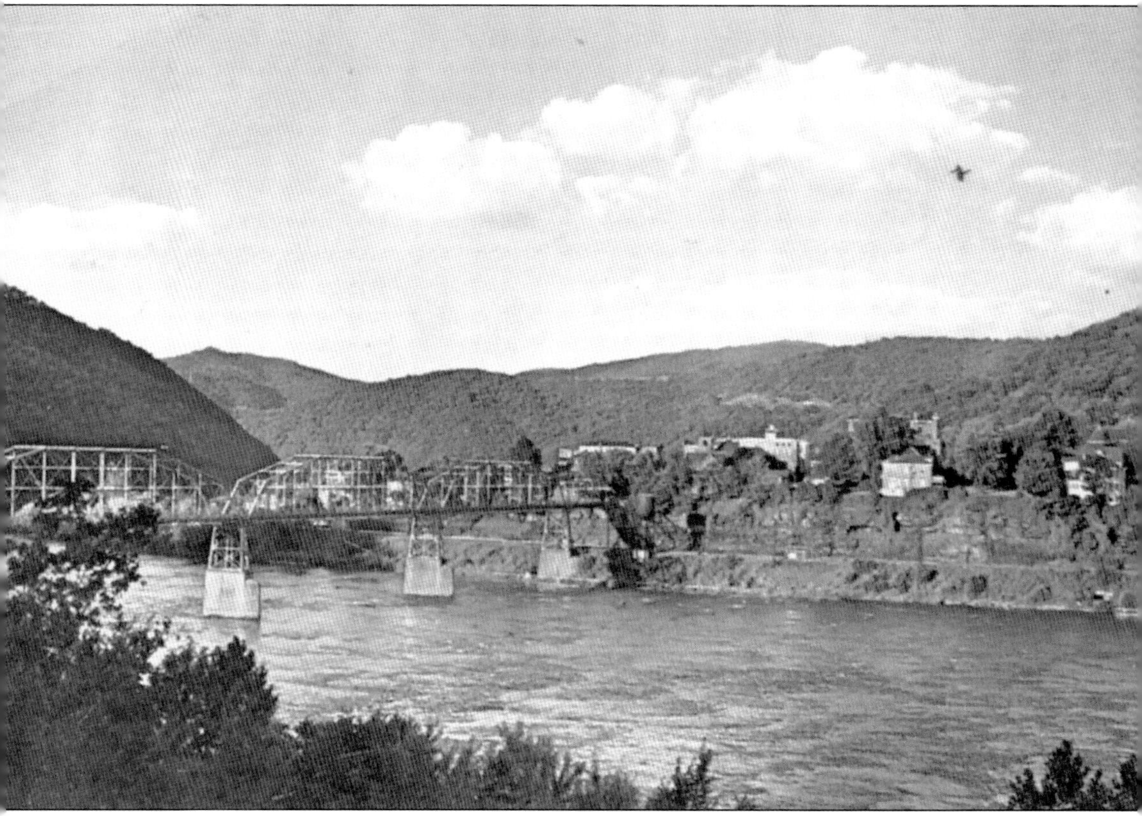

ANOTHER VIEW OF BRIDGE. A mile south of Hinton is the Bluestone Dam and Reservoir and Bluestone State Park. The bridge closed in 1967 or 1968. (Courtesy of John Kesler.)

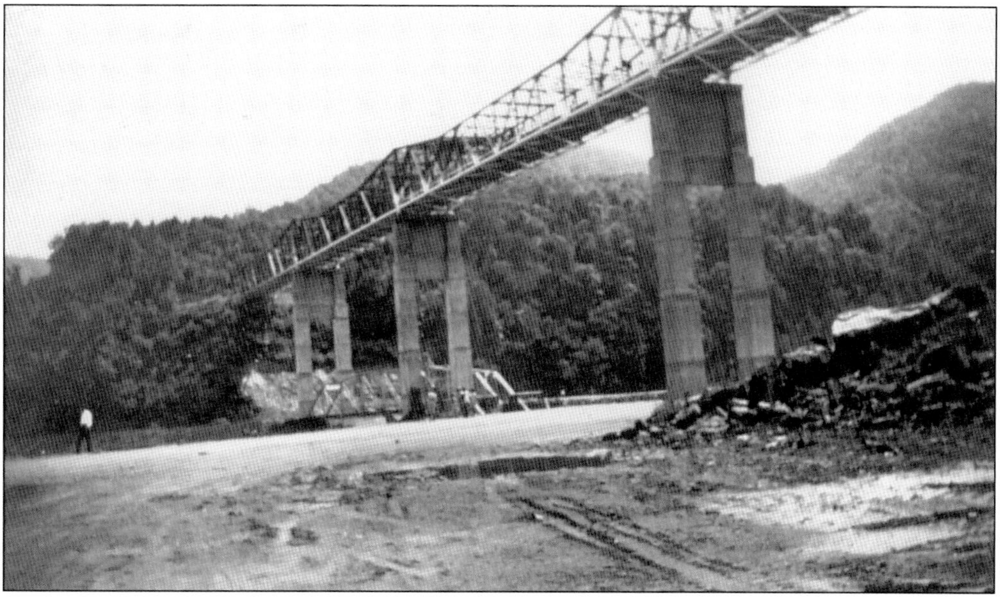

Bluestone Bridge Under Construction. When the last span of the bridge was being built, it fell into the river, killing five workers and injuring four others. (Courtesy of John W. Kesler.)

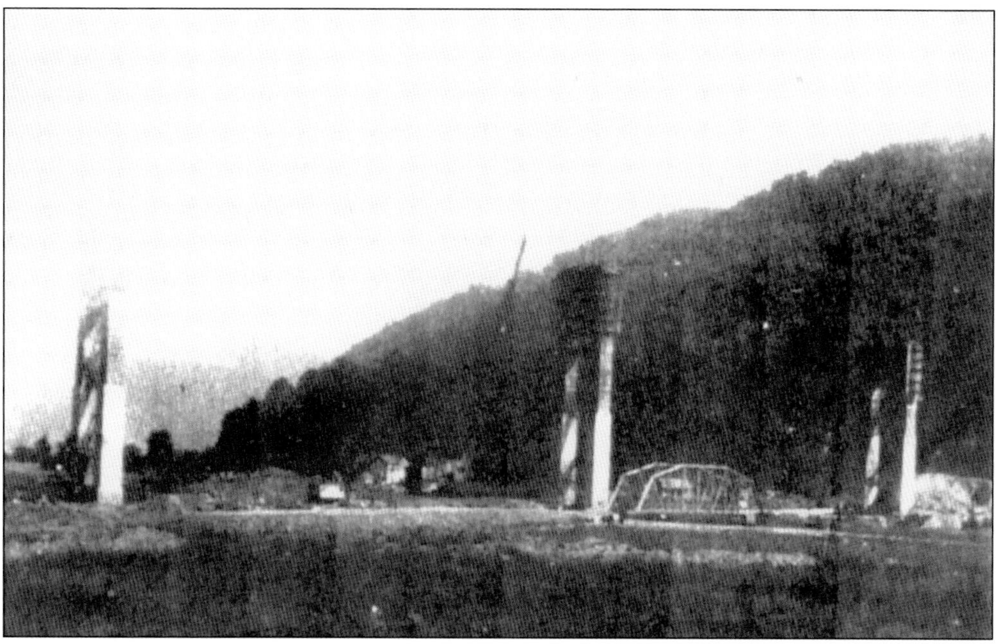

Building Bluestone Bridge for the Second Time. Pictured here is the bridge under construction in 1948, after the accident. It is now named Lilly Bridge for the village of Lilly, which stood three miles from this site. (Courtesy of John W. Kesler and Betty Cooper.)

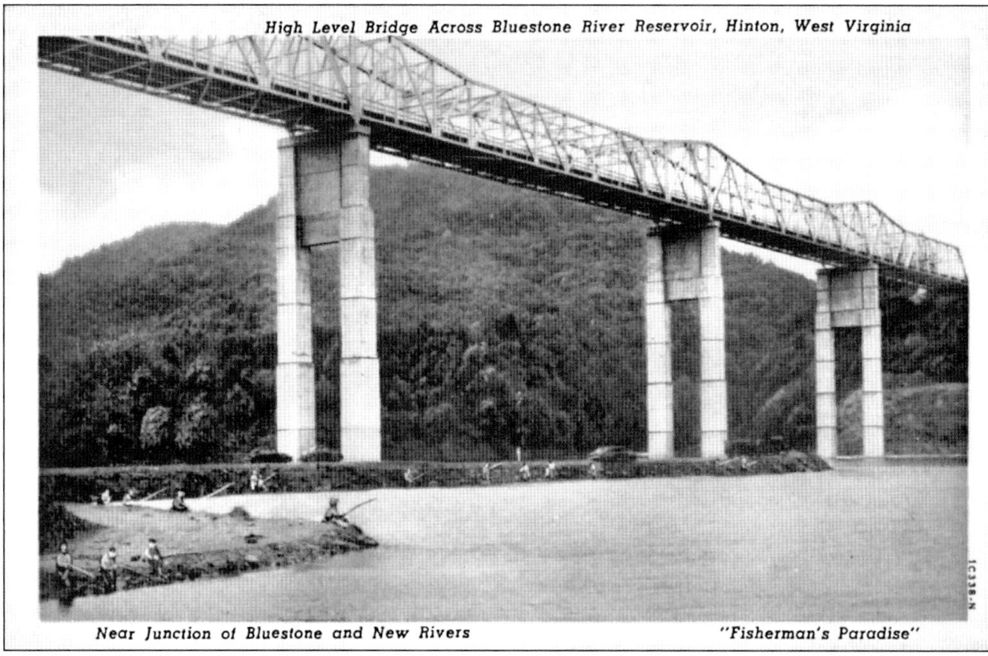

BRIDGE ACROSS BLUESTONE RIVER RESERVOIR. This was the highest bridge in West Virginia before the New River Gorge Bridge was built in 1977. (Courtesy of Margaret Martin.)

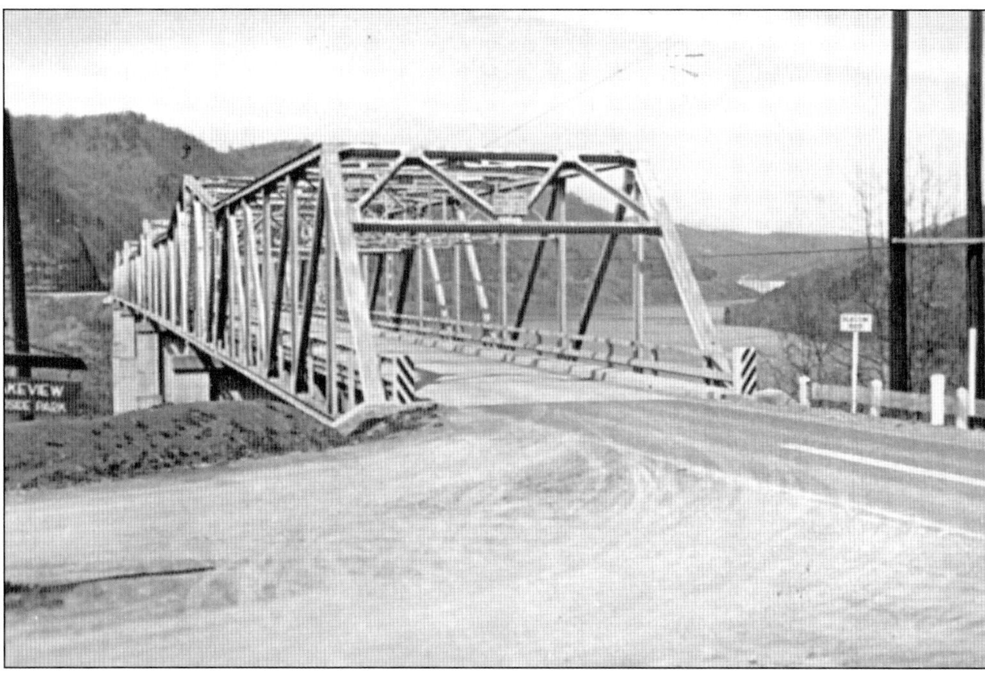

BLUESTONE BRIDGE. Located five miles south of Hinton on Route 20, this bridge stretches across Lake Bluestone. In the background can be seen the Bluestone Dam. (Published by Monroe and Creed of Hinton; courtesy of Dot Turman.)

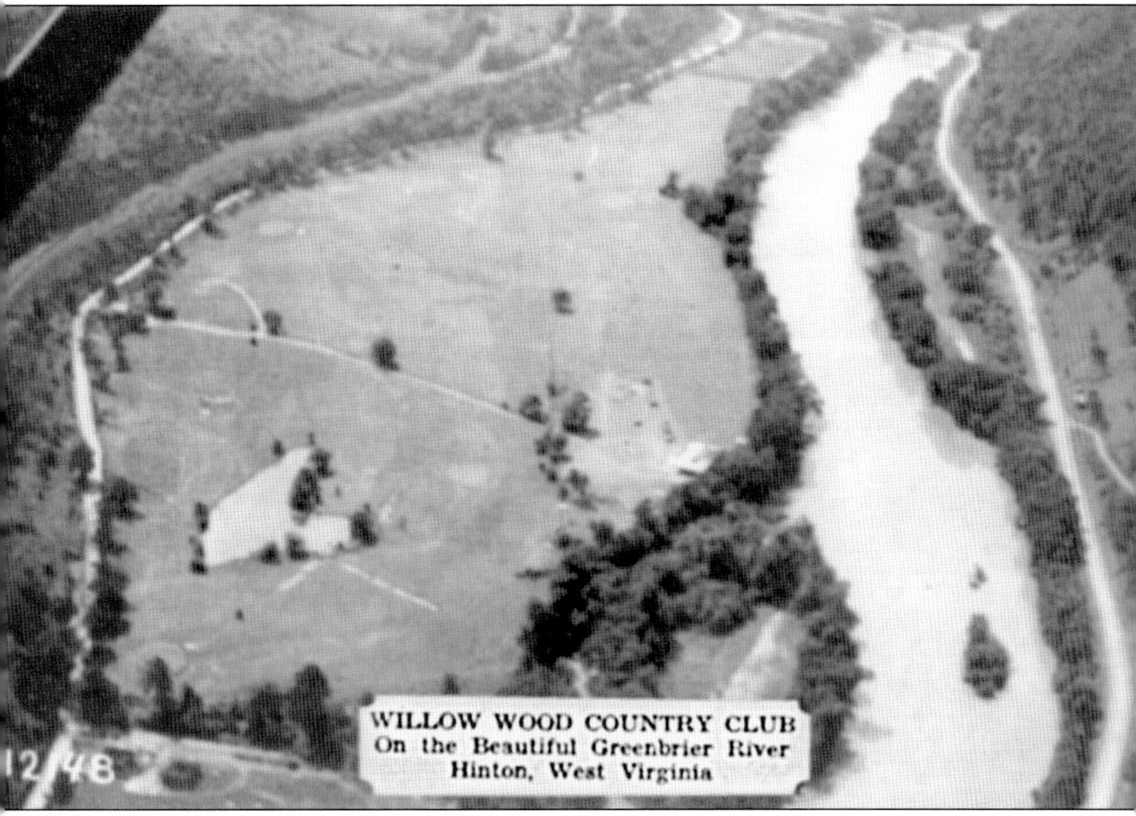

WILLOW WOOD COUNTRY CLUB. The Willow Wood Country Club was formed in 1938 by a group of Hinton businessmen. Here it is pictured in 1948 on the beautiful Greenbrier River. In May 1945, Elks Lodge bought a controlling interest in the club. (Courtesy of Thomas N. Clark.)

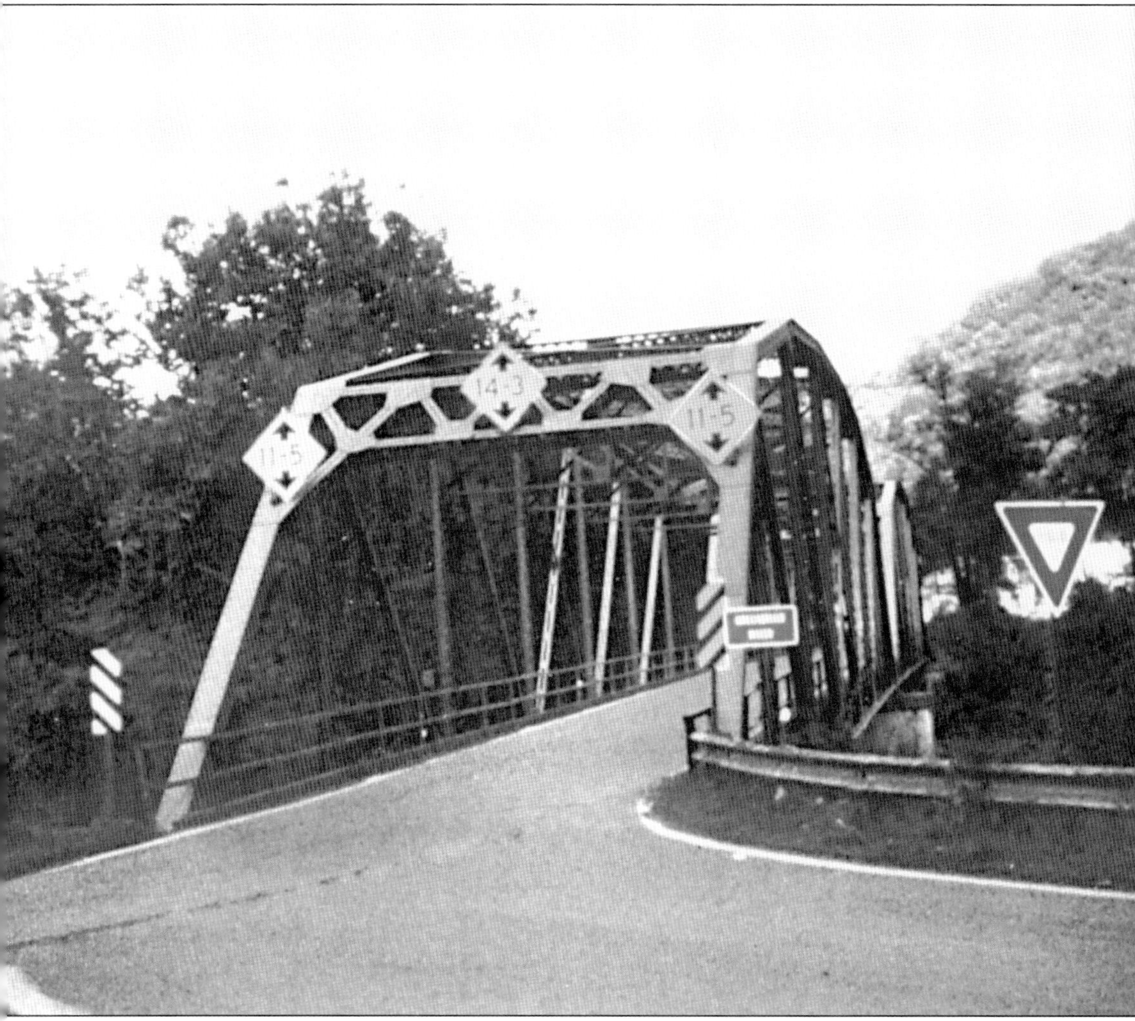

Willow Wood Bridge. This bridge is located six miles west of Hinton on Routes 3 and 12. (Courtesy of Dot Turman.)

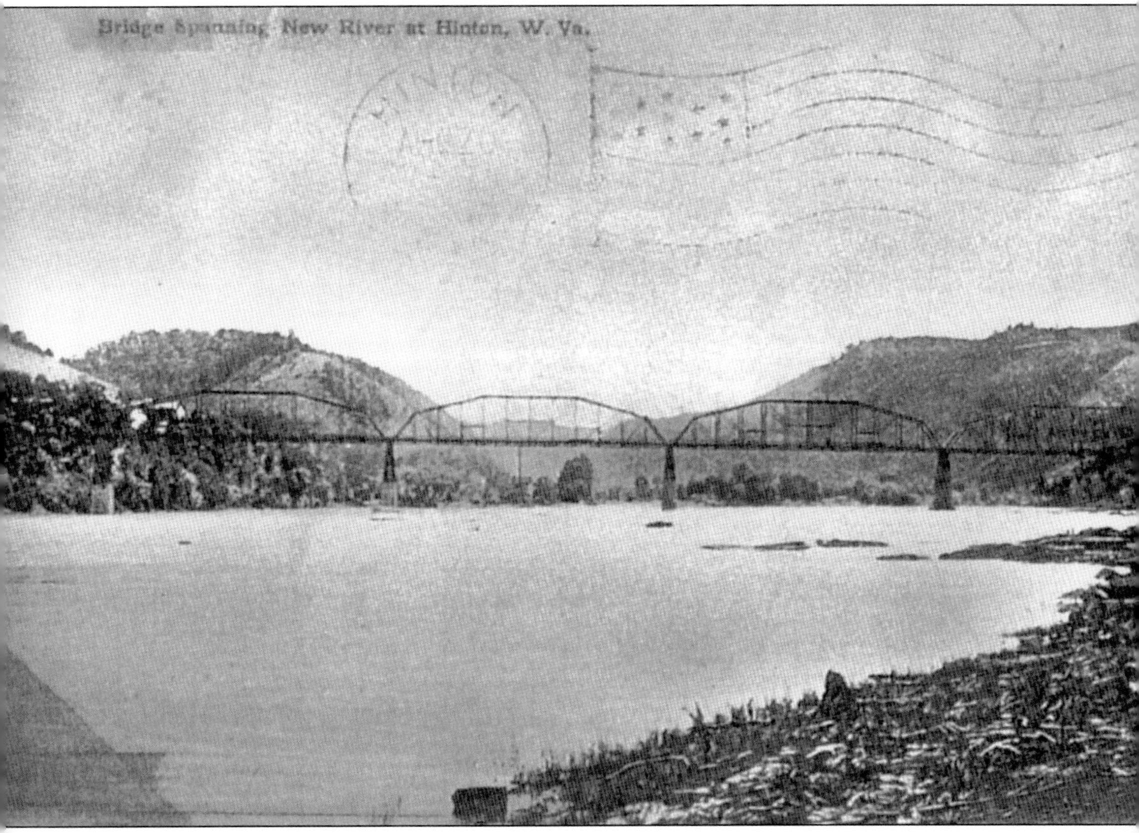

HINTON TOLL BRIDGE. Completed in 1906, the bridge's pedestrian tolls were 5¢ one way and 10¢ round-trip. Tolls were done away with in 1935, and the bridge was dismantled in 1976. The photograph was taken by the National Park Service. (Courtesy of Betty Cooper.)

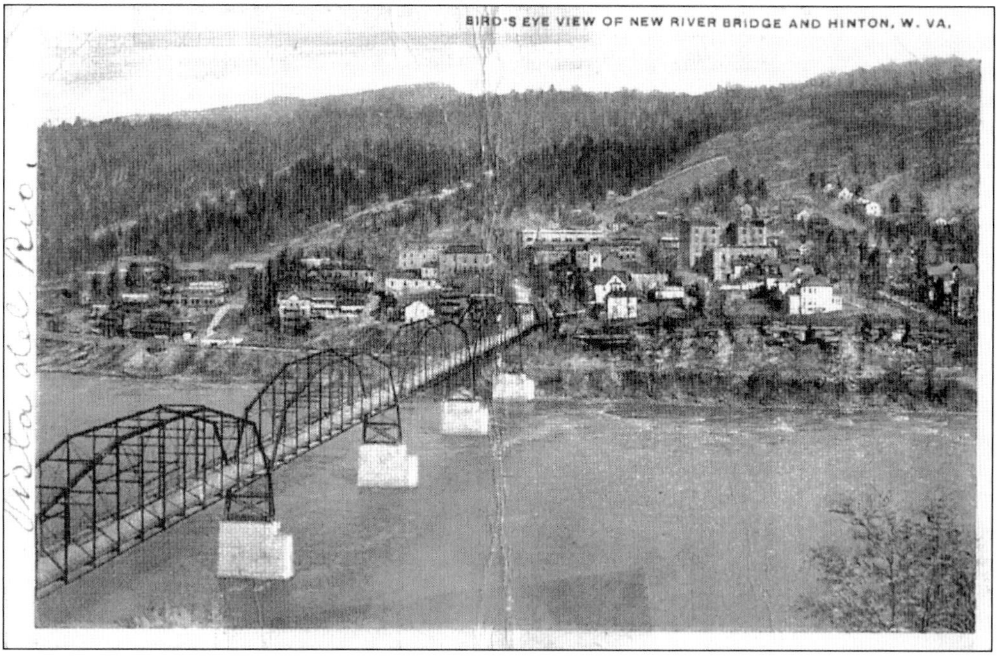

HINTON TOLL BRIDGE. Built by the West Virginia Bridge and Construction Company, this bridge was started in March 1905 and finished in August 1906. Until cars became popular, the bridge showed little profit. But in the 1920s and 1930s, annual revenue was said to have been more than $50,000.

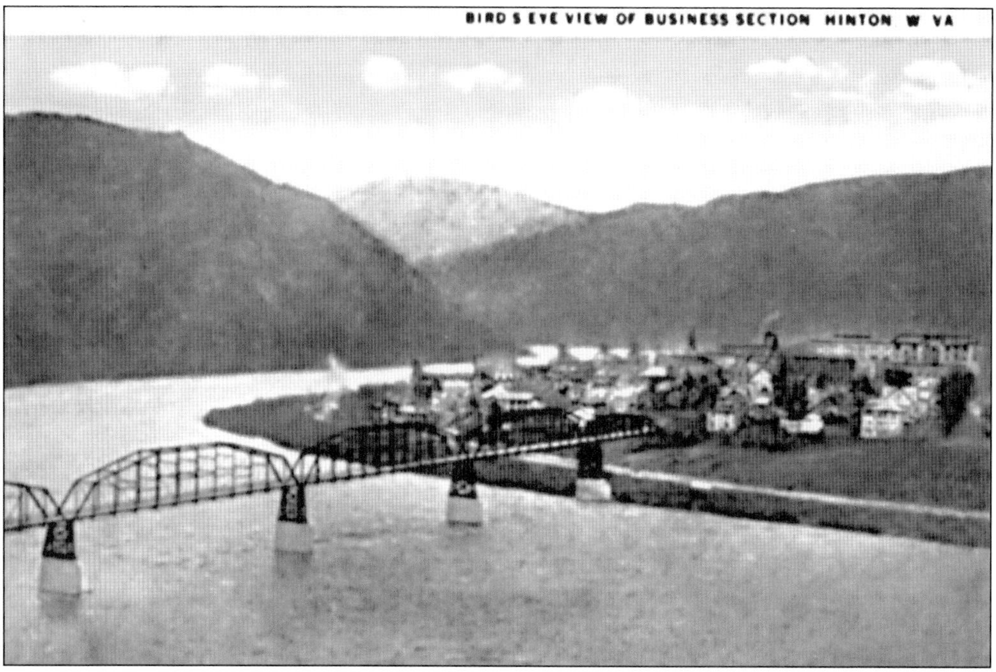

BIRD'S EYE VIEW OF BUSINESS SECTION OF HINTON. This postcard focuses on the bridge. The courthouse is not visible in this picture. (Courtesy of Thomas N. Clark.)

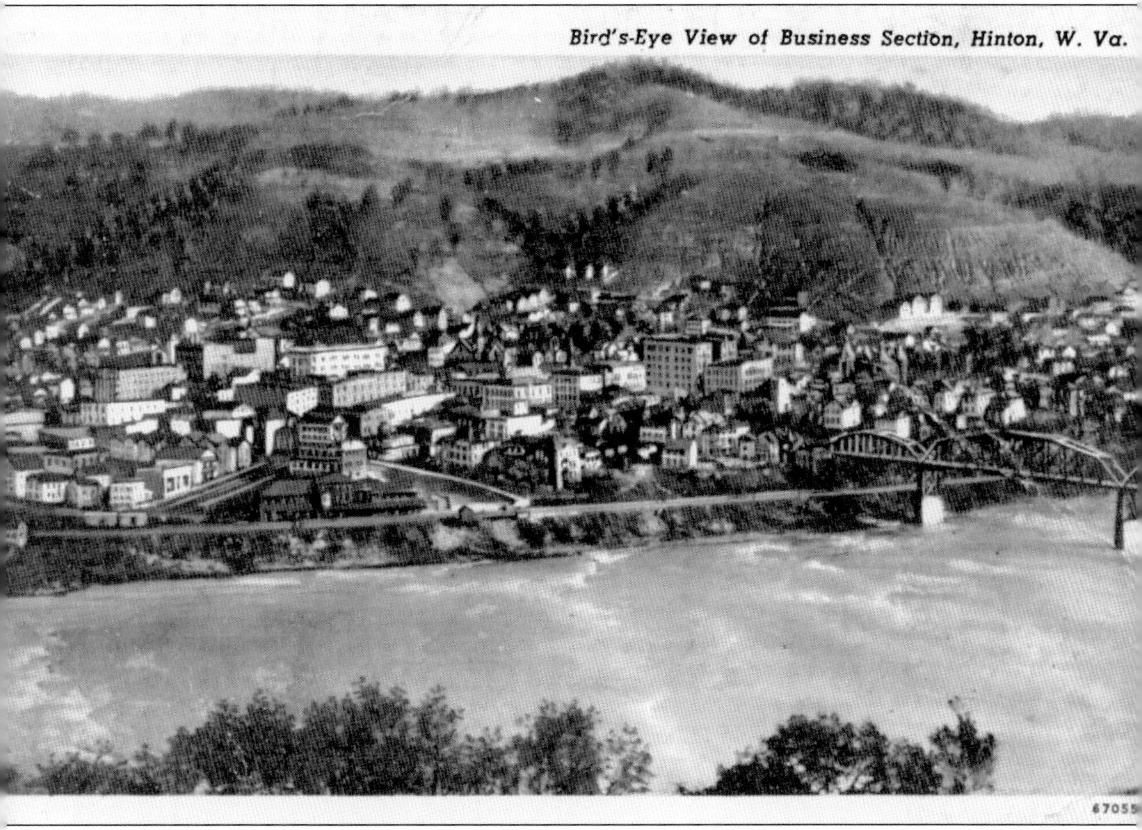

HINTON'S BUSINESS SECTION. This card, with a mailing date of 1950, depicts the courthouse with its towers at right. (Courtesy of Bob Evans.)

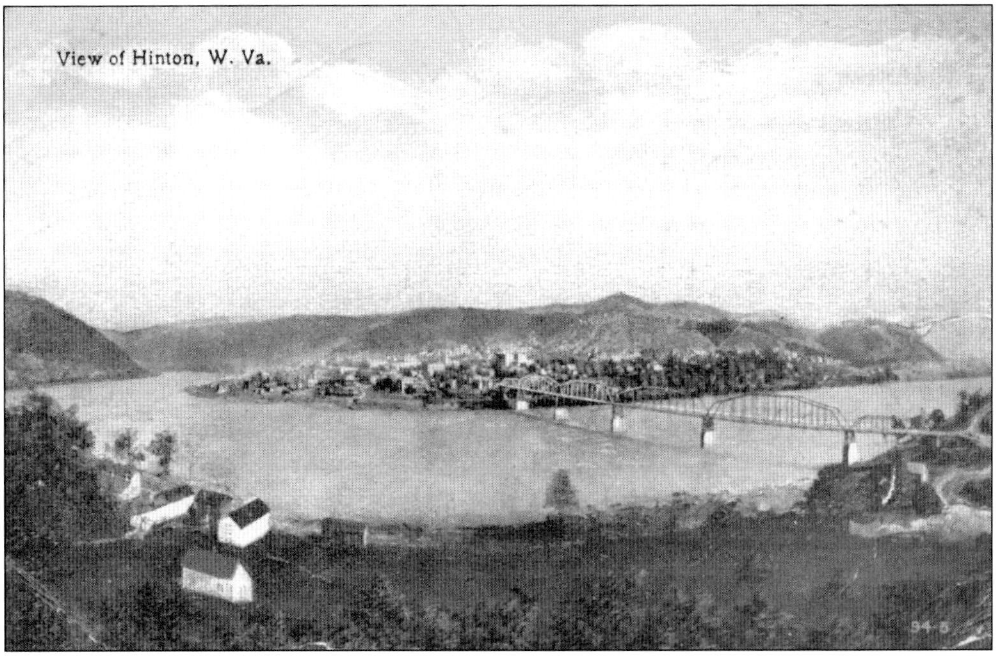

ANOTHER VIEW OF HINTON AND THE NEW RIVER. Look to the left for the neighboring communities of Madam's Creek and Brooklyn. Today, in 2005, Restwood Cemetery is located on this road. (Courtesy of Margaret Martin.)

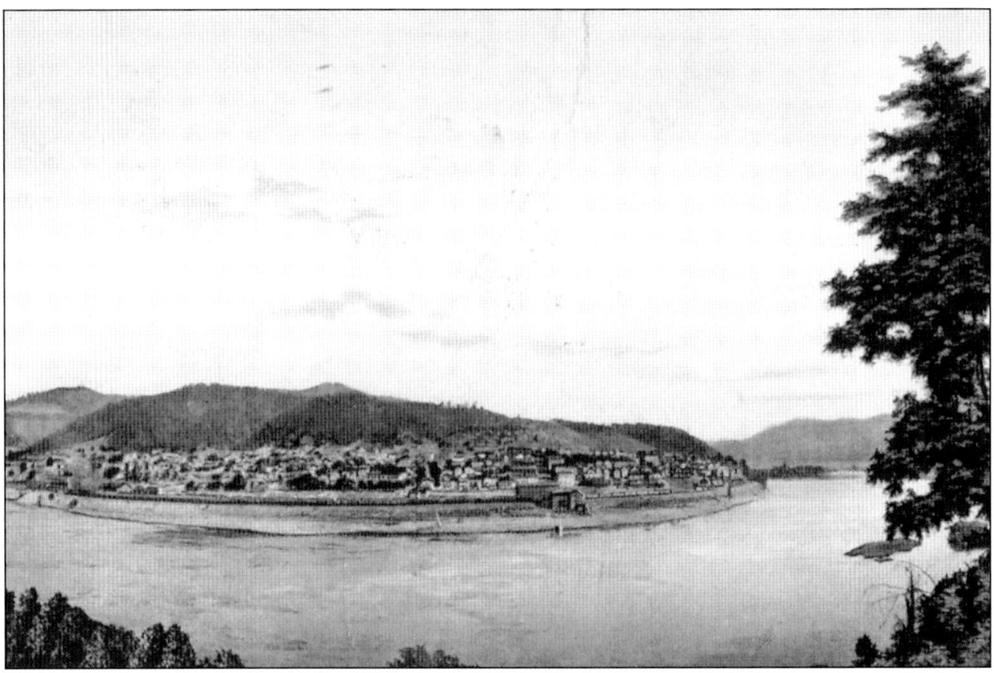

BIRD'S EYE VIEW OF HINTON AND THE NEW RIVER. This card shows the scene in 1908, before the Hinton Toll Bridge was built. (Courtesy of Thomas N. Clark.)

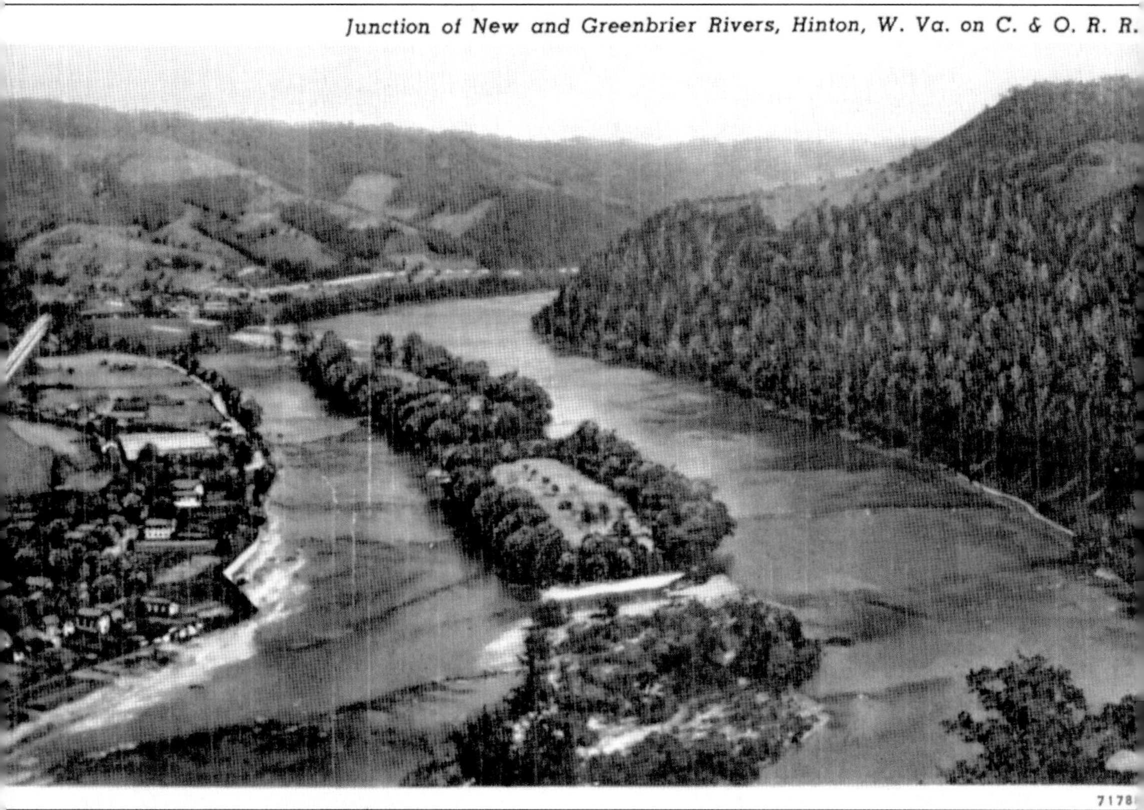

CONFLUENCE OF THE NEW AND GREENBRIER RIVERS AT HINTON ON THE C&O RAILROAD. The scene dates from before the construction of the Bluestone Dam and the Bellepoint New River Bridge. The Bellepoint community is on the left. (Courtesy of Margaret Martin and Thomas N. Clark.)

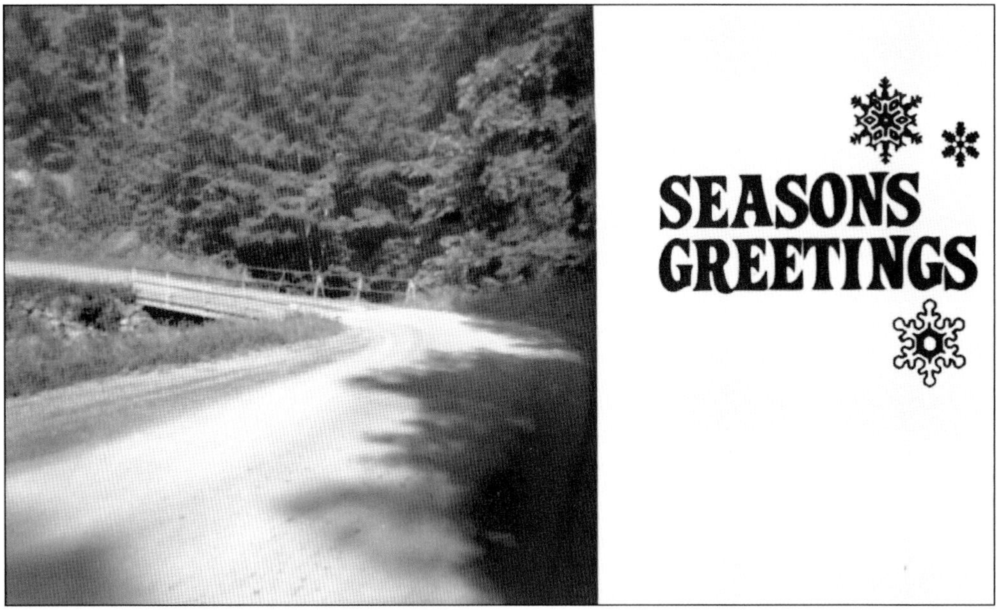

Old Wooden Bridge over Little Wolf Creek at Buck. This bridge was dismantled and replaced around 1974. (Courtesy of Dot Turman.)

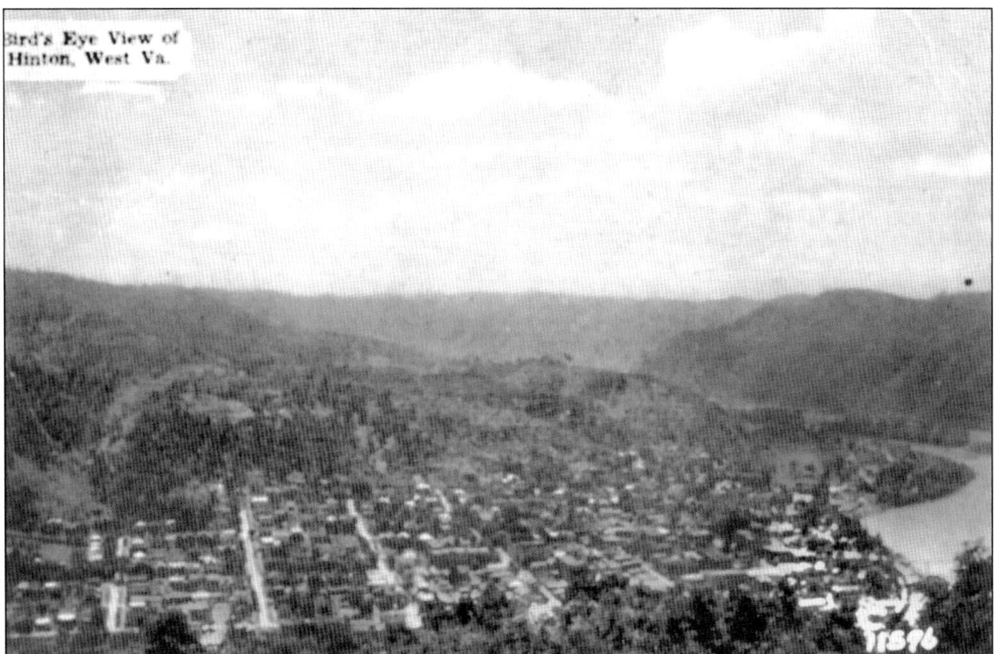

Overview of Hinton. This is an old aerial view of early Hinton showing the layout of the streets. (Courtesy of John W. Kesler; another card with the same view comes from Thomas N. Clark.)

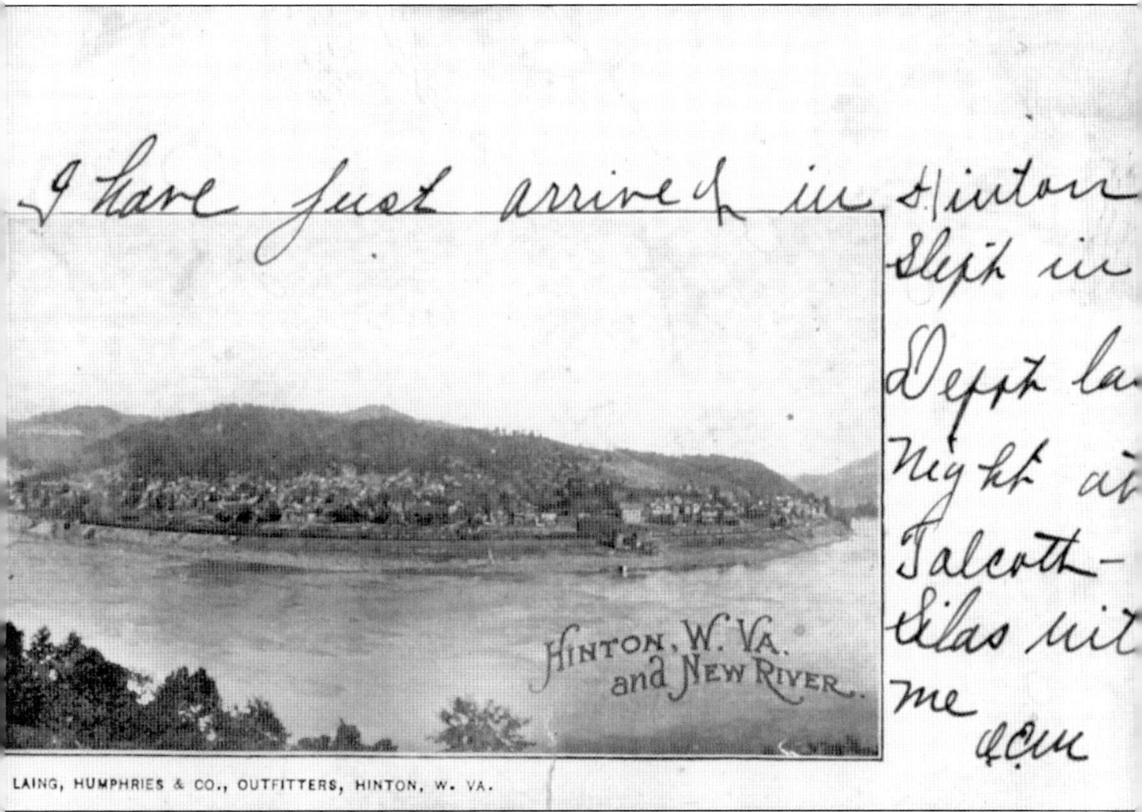

BIRD'S EYE VIEW OF HINTON AND THE NEW RIVER. The message on the card reads: "I have just arrived in Hinton. Slept in depot last night. Silas with me." It is signed O. E. W. (Courtesy of Margaret Martin.)

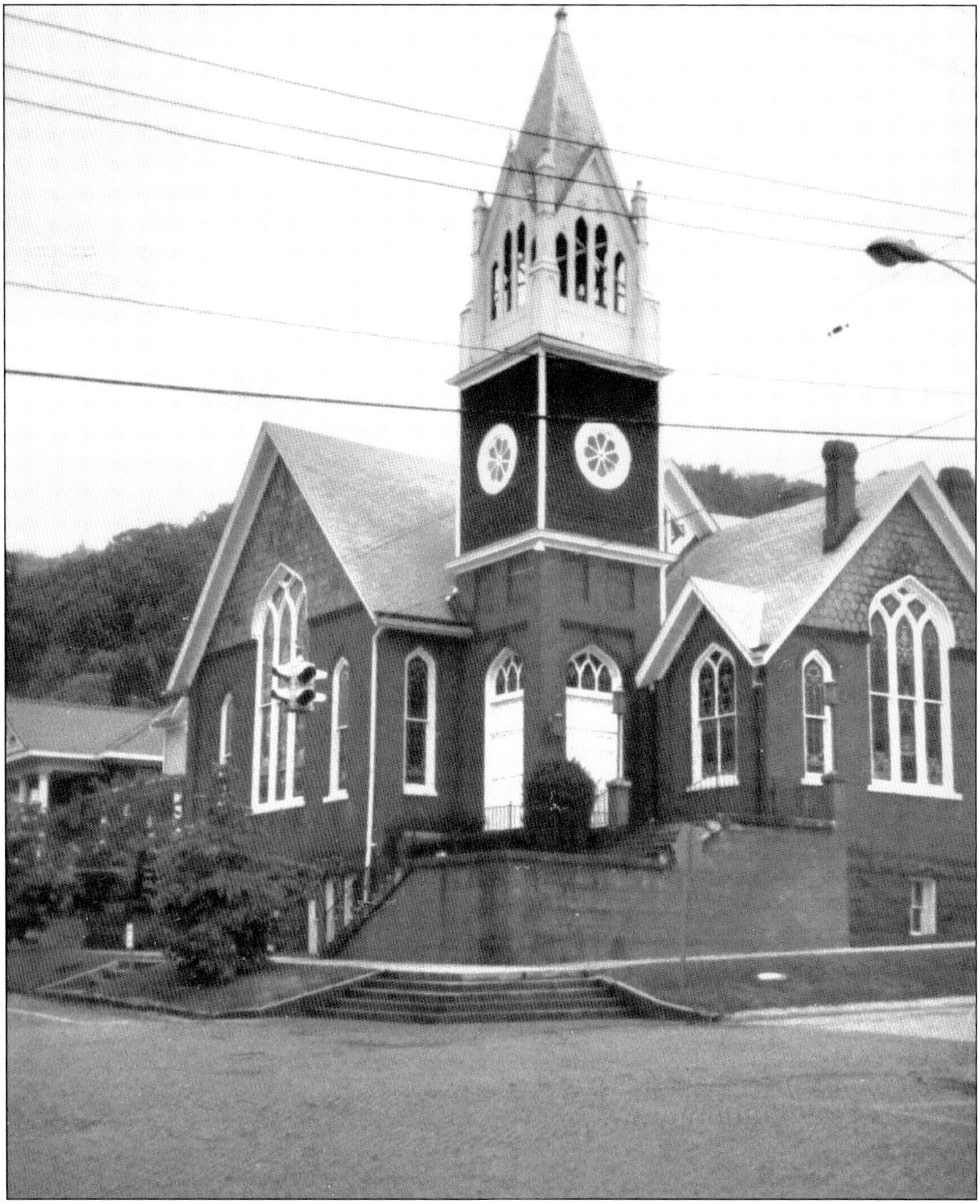

First United Methodist Church of Hinton. The First United Church of Hinton had its origins in 1872. The congregation worshipped with three other denominations in the temporary courthouse and in the C&O Railroad Station until the church was built. (Courtesy of Dot Turman.)

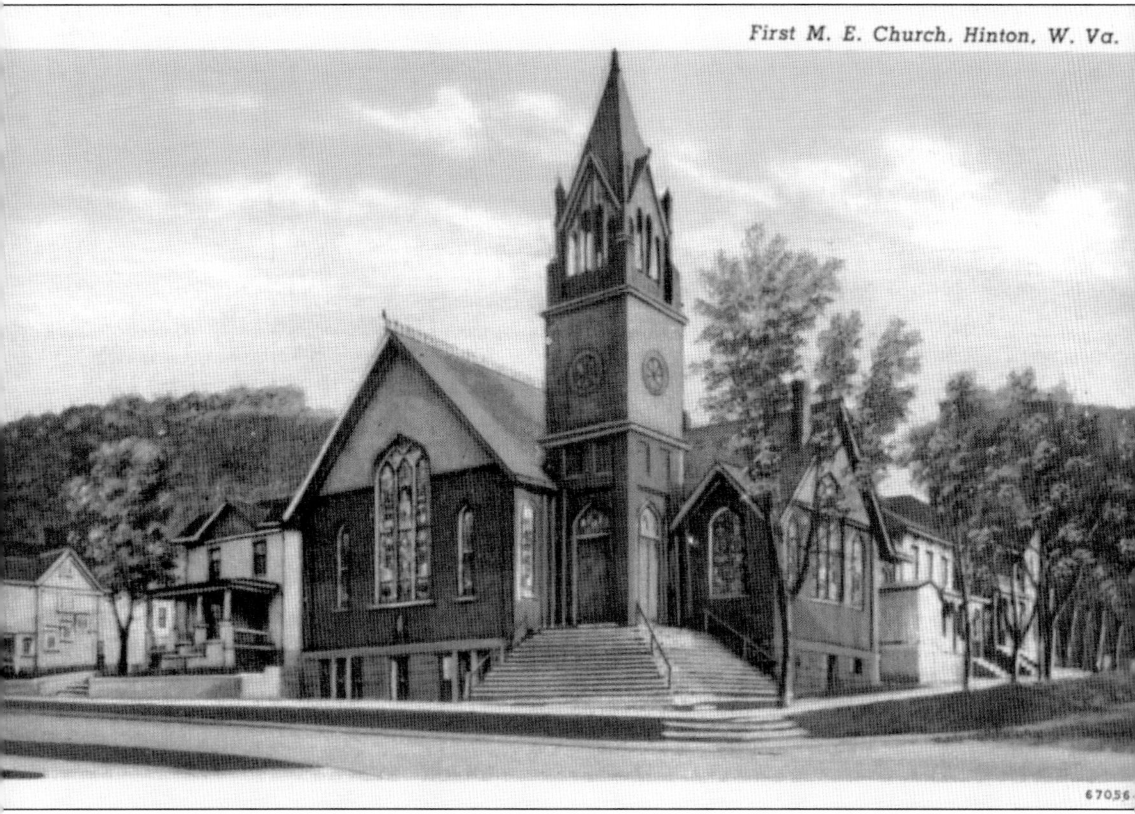

First Methodist Church in Hinton. This image shows the parsonage at the left and the old James Home at the right. (Courtesy of Virginia Gadd and Thomas N. Clark.)

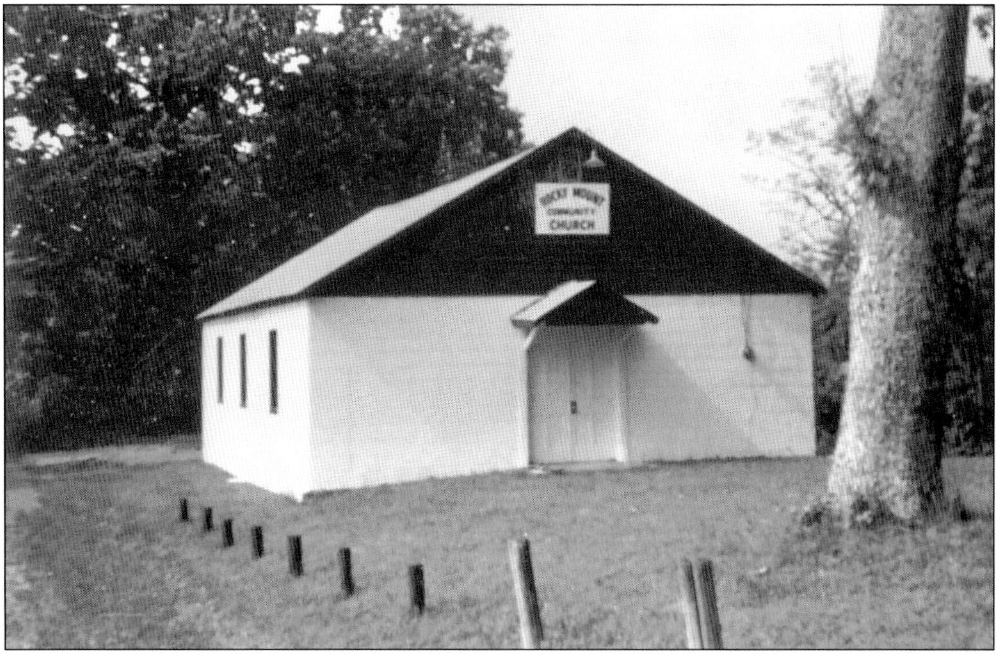

ROCKY MOUNT COMMUNITY CHURCH, PIPESTEM. Members of the Rocky Mount Baptist Church built three meeting houses in the Pipestem area. One has been replaced by a cinderblock building that has been enlarged and covered with aluminum siding. It is near the Rocky Mount Cemetery and is used by the Rocky Mount Community Church. (Courtesy of Dot Turman.)

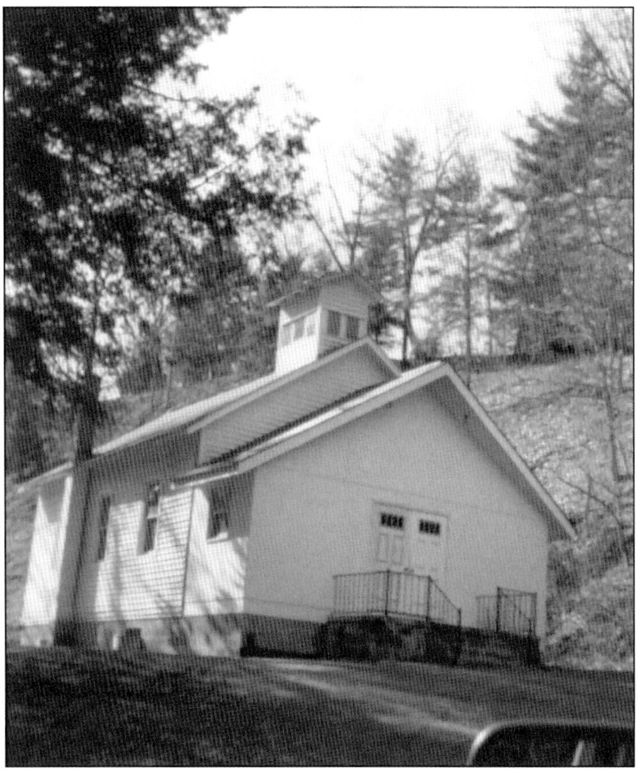

SPRUCE RUN CHAPEL. Located between Hinton and Forest Hill, this church was founded by Rev. Harry Peyton. (Courtesy of Dot Turman.)

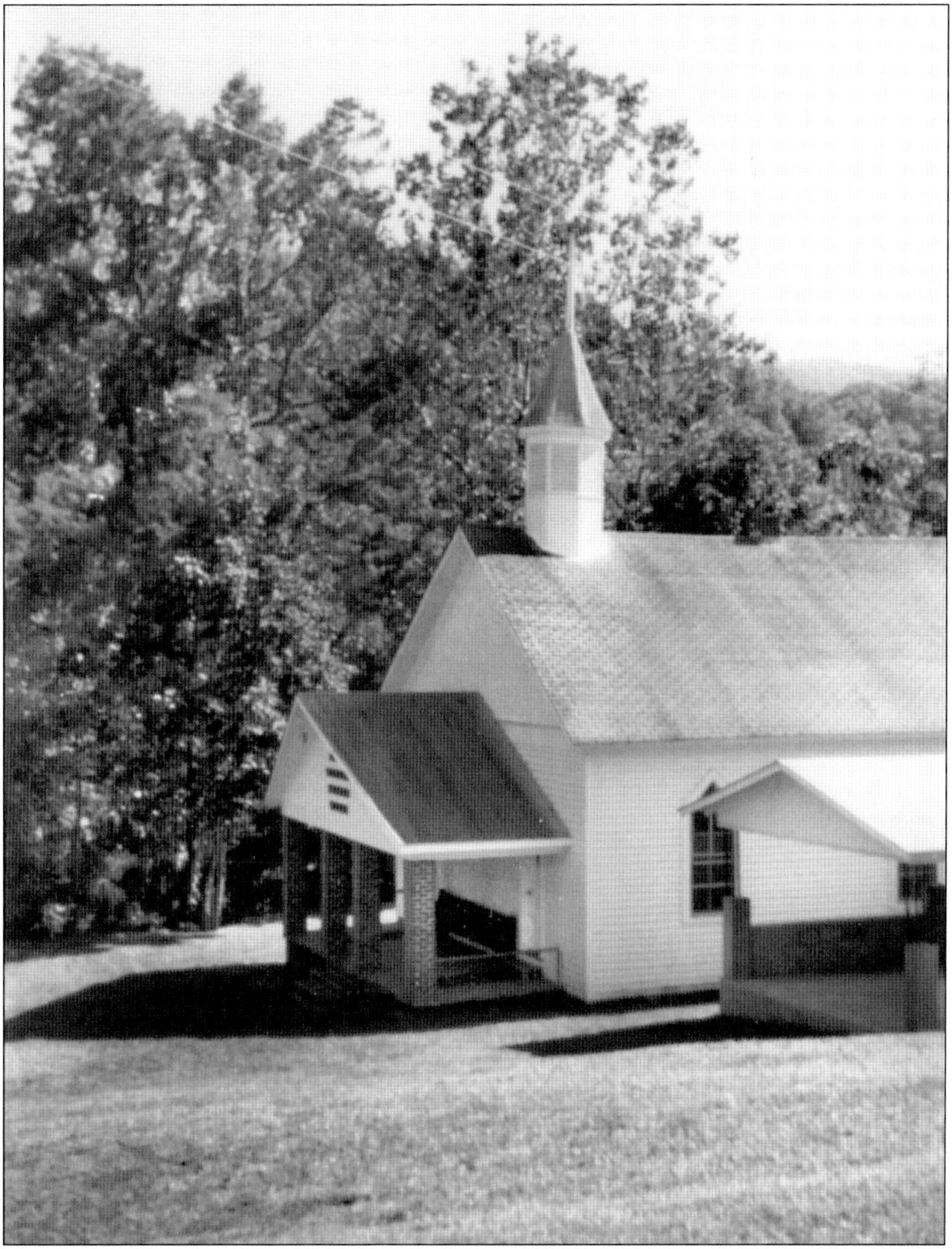

Wolf Creek Missionary Baptist Church. The Wolf Creek Missionary Baptist Church is located in the town of Buck, and its pastor is Eddie Harris. (Courtesy of Dot Turman.)

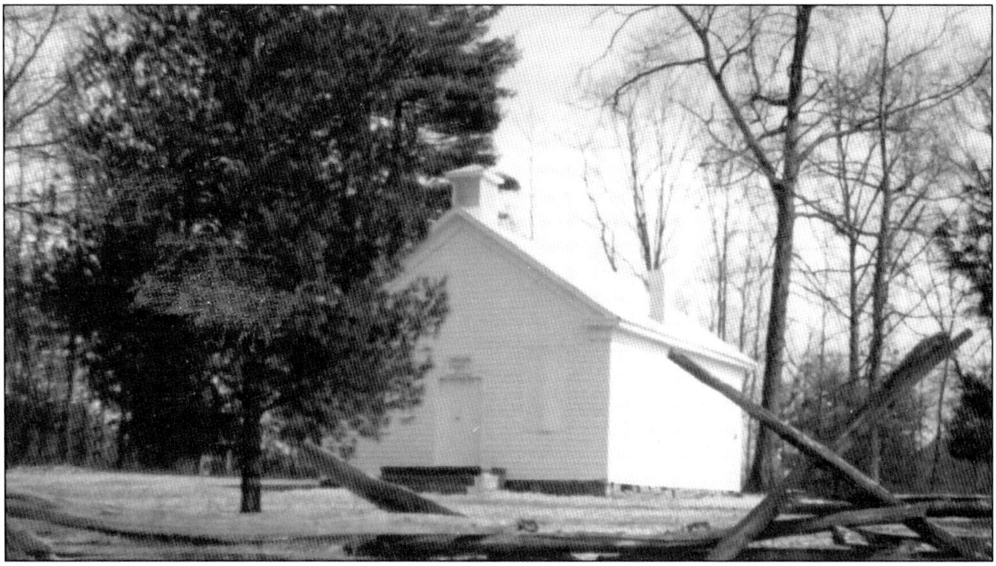

JORDAN'S CHAPEL ON TRUE ROAD. The church has great significance for United Methodists in Mercer and Summers Counties. Built in 1852, Jordan's Chapel was the mother church of all the Methodist churches in the area. Gordon and Thomas Jordan provided the land and lumber for the building. This postcard was taken from the 2001 Homecoming Program. (Courtesy of Dot Turman.)

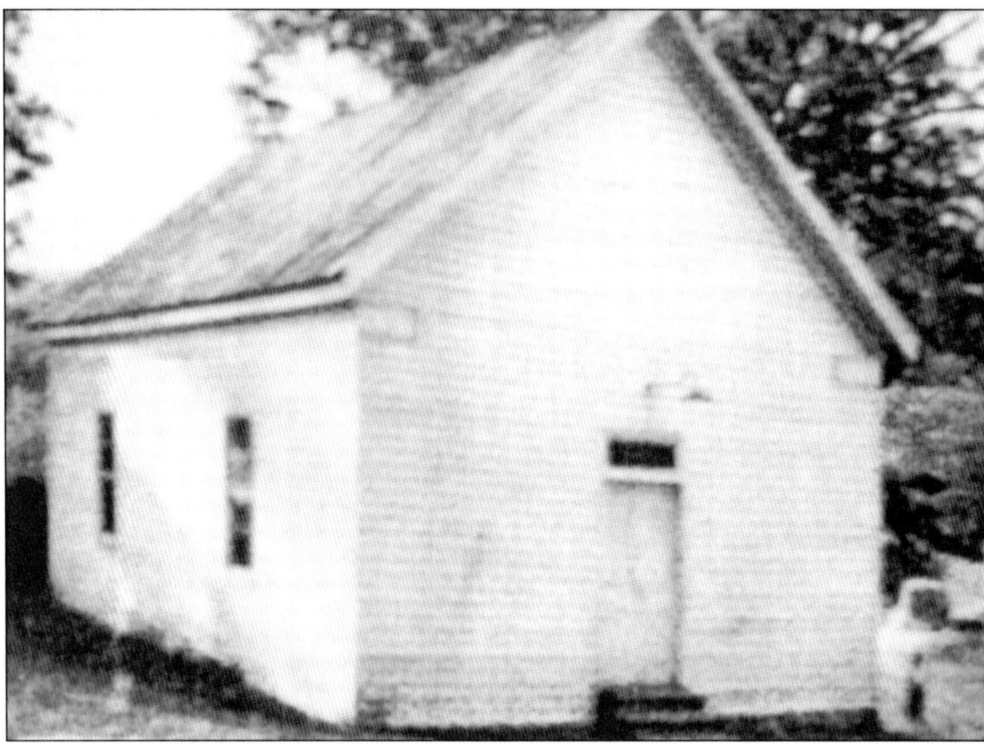

MOUNT ZION METHODIST CHURCH. George F. and Mahala Wikel deeded land for a church to the church trustees. The church congregation worshipped in the old log church for several years. The present building was built around 1885. (Courtesy of Glenna Harvey Saunders.)

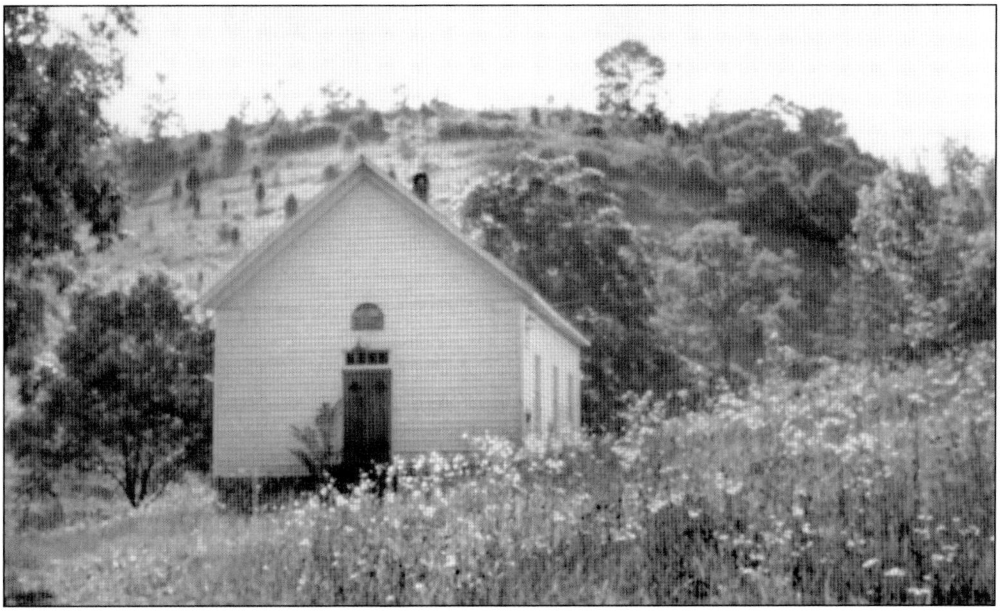

Hill's Chapel in Buck. Built in 1885, the church's original trustees were Samuel Huffman, J. P. Smith, John C. Ballard, Newton Smith, M. A. Wikel, John W. Wikel, John W. Allen, John A. Allen, Giles Thomas Lowry, and James A. Foster. The church has been torn down. (Courtesy of Dot Turman.)

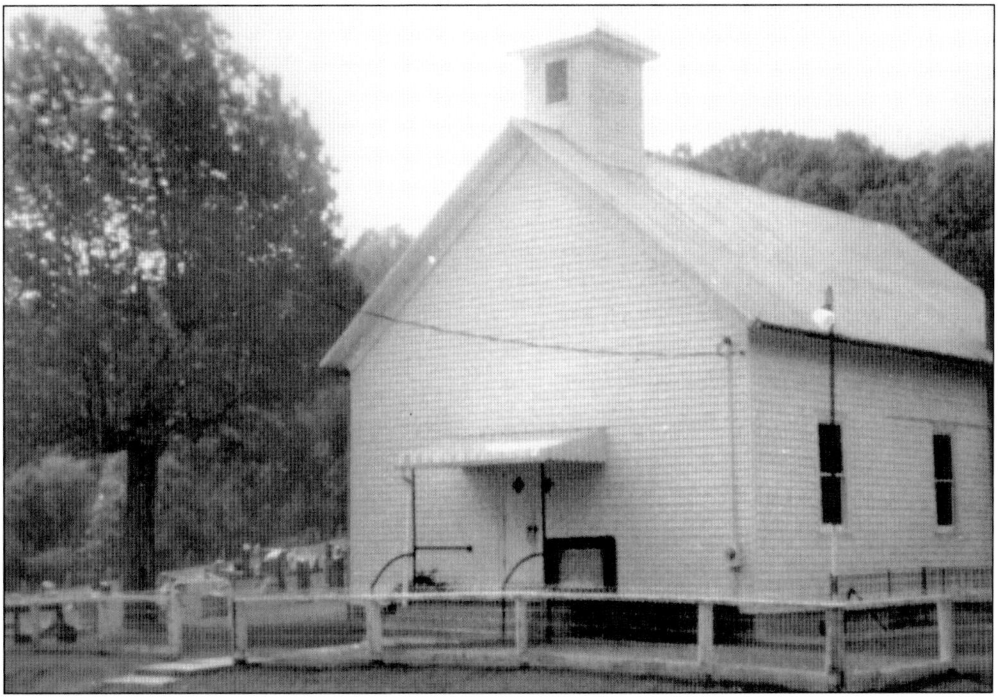

Roles Chapel, Missionary Baptist Church. John Roles gave land for a church and a cemetery. Members of the Roles Chapel Church adopted the covenant of the Missionary Baptist church in 1899. This is a small, nice, country church. From it, five ministers have been called to serve. (From the collection of the late Verona Canterberry.)

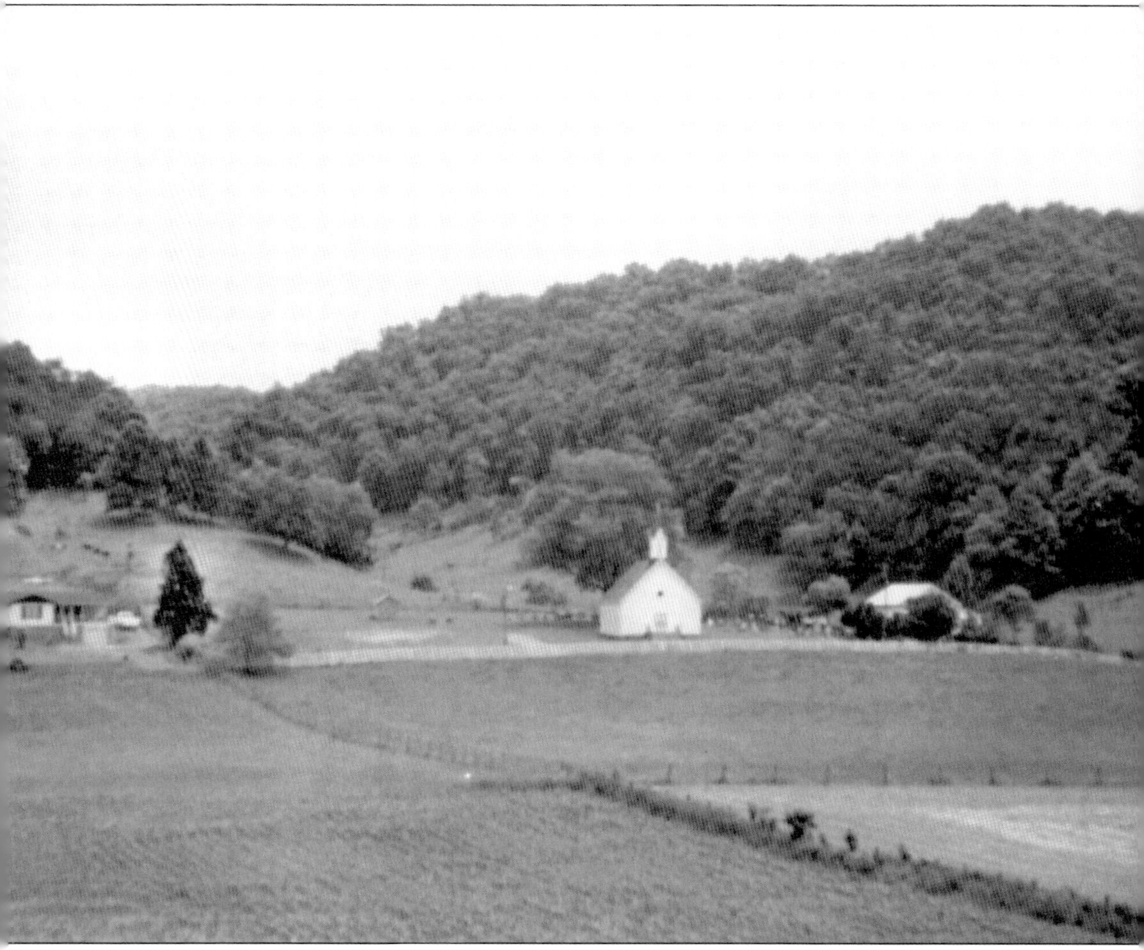

RED SULPHUR SPRINGS CHURCH. This charming country church, with its adjoining cemetery, is located near the Summers/Monroe County line. It was established in 1898. It is situated near the old Red Sulphur Springs Resort Hotel and its healing waters. (Courtesy of Dot Turman.)

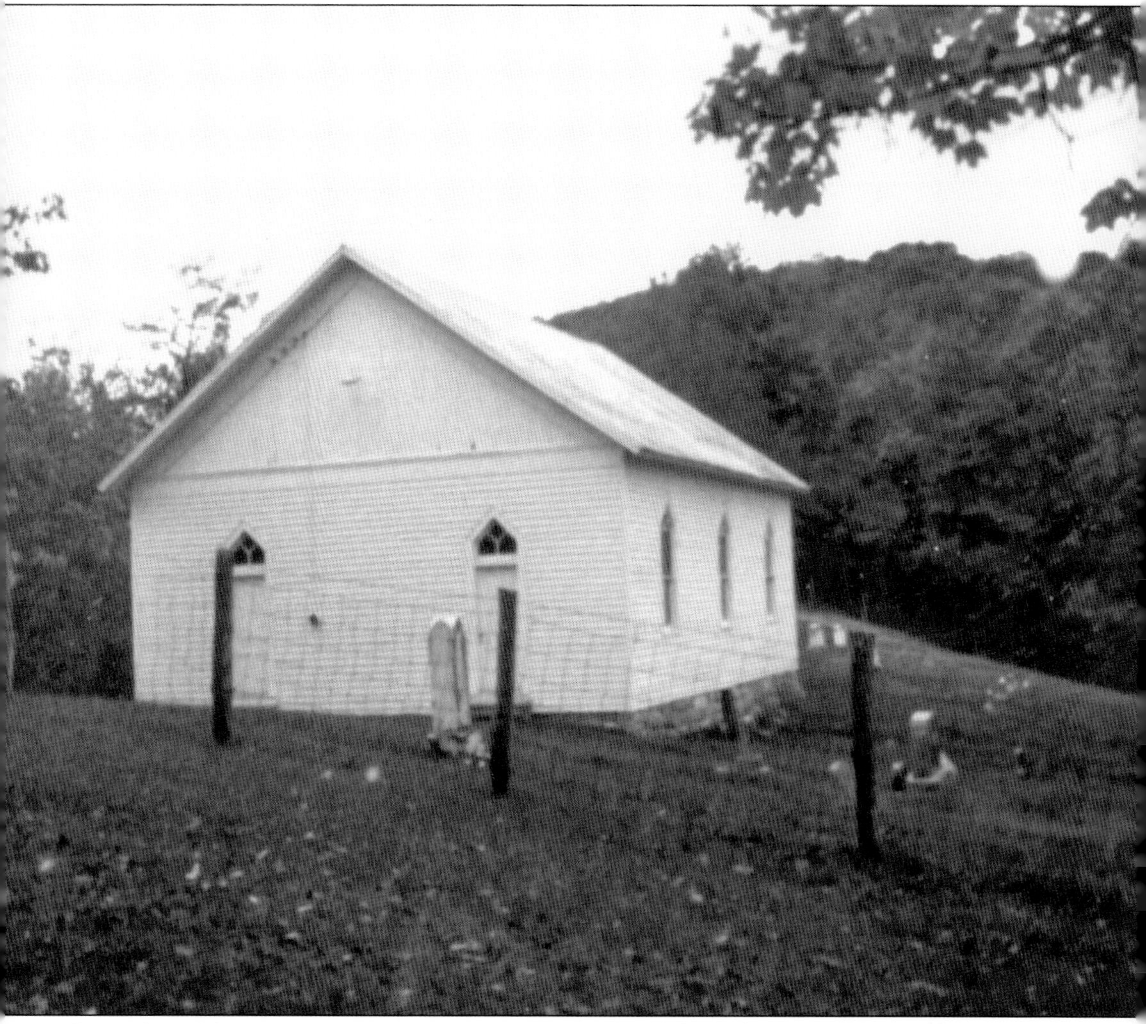

LOW GAP METHODIST EPISCOPAL CHURCH. Located on the New River Hills, this is a pre–Civil War church. The steeple was torn down in the 1950s. This view shows the front of the church. (Courtesy of Dot Turman.)

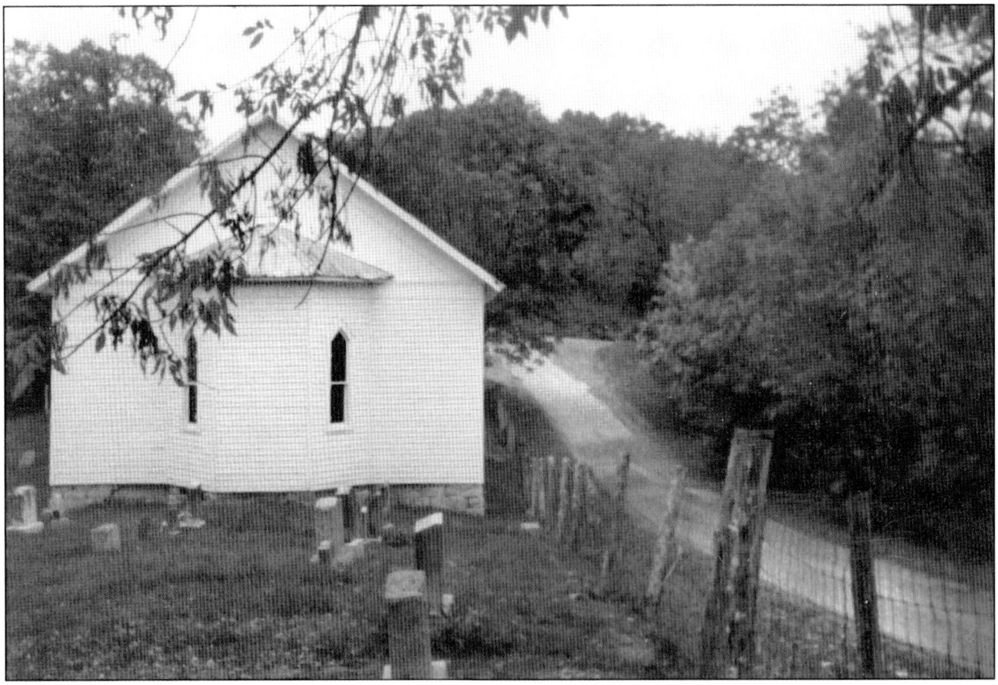

REAR VIEW OF LOW GAP CHURCH. Elizabeth Allen, who gave the land for the church, is buried in this cemetery. (Courtesy of Dot Turman.)

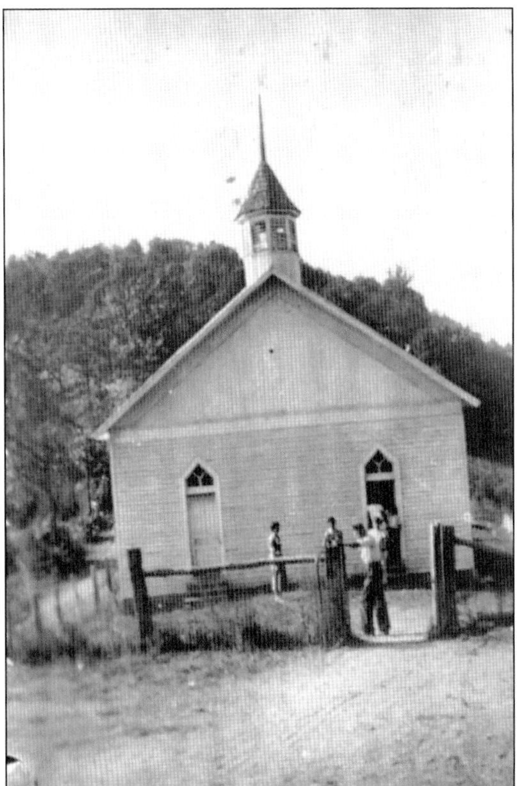

EARLY PICTURE OF LOW GAP CHURCH. Note the steeple and the well-worn path. The original church was built of logs and was called Mount Lebanon. (Courtesy of Dot Turman.)

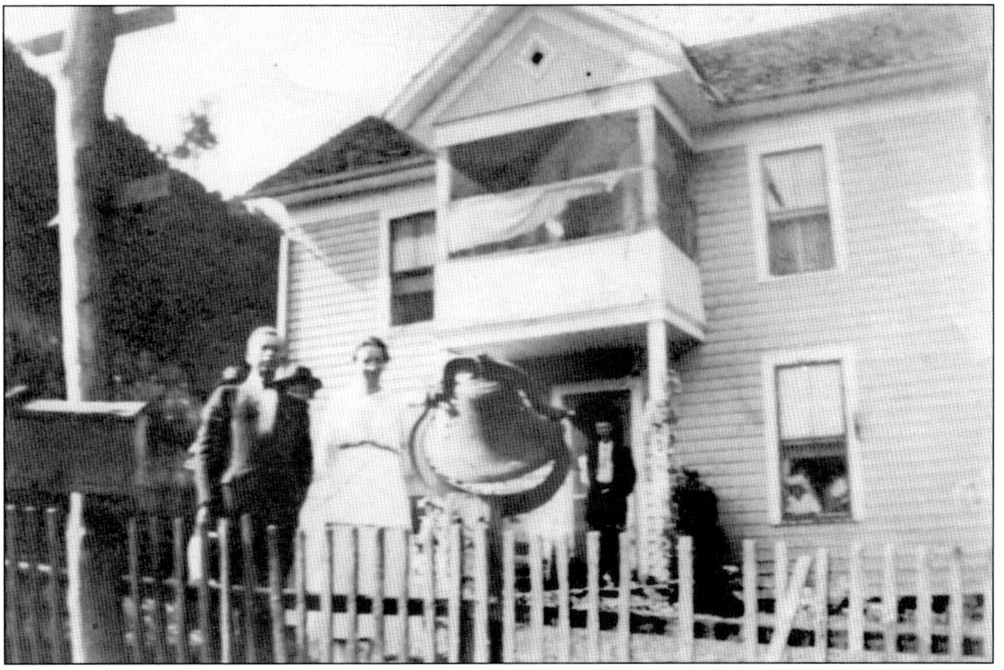

OLD METHODIST PARSONAGE AT BUCK. This is Methodist minister Reverend Redding and wife in 1918, standing on the porch of the parsonage. Rev. C. N. Neff is in the background. Buck was on the Forest Hill Charge, a group of churches that shared a circuit-riding minister. Note the old bell, which hung on the gatepost for many years. (Courtesy of Dot Turman.)

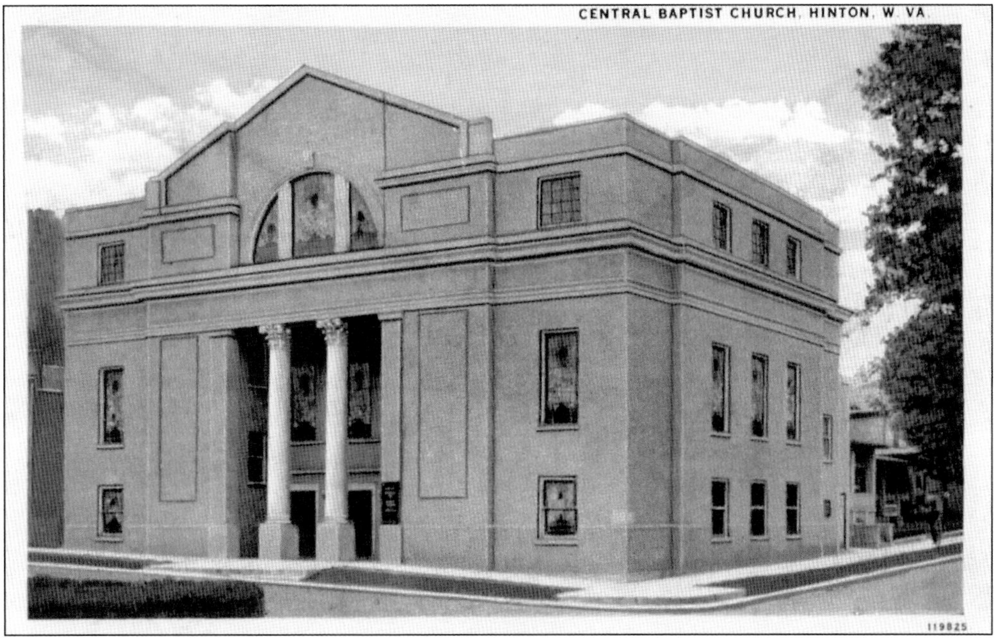

CENTRAL BAPTIST CHURCH. This congregation was organized in Bruce Hall in 1894, and the building later was converted into the Hotel Miller. This yellow-brick church was built in 1907. (Courtesy of Thomas Clark, Bonnie Duncan, Margaret Martin, Amy Parker, and Virginia Gadd.)

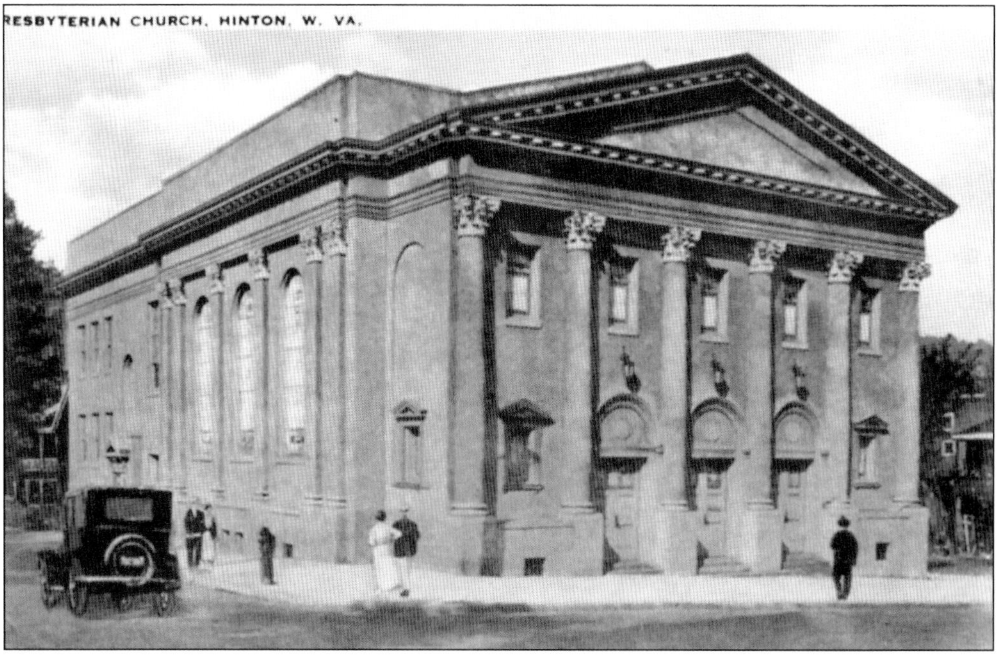

PRESBYTERIAN CHURCH, HINTON, *c.* 1922. A congregation of six members organized in June 1874. The present building was completed in 1922, during the construction of the Bluestone Dam. At its height, membership reached nearly 400 communicants. (Courtesy of Thomas N. Clark.)

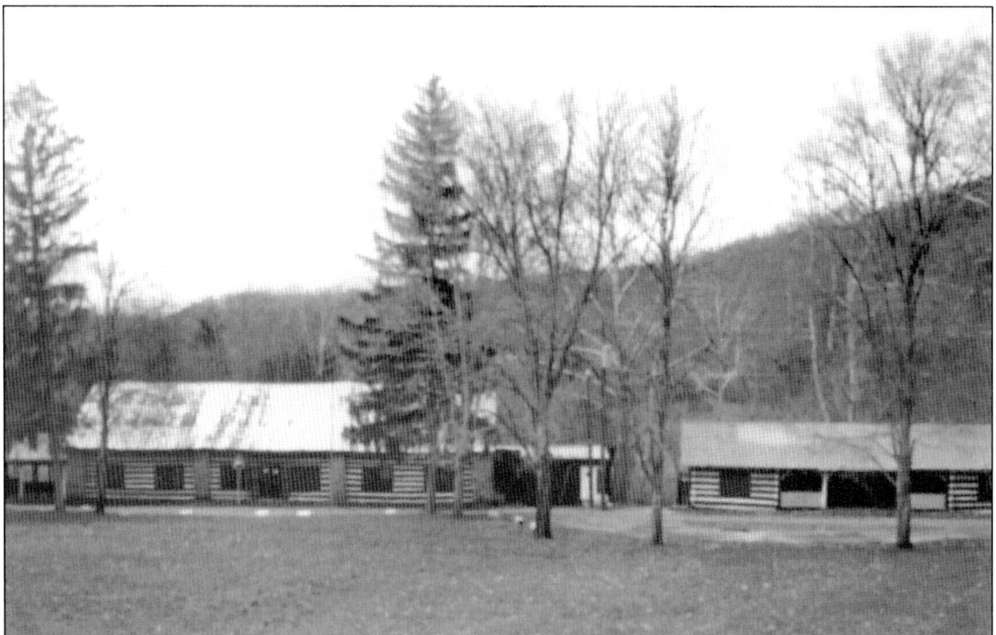

CAMP SUMMERS, NEAR HINTON. A. L. Campbell, a pioneer resident of Summers County, donated 25 acres of land, and this camp, located on the banks of the Greenbrier River, was built at a cost of $2,500. (Courtesy of Dot Turman.)

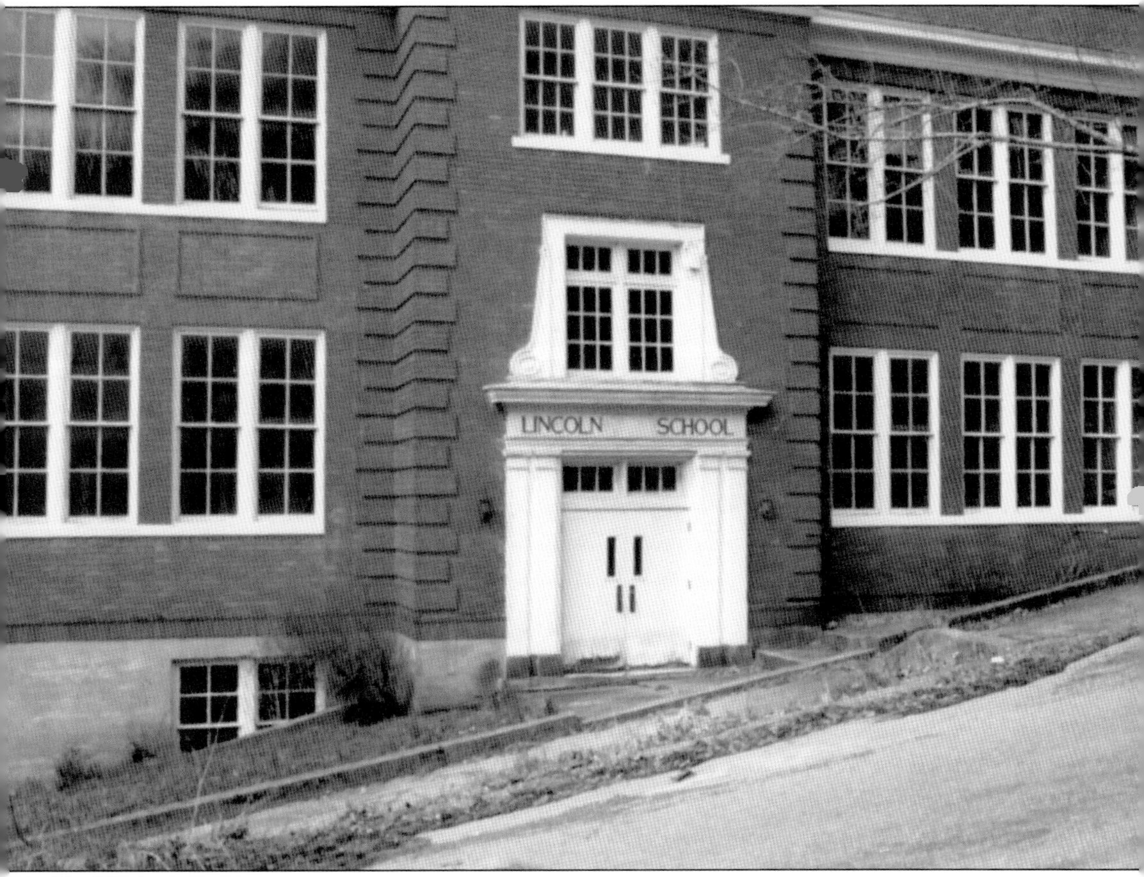

LINCOLN SCHOOL ON HILL STREET IN HINTON. The school, which existed from 1897 to 1963, was first located on James Street and was a wood-framed building. It was replaced in 1926 with a brick building with eight classrooms, an auditorium, a gymnasium, a basement, and two offices. (Courtesy Everett Crawford.)

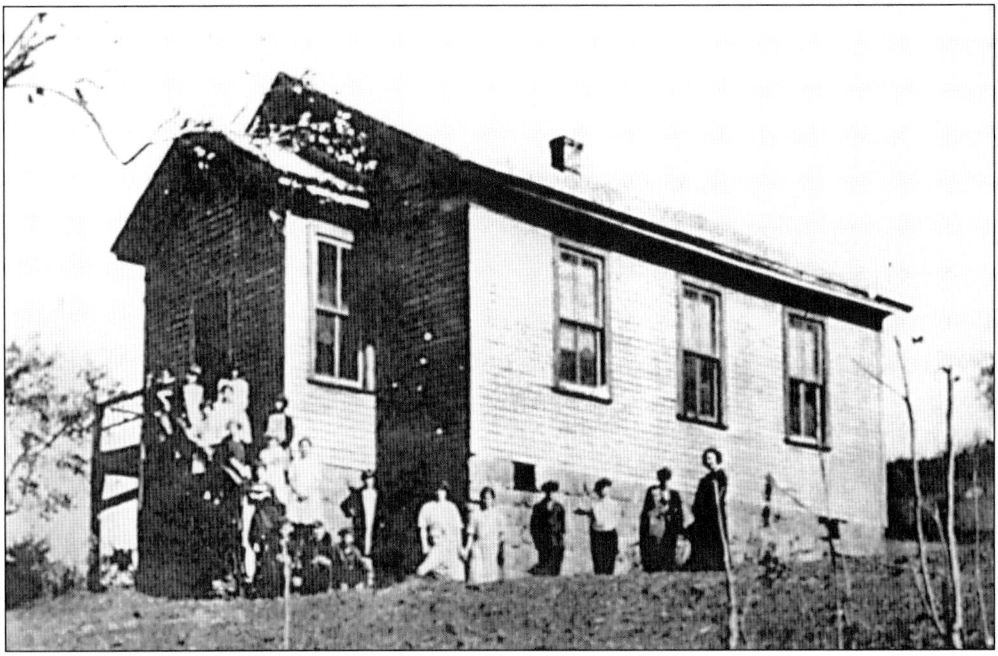

BELLEPOINT ON THE HILL AND THE CHICKEN COOP. These two schools (above and below, respectively) consolidated to form the Bellepoint Elementary School in 1924. (From *The Dart*, official yearbook of Hinton High School.)

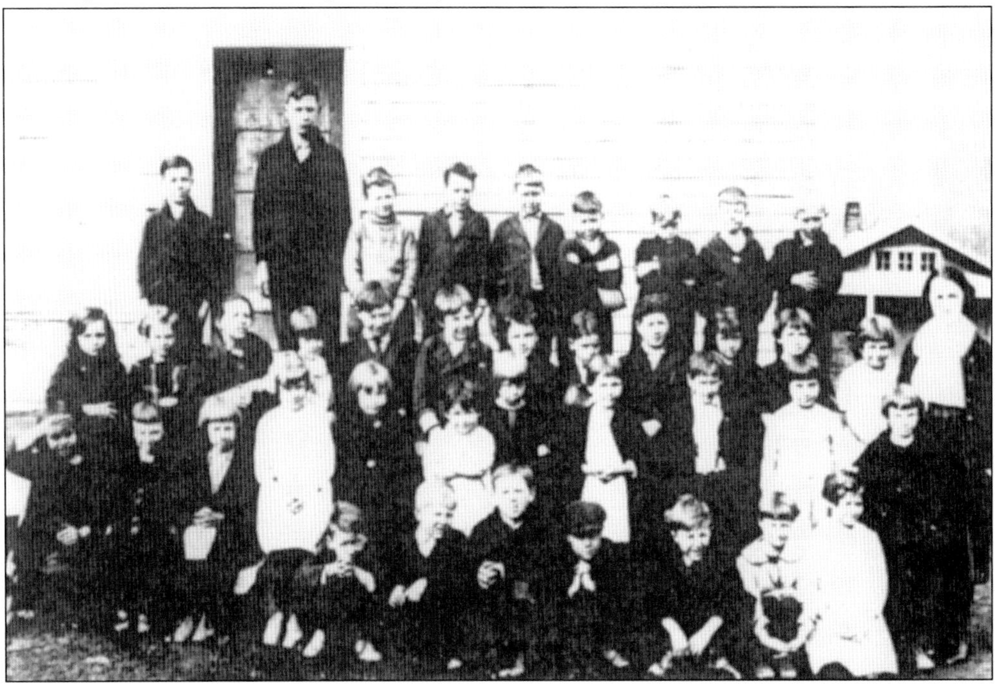

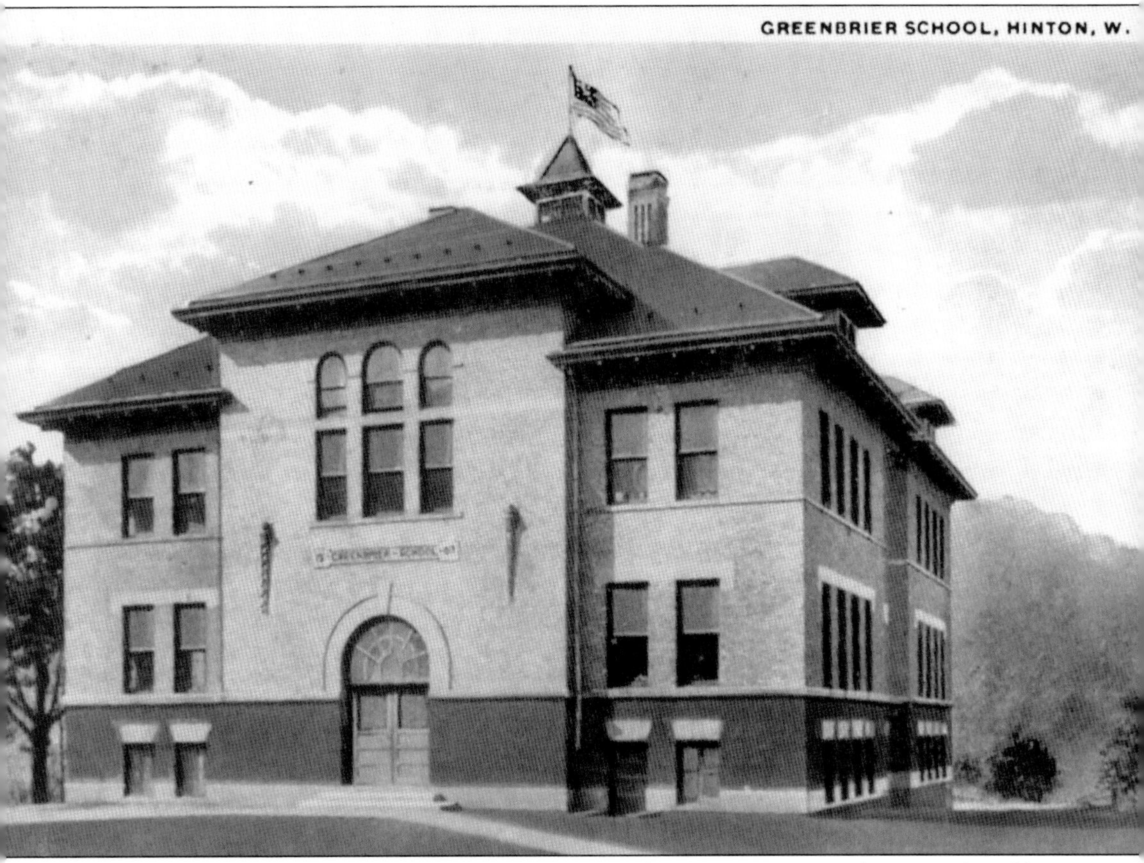

GREENBRIER SCHOOL. This building was constructed by West Virginia Architects and Builders, who submitted a bid of $18,500. However, the school board asked that all the arches over the windows be built of Indiana limestone and all the interior wood be made of oak, so that increased the price. In 1907, the total came to $21,000. (Courtesy of Fred Long.)

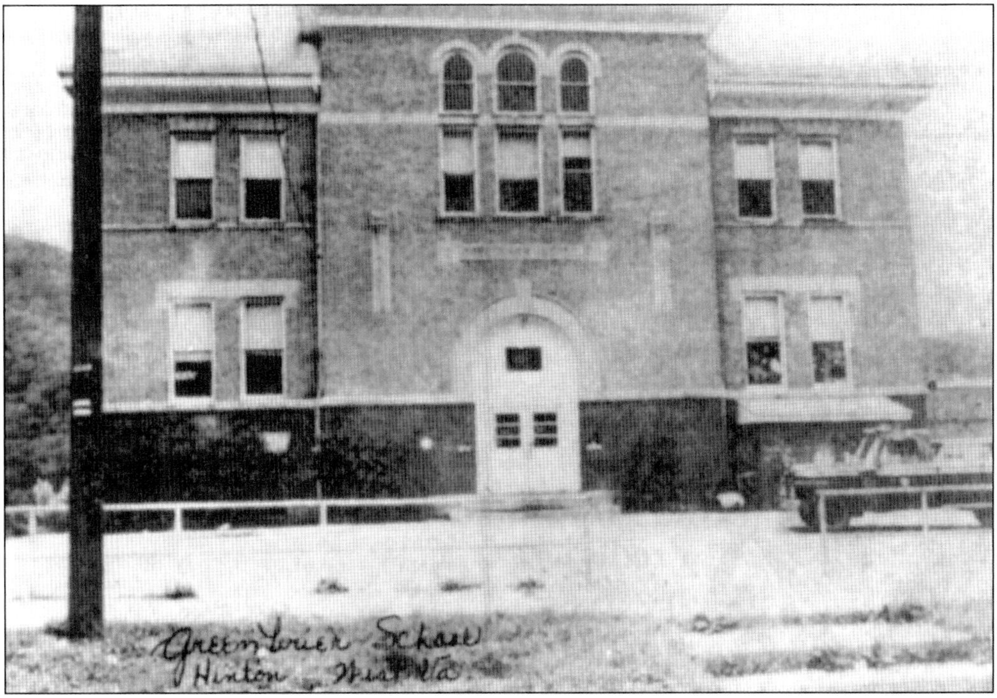

GREENBRIER SCHOOL. This was the last picture taken before the demolition of the school. The board of education voted to raze the school to make room for playground equipment at the new Hinton Area Elementary. (Courtesy of Fred Long.)

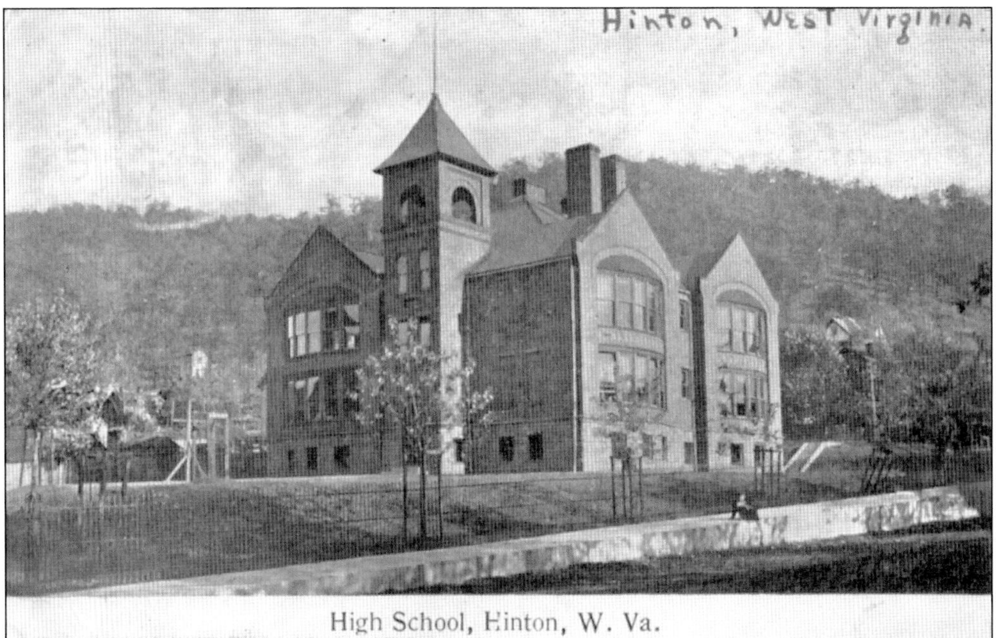

HINTON HIGH SCHOOL. The high school is pictured here in 1921. Later it was called Central School, but it eventually burned in 1940. (Courtesy of Bonnie Duncan and Margaret Martin.)

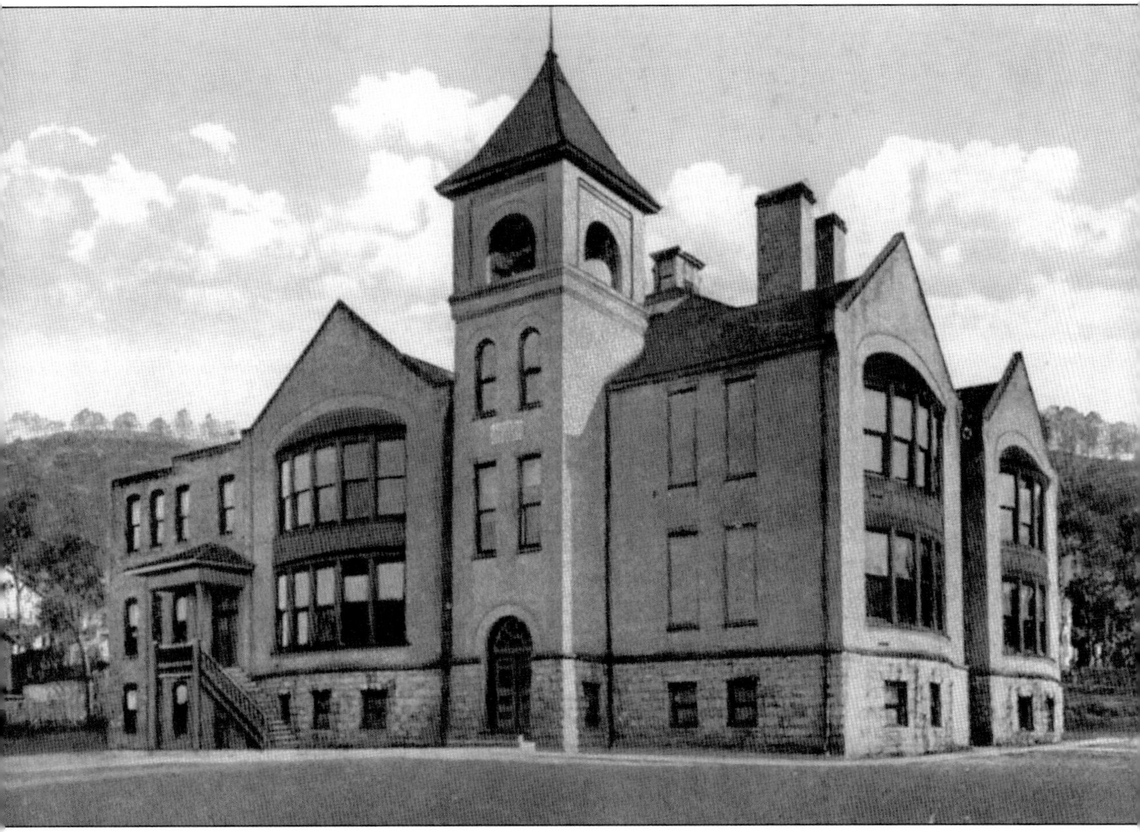

HINTON HIGH SCHOOL. The building also once served as Summers Middle School. (Courtesy of Thomas N. Clark.)

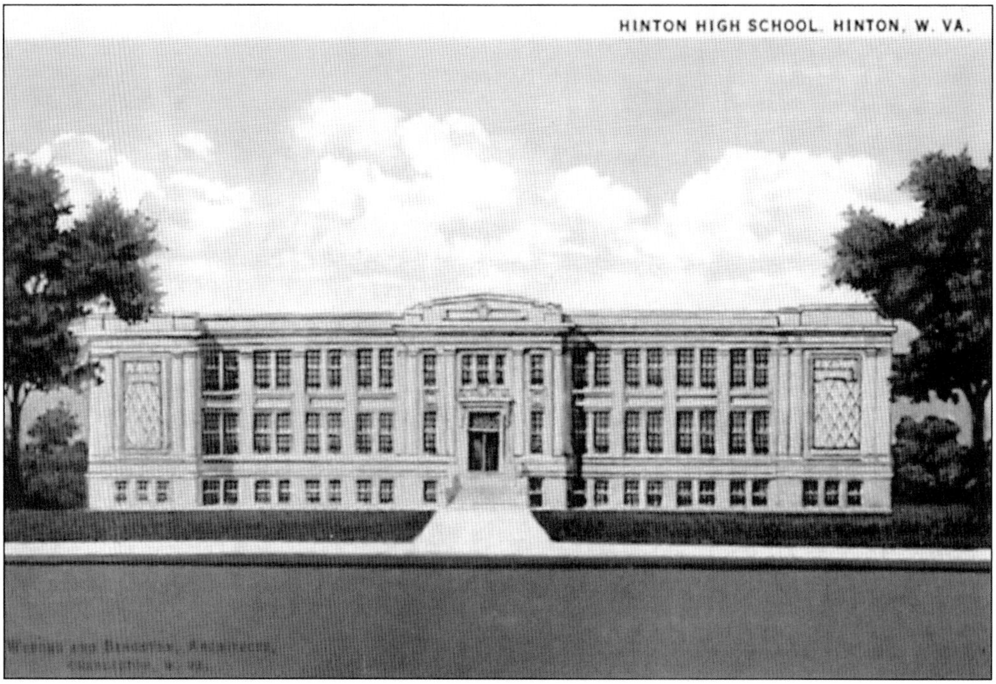

HINTON HIGH SCHOOL. This postcard shows Hinton High School in Hinton, West Virginia. (Courtesy of Thomas N. Clark.)

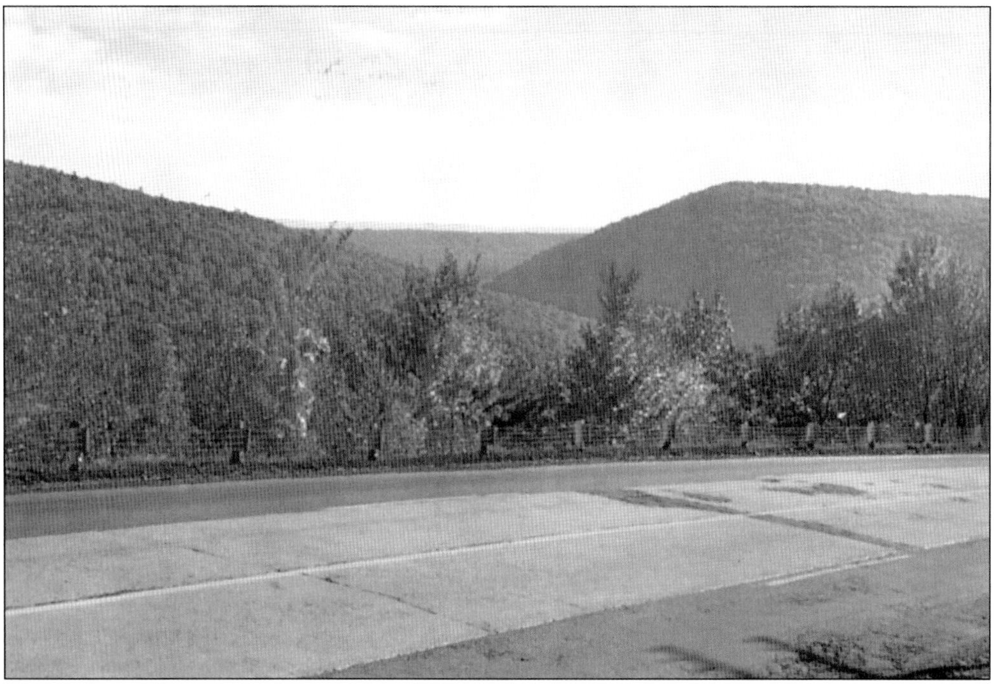

COME TO HINTON, WEST VIRGINIA. Pictured here is one of the highways leading into Summers County. With its autumn foliage and flowers, this road is one of the county's prettier sights at that time of the year. (Photographer unknown.)

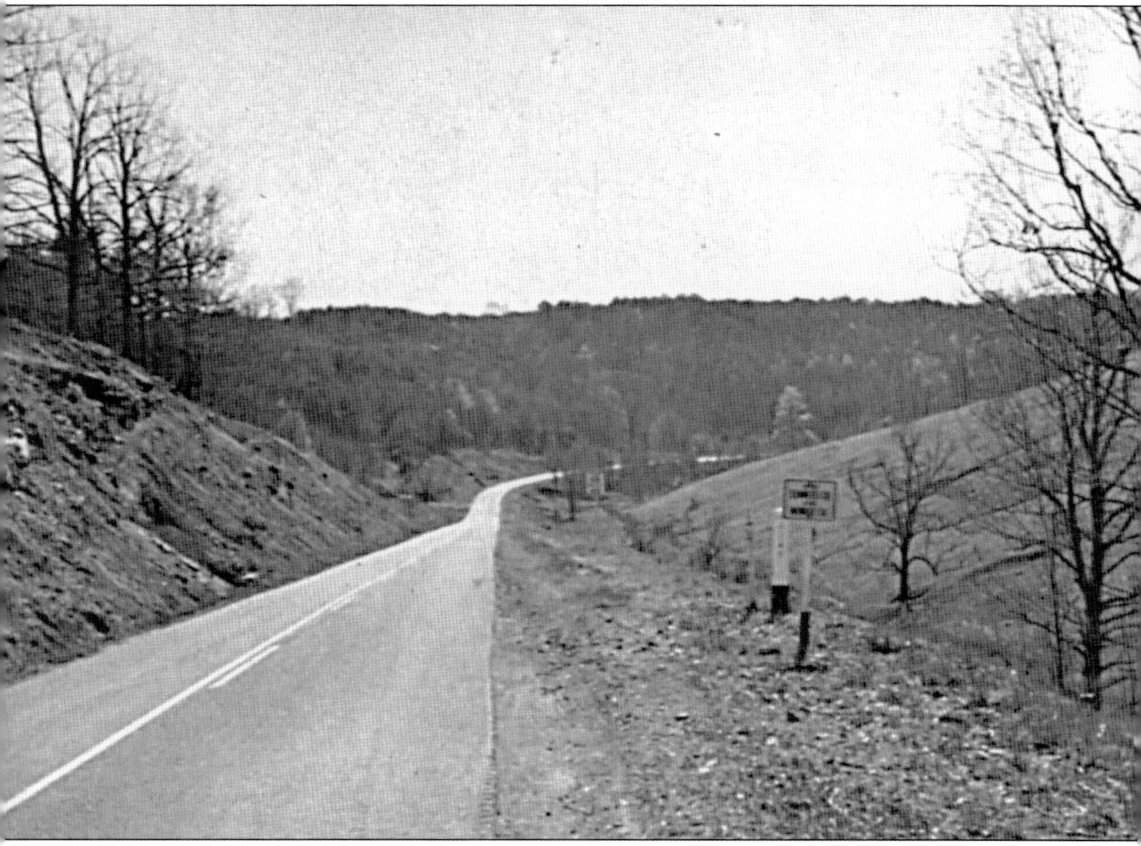

ENTERING SUMMERS COUNTY ON ROUTE 12 HEADED NORTH. The highway sign pictured as drivers are leaving Monroe County gives historical information about the formation of Summers County in 1871. (Published by Monroe and Creed, Hinton.)

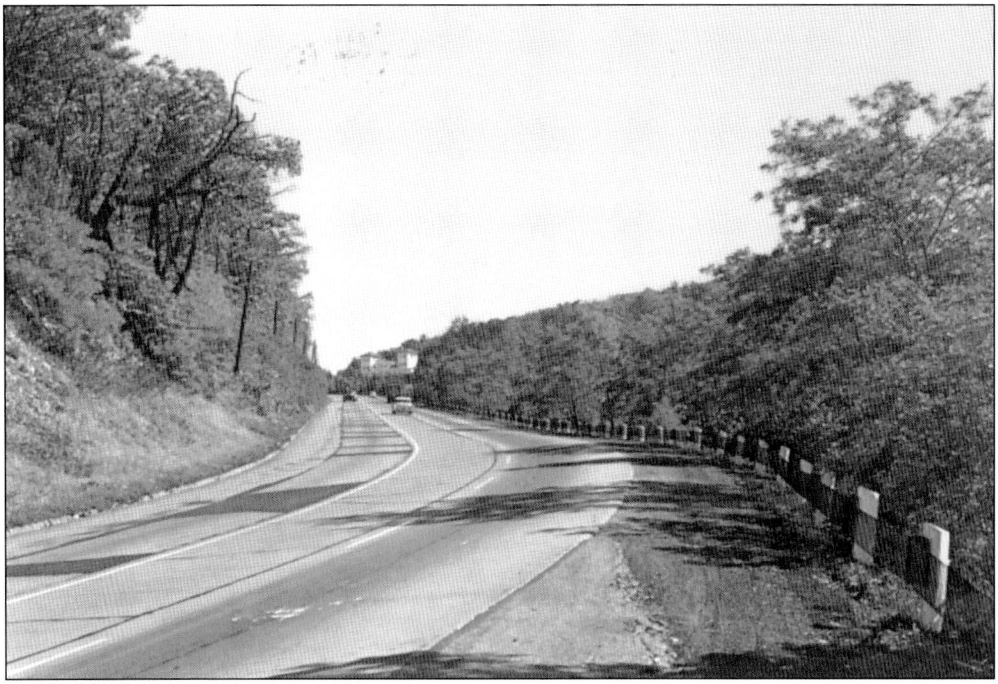

ANOTHER CARD PLEADING WITH YOU TO COME TO HINTON. It's a lovely card, but most native West Virginians need no urging to come home at every opportunity. (Photographer unknown.)

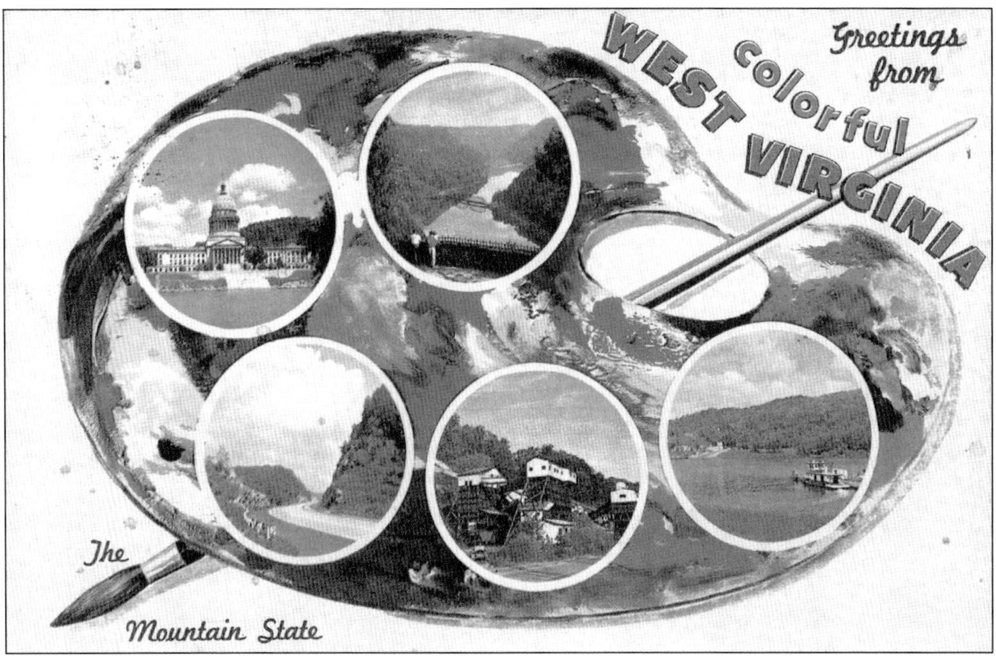

PALETTE OF THE MOUNTAIN STATE. Clockwise from upper left are the West Virginia State Capitol Building in Charleston, a view of New River Canyon from Hawk's Nest, an Ohio River ferry, a coal mining scene, and a curve on the West Virginia Turnpike.

Two

TALCOTT

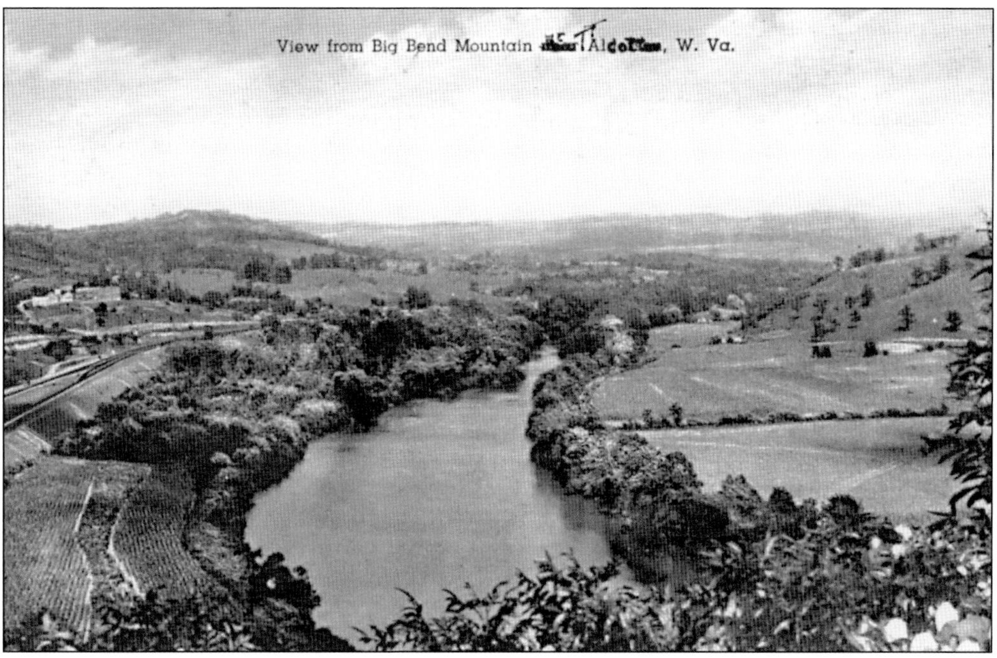

VIEW OF TALCOTT, WEST VIRGINIA, FROM BIG BEND MOUNTAIN. Photographer Richard Ford was a member of the Ford family of medical fame. Big Bend was the mountain through which the Great Bend Tunnel (also called the Big Bend Tunnel) was drilled at the cost of so many lives. (Courtesy of Margaret Martin.)

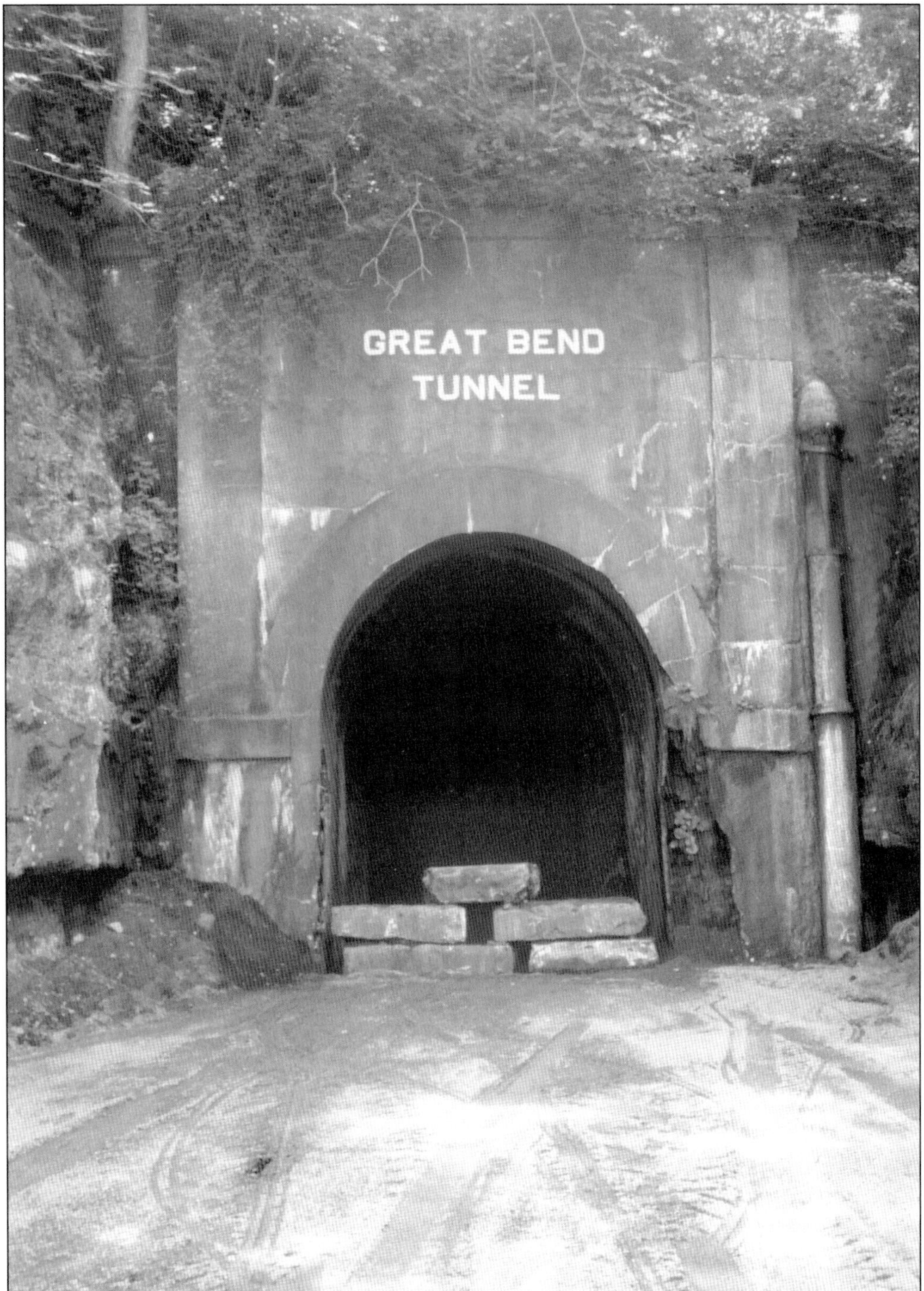

GREAT BEND TUNNEL, TALCOTT. The Great Bend Tunnel of the C&O Railroad was started in 1870 and completed three years later. It is over a mile long and is the setting of the ballad *John Henry—The Steel-Drivin' Man*. It was here that John Henry defeated the steam drill. (Courtesy of Margaret Martin.)

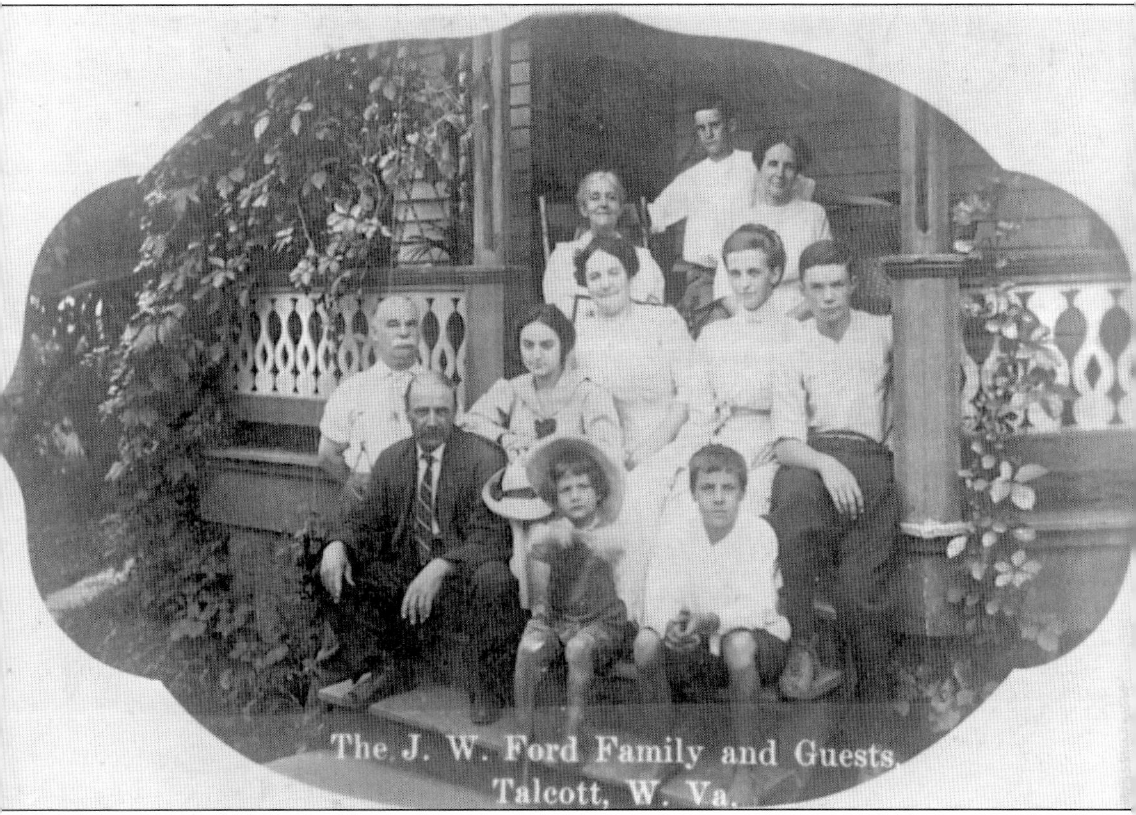

DR. JAMES WALLER FORD FAMILY AND GUESTS. Pictured from left to right are (first row) Dr. J. W. Ford; Jim Ford; and Bob Ford; (second row) Silver Gloss Gilfillan; Margaret Ford; Mrs. Lena Ford; Miss Margaret Moncure; and Bill Ford; (third row) Mrs. Knight, who is the mother of Mrs. Ford and Mrs. Hepburn; George Hepburn; and Mrs. Minnie Hepburn. The elder Dr. Ford was killed by his horse. (Courtesy of Margaret Martin.)

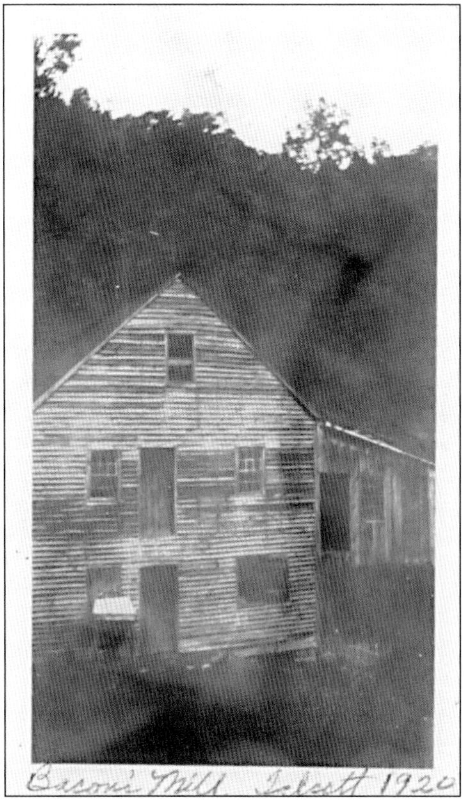

BACON'S MILL, TALCOTT. One of the first buildings to be built at Rollinsburg was Fluke's Mill, later to be known as Bacon's Mill. This picture shows the second mill, rebuilt around 1853 after a fire. The image comes from the Memorabilia Room in Talcott. (Courtesy of John Kesler.)

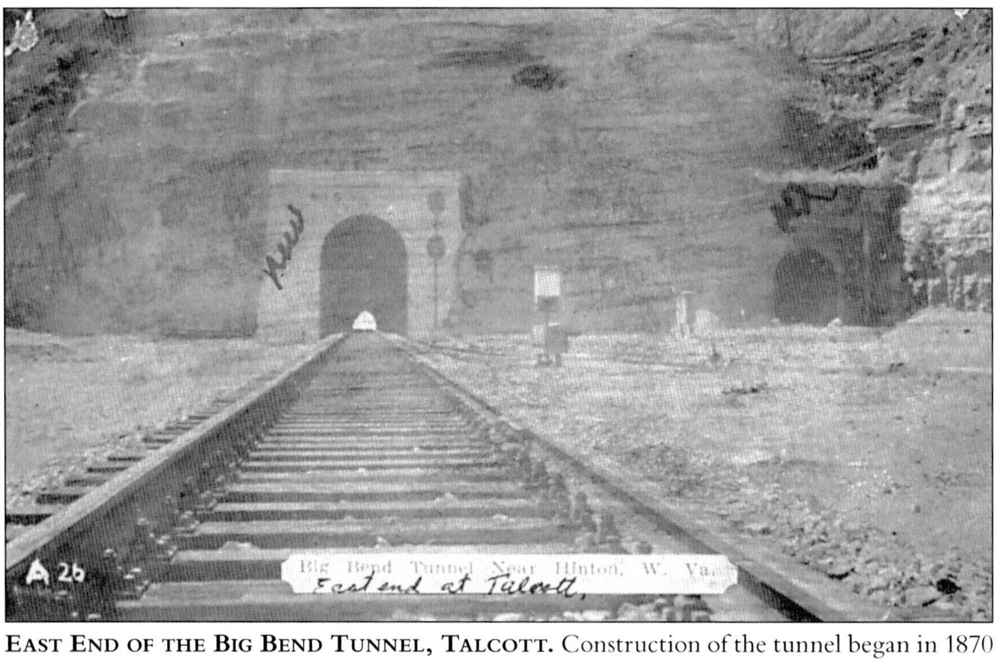

EAST END OF THE BIG BEND TUNNEL, TALCOTT. Construction of the tunnel began in 1870 and proceeded from both ends and from three shafts. Steam engines of 30 horsepower were used for hoisting out debris. This image is from the brochure created by the John Henry Days Committee. (Courtesy of Margaret Martin.)

TUNNEL ENTRANCE. This is believed to be the entrance to the Little Bend Tunnel. (Courtesy of John Kesler and Margaret Martin.)

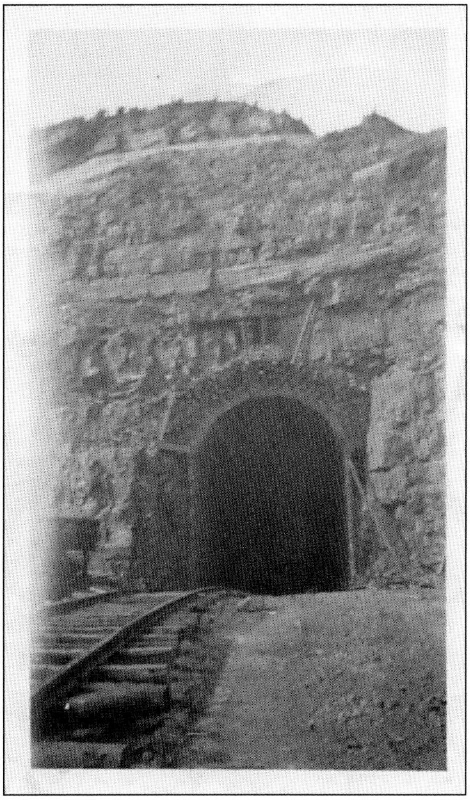

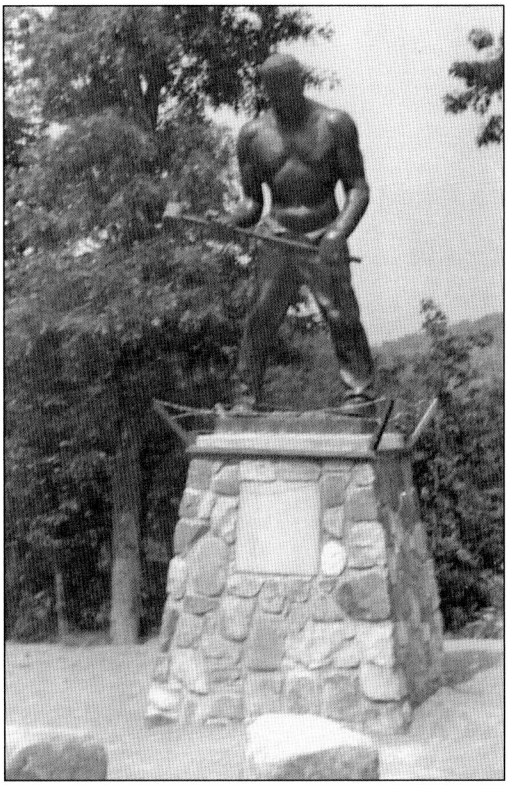

STATUE OF JOHN HENRY, THE STEEL-DRIVIN' MAN. The bronze statue of John Henry has recently been painted black to cover the scars of vandalism. (Courtesy of Dot Turman.)

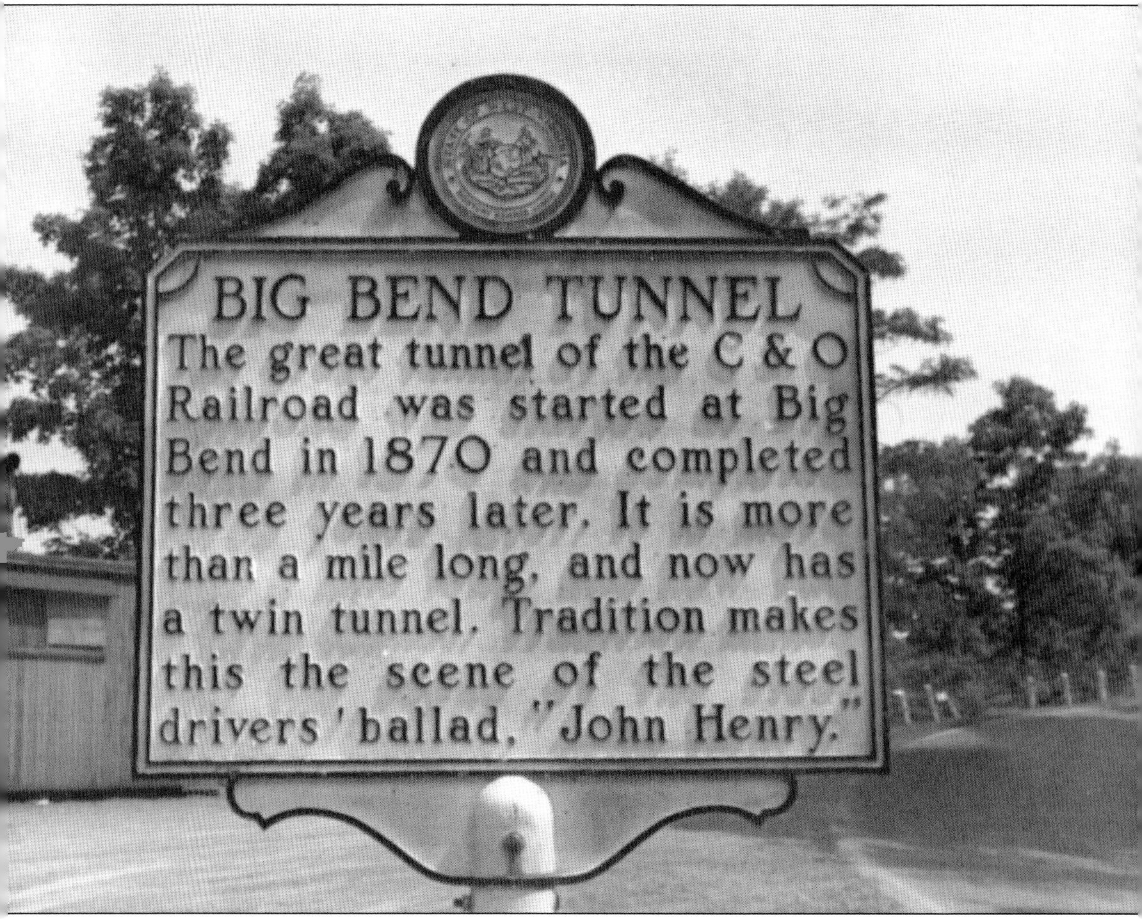

HISTORICAL HIGHWAY MARKER NEAR TALCOTT. More than one mile of red shale was cleared through Big Bend Mountain for the tunnel. Driving steel by hand was dangerous, and reports say that one in five men was killed as rock crashed down upon them. (Courtesy of Dot Turman.)

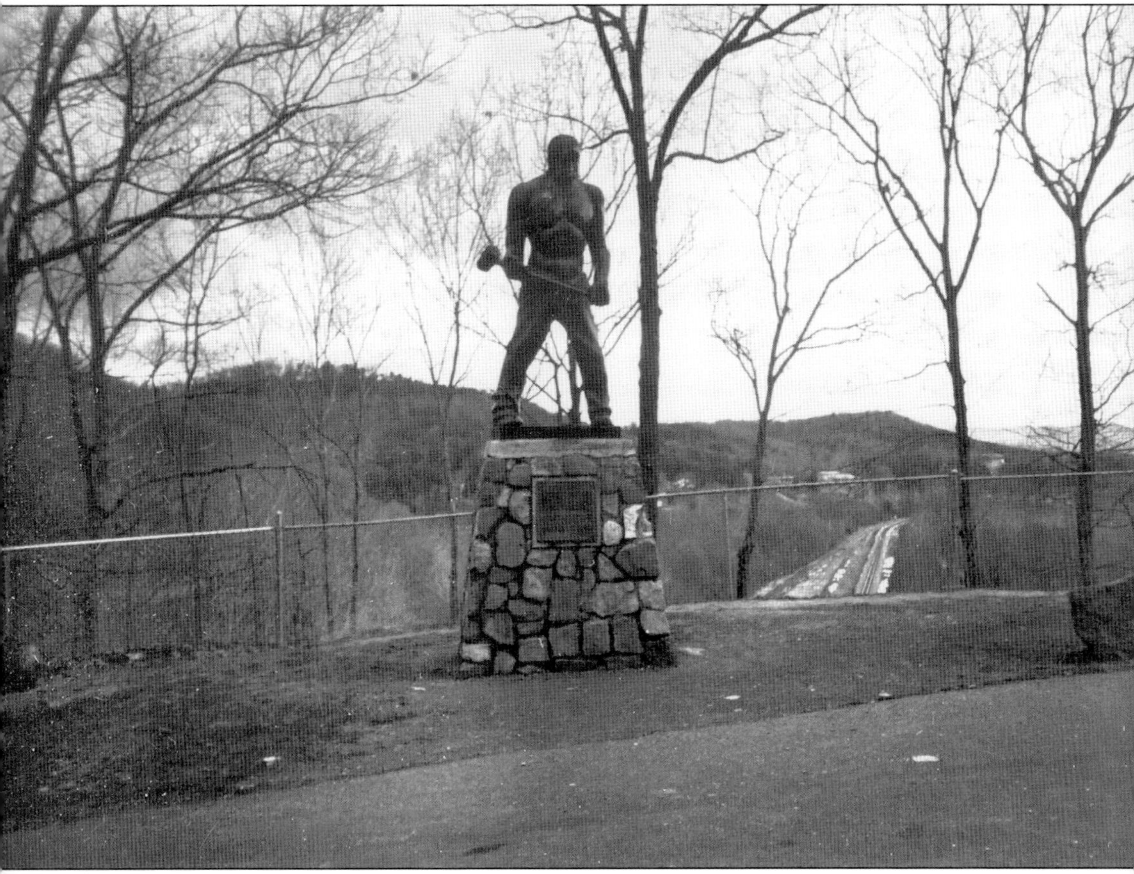

JOHN HENRY STATUE AT NIGHT. The statue has been vandalized many times, but it is still standing because of the rescue efforts of the people of Talcott. (Courtesy of Dot Turman.)

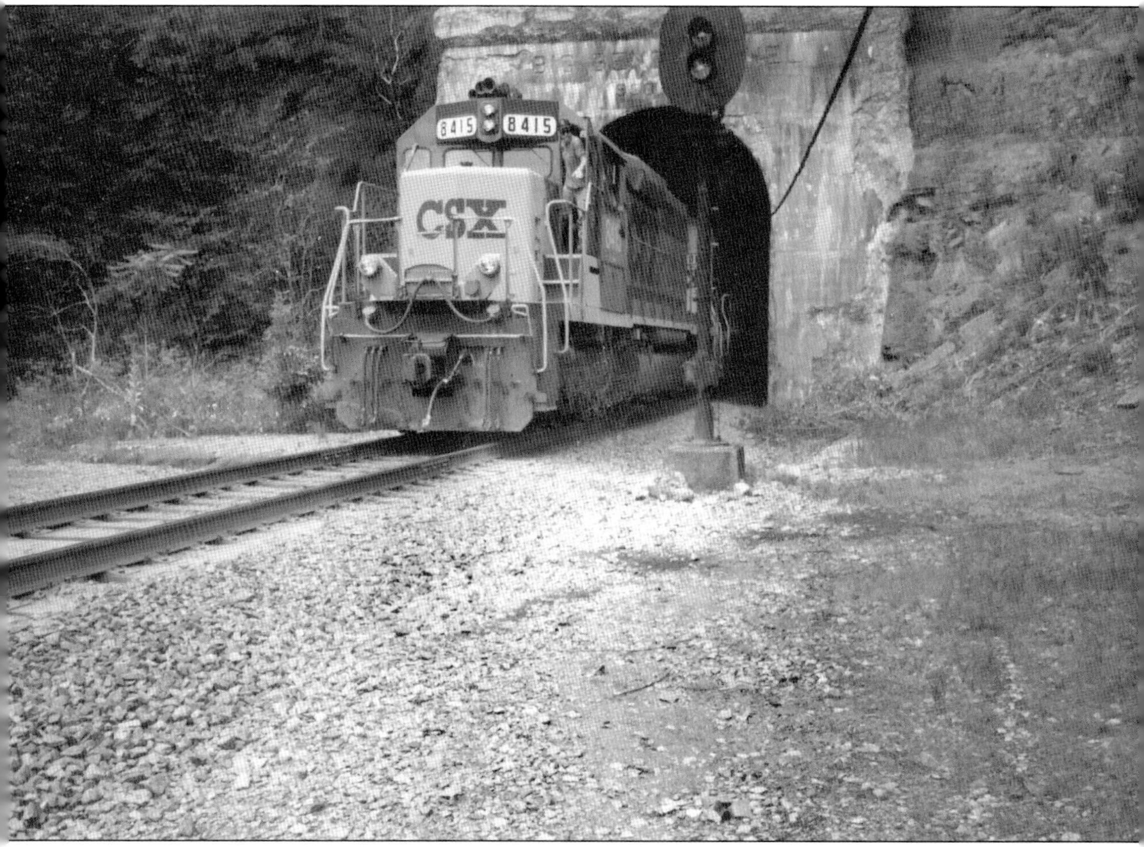

CSX LOCOMOTIVE. Emerging from the Big Bend Tunnel for a photograph during the first John Henry Days celebration in Talcott in 1996, this train brings back memories. (Courtesy of Margaret Martin.)

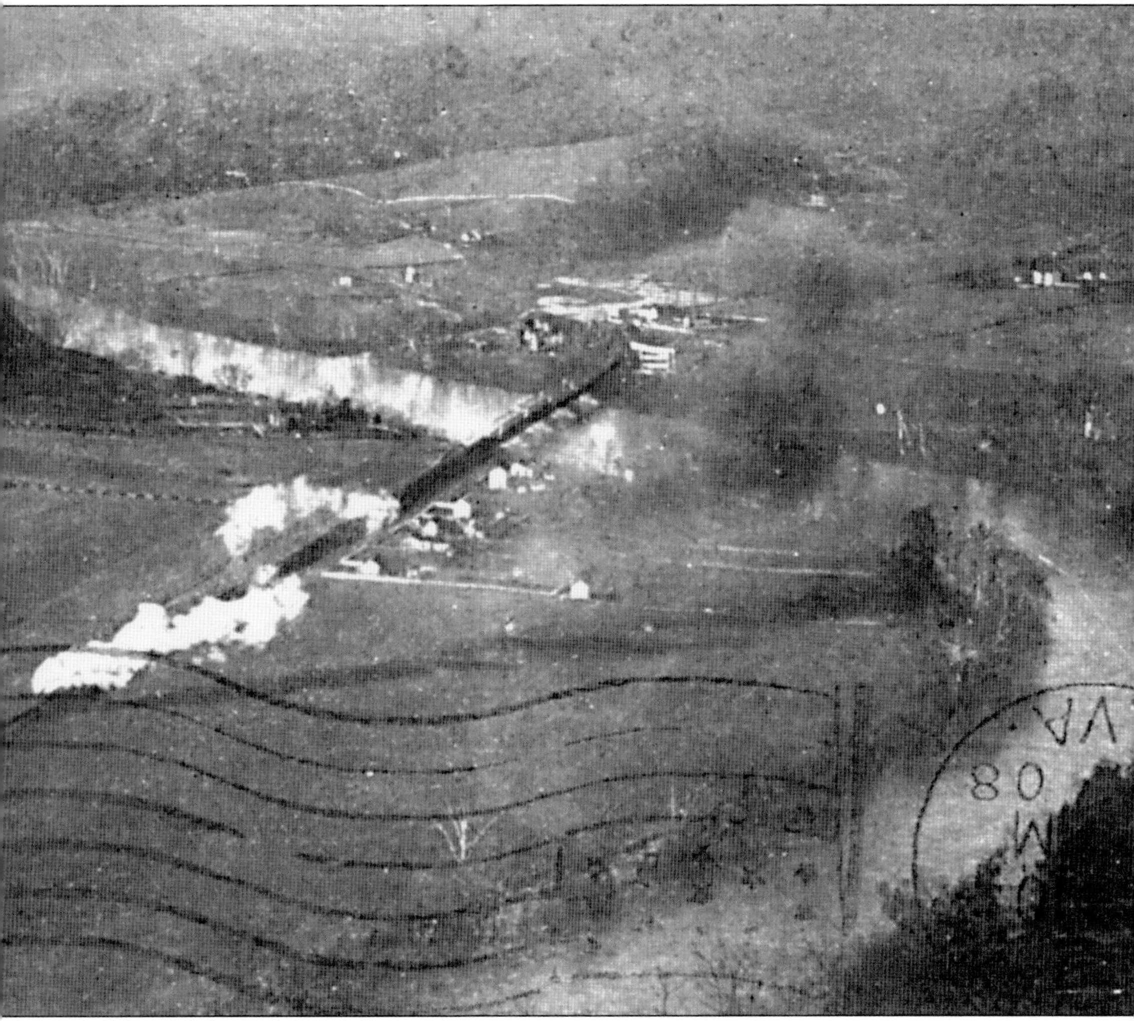

AN AERIAL VIEW OF LOWELL. Lowell is the oldest community in Summers County. Some pioneer names were Graham, Gwinn, See, VanBibber, Keller, and Hinchman. Lowell was once the terminal for the stagecoach to Red Sulphur Springs. (Courtesy of Margaret Martin.)

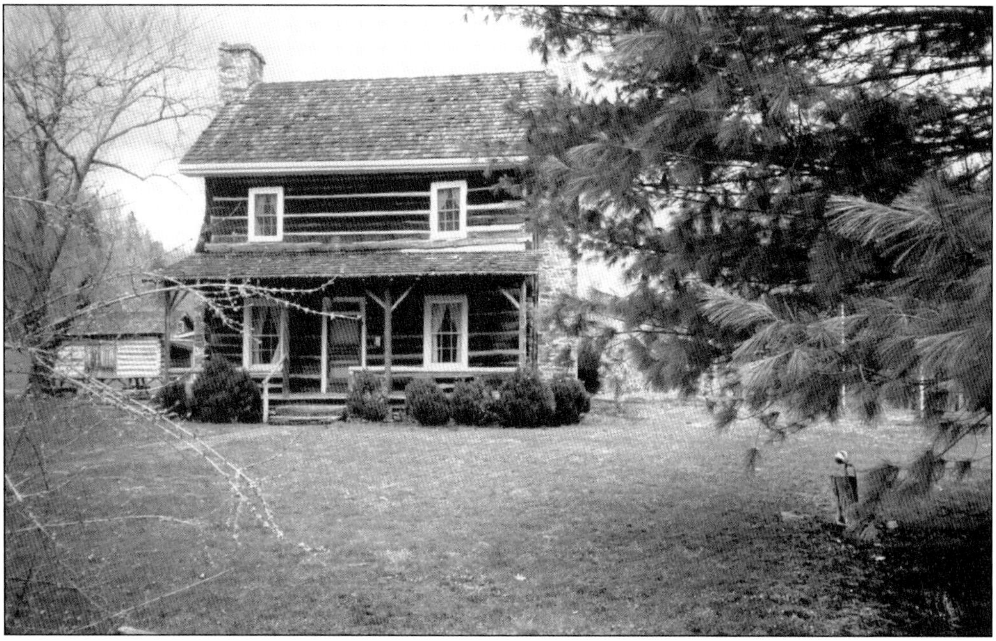

GRAHAM HOUSE, LOWELL. The Graham House is one of the oldest and most historic homes in West Virginia. It is a three-story log house built by Col. James Graham in 1772. The home is on the National Register of Historic Places. (Courtesy of Dot Turman.)

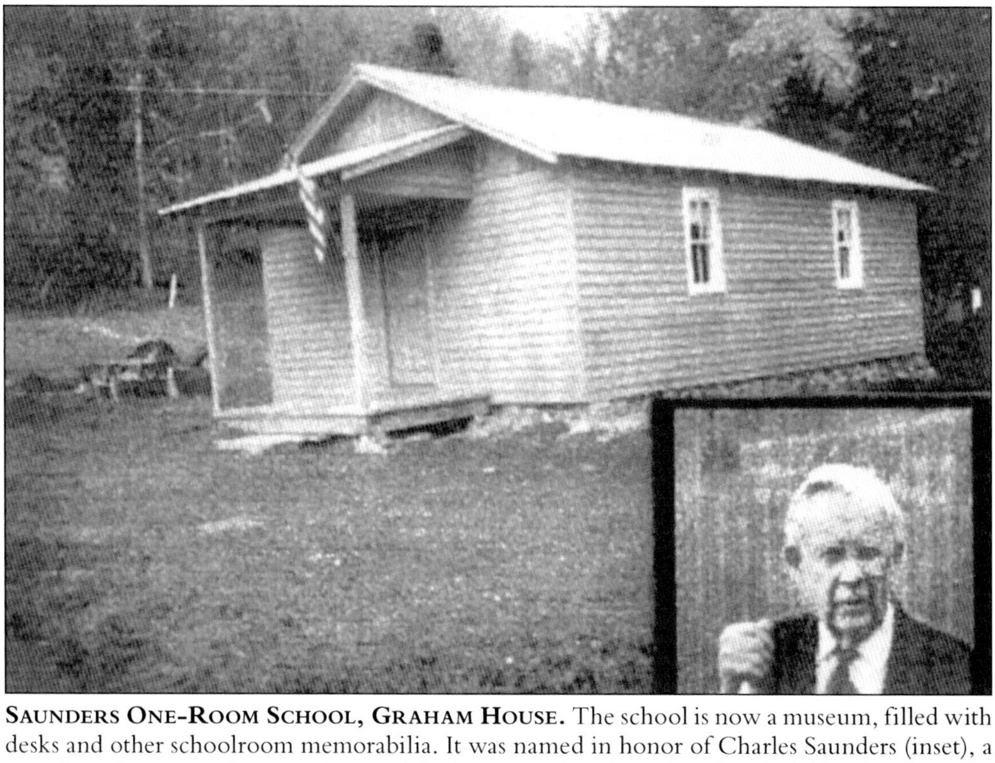

SAUNDERS ONE-ROOM SCHOOL, GRAHAM HOUSE. The school is now a museum, filled with desks and other schoolroom memorabilia. It was named in honor of Charles Saunders (inset), a prominent Summers County educator. The image is taken from the school's dedication program. (Courtesy of Margaret Martin.)

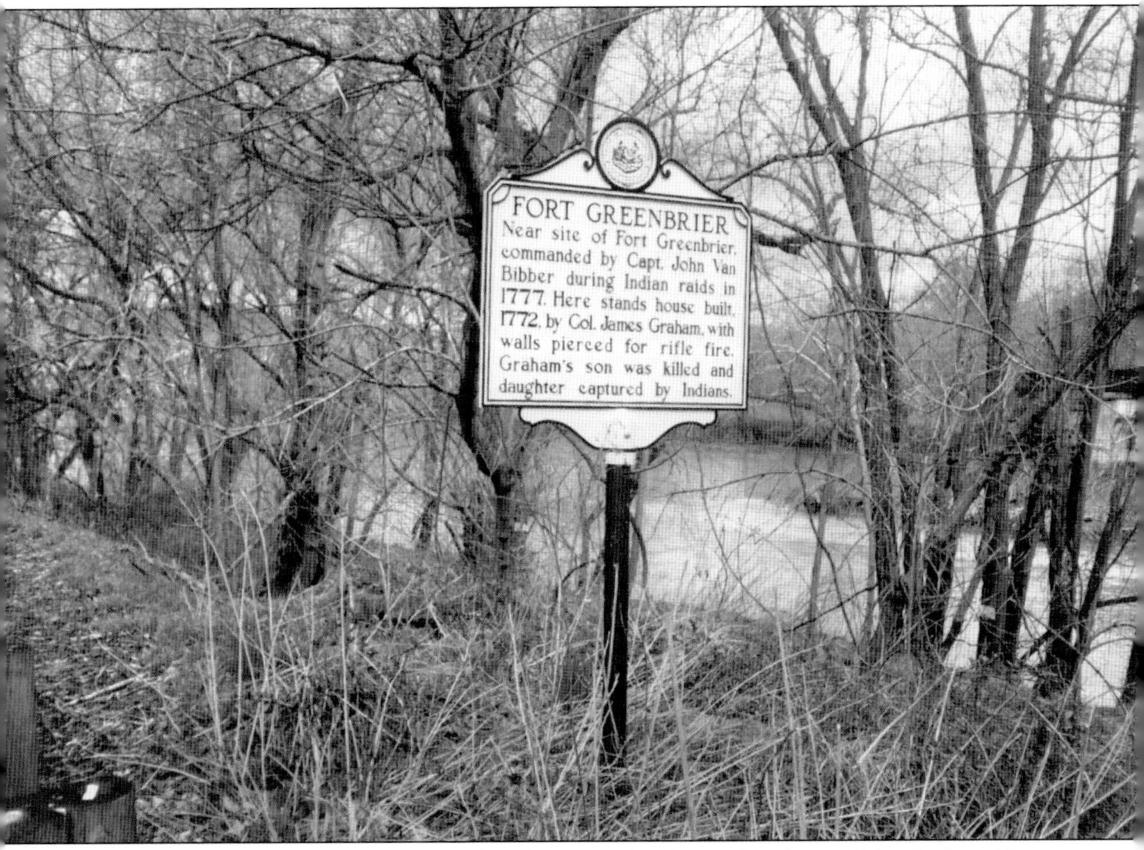

HISTORICAL MARKER. This historical highway marker located in front of the Graham House at Lowell notes the site of Fort Greenbrier during Native American raids in 1777. (Courtesy of Dot Turman.)

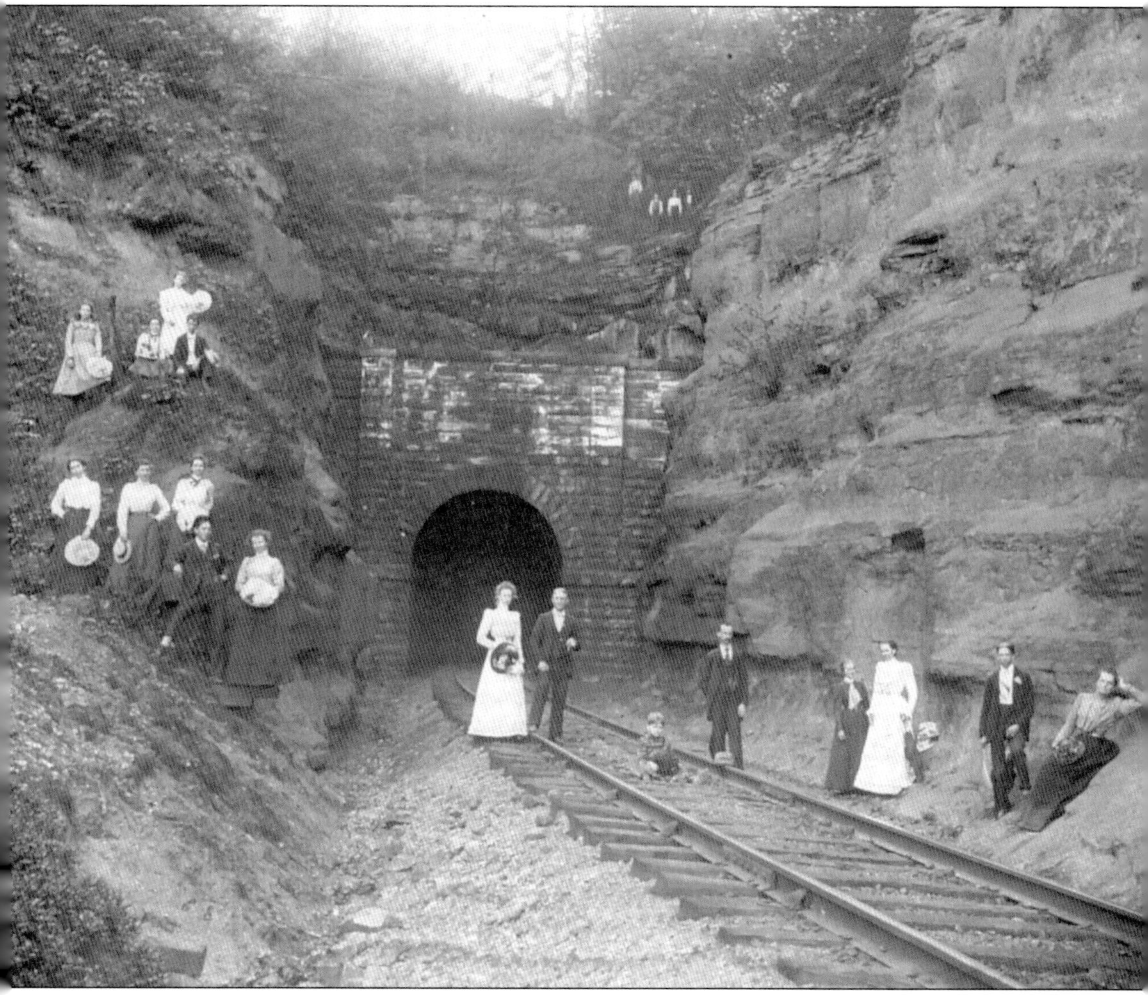

NEIGHBORHOOD GROUP, GREAT BEND TUNNEL, *c.* 1900. Pictured here from left to right are (at the top of the hill) Rosa Jones, Rena Jones, Fannie Huston Rhodes, and unidentified; (farther down the hill) three unidentified women, one unidentified man, and Amy Jones Miller; (on the track) Maggie Jones Eades, an unidentified man, and an unidentified child; (on the side of the track) F. W. Jones, Nora Gillespie Lively, Edna Keaton, unidentified, and Carrie Hill Grimes Howell. (Courtesy of Margaret Martin.)

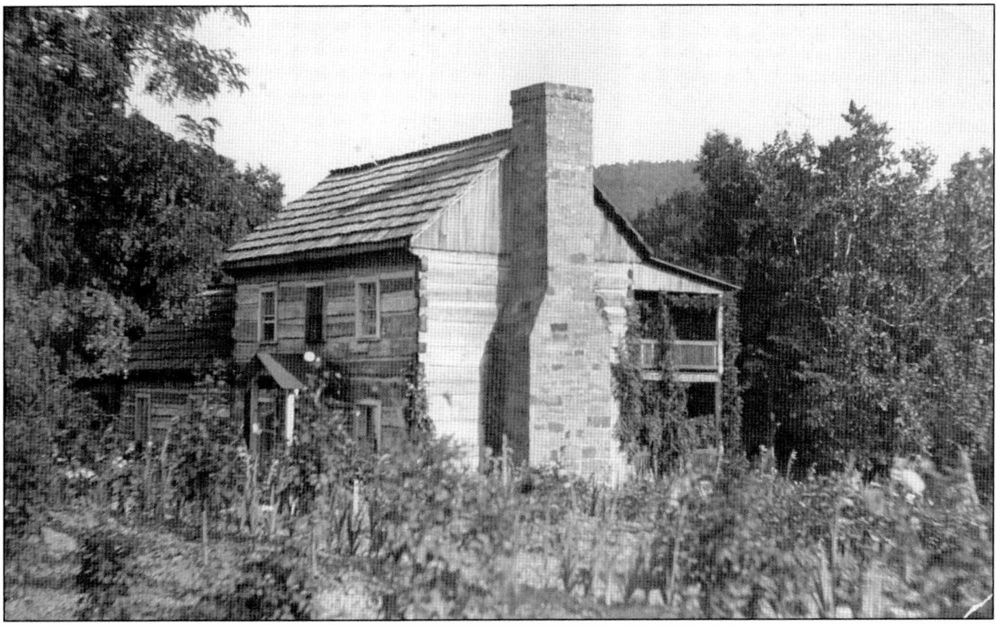

GILLESPIE HOME. Arrowheads were found in the walls of this old home when it was torn down. Sarah Alderson Woodson, great-grandmother of John Kesler, lived and died in this house. (Published by Gem Studios, Beckley, West Virginia; courtesy of John Kesler.)

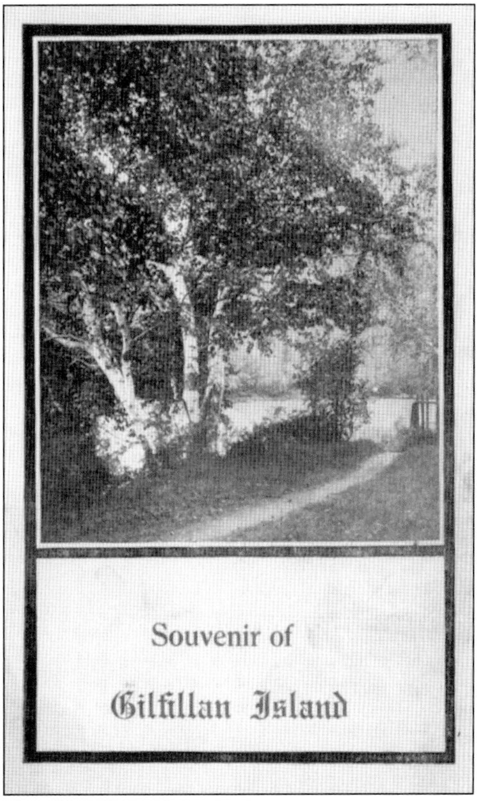

GILFILLAN ISLAND. S. G. Gilfillan was a businessman who had a home and a store on the island. Gilfillan's son-in-law, a Mr. Davis, was the next owner of the island. (Courtesy of Margaret Martin.)

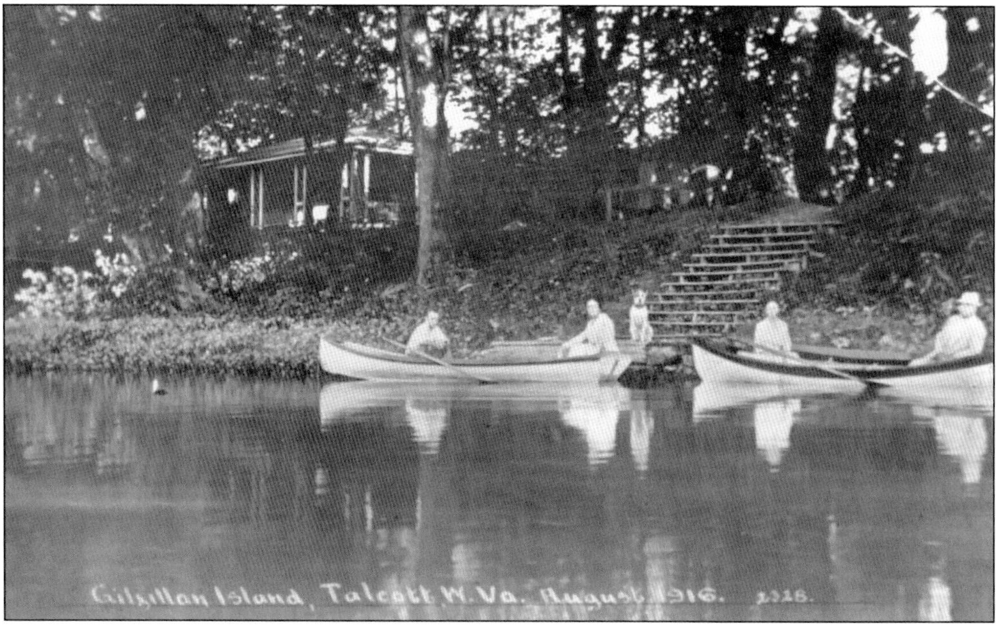

Boating Party on Gilfillan Island. Note the nice cabins and the steps leading up to land. The card is dated 1916. (Courtesy of Margaret Martin.)

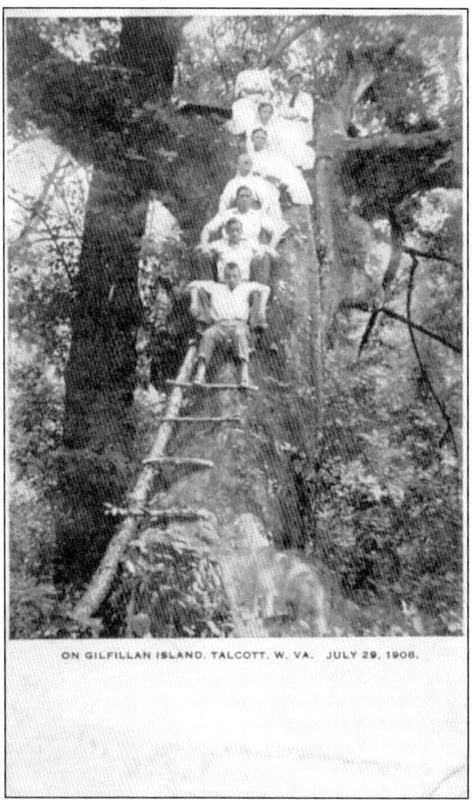

A Group of Young People on Gilfillan Island. Cross your fingers and hope that ladder holds. The message on the card reads, "Please quote me by return mail correct possible prices by mail on 1 dozen or 1/2 dozen white watch fobs." It is signed, "Silver Gloss Gilfillan." (Courtesy of Memorabilia Room in Talcott.)

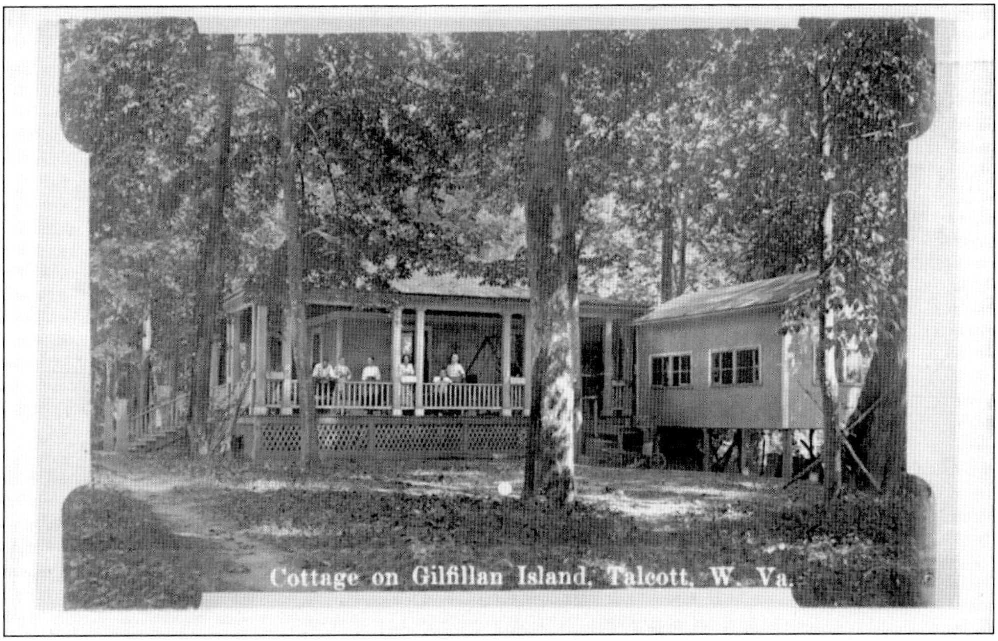

COTTAGE ON GILFILLAN ISLAND. The island was full of cottages, homes, and summer camps. Some of the visitors came from Ohio. (Courtesy of Margaret Martin.)

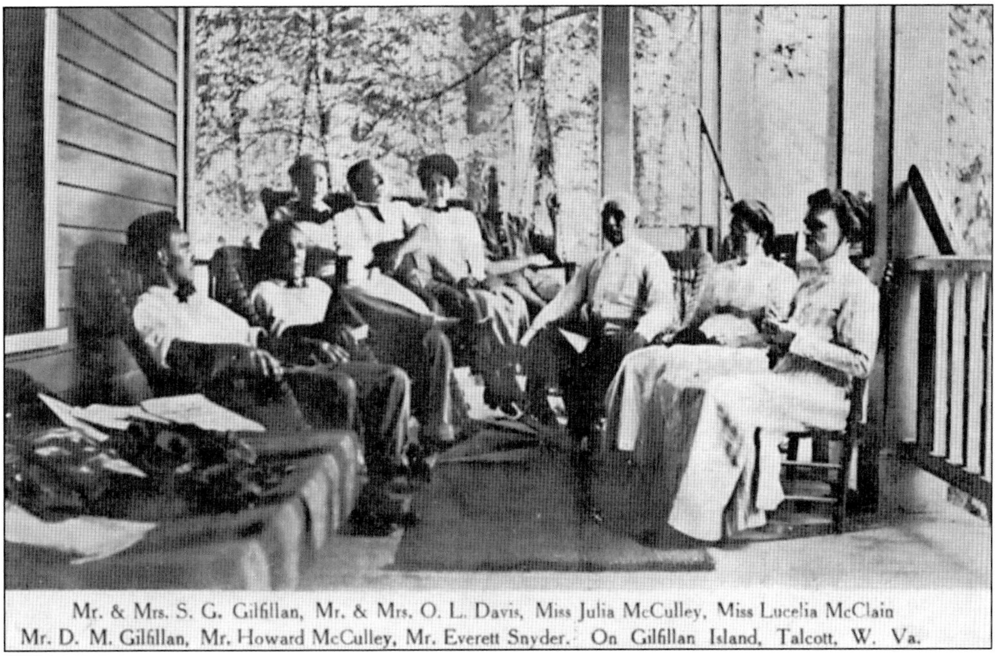

HOUSE PARTY AT THE S. G. GILFILLANS' HOME. The guests' names, in no particular order, are Mr. and Mrs. S. G. Gilfillan, Mr. and Mrs. O. L. Davis, Miss Julia McCulley, Miss Lucelia McClajn, Mr. D. M. Gilfillan, Mr. Howard McCulley, and Mr. Everett Snyder. (Courtesy of Margaret Martin.)

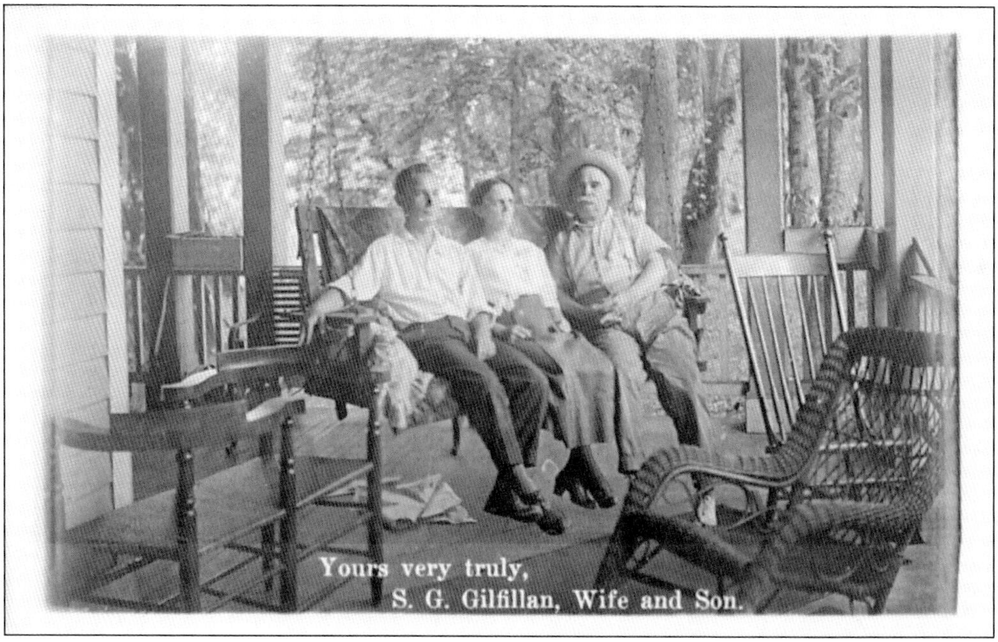

MR. SILVER GLOSS GILFILLAN, WIFE, SON. The Gilfillans owned the island and lived there year-round. They were active in the community life of Talcott. (Courtesy of Margaret Martin.)

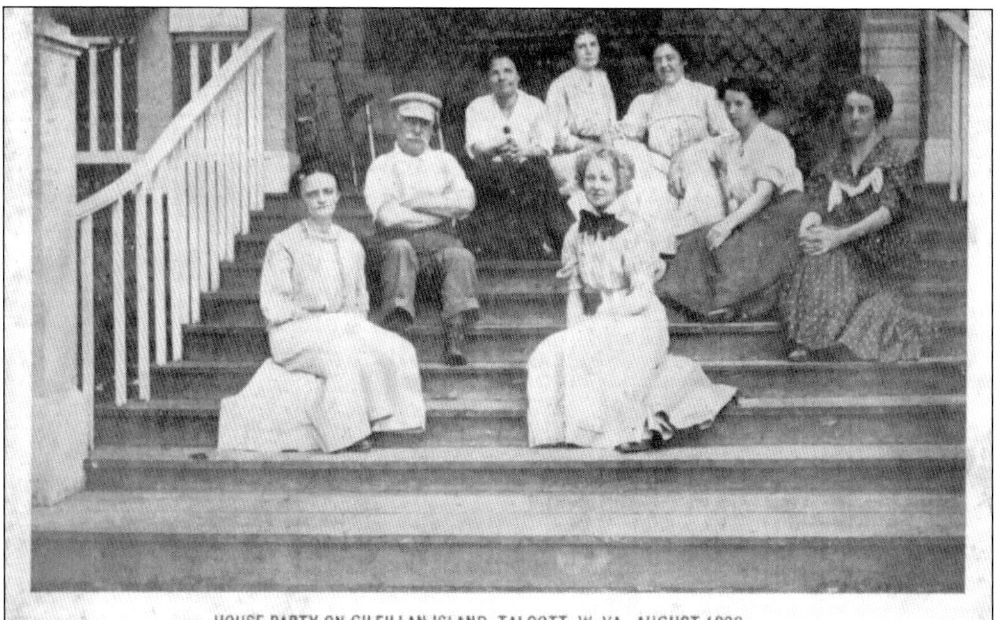

HOUSE PARTY ON GILFILLAN ISLAND, 1909. The guests are not identified except for S. G. Gilfillan, the gentleman sitting second from left. (Courtesy of Margaret Martin.)

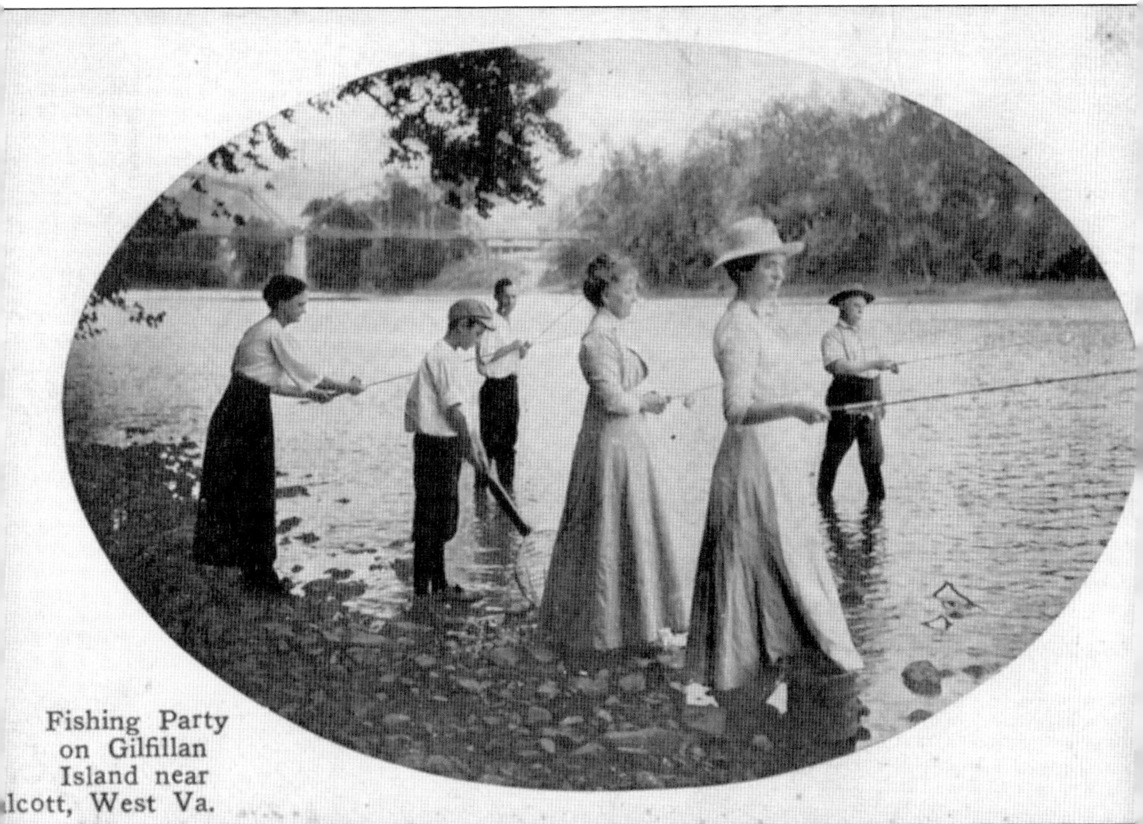

FISHING PARTY ON GILFILLAN ISLAND. The people are unidentified except for Mr. Gilfillan, the gentleman farthest out in the water. He was the owner of the island. Note the bridge and the cabin in the background. (Courtesy of Margaret Martin.)

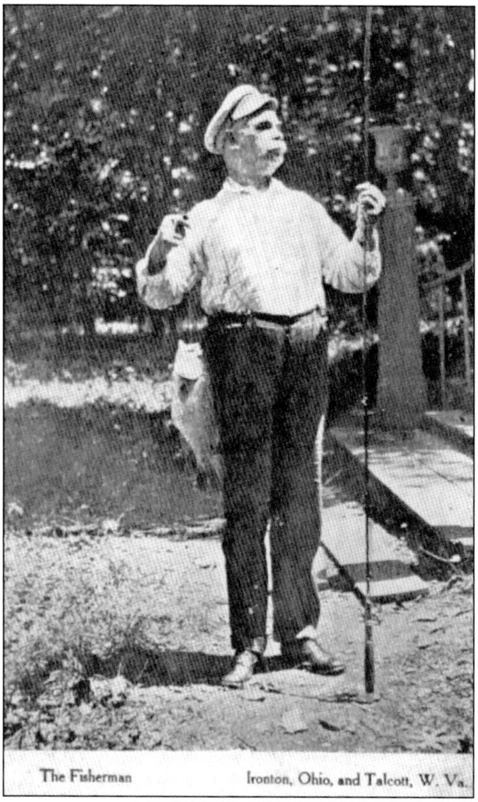

THE PROUD FISHERMAN. S. G. Gilfillan of Ironton, Ohio, and Talcott, West Virginia, loved to fish and boat off his own island. It looks like this fish is a "keeper." (Courtesy of Margaret Martin.)

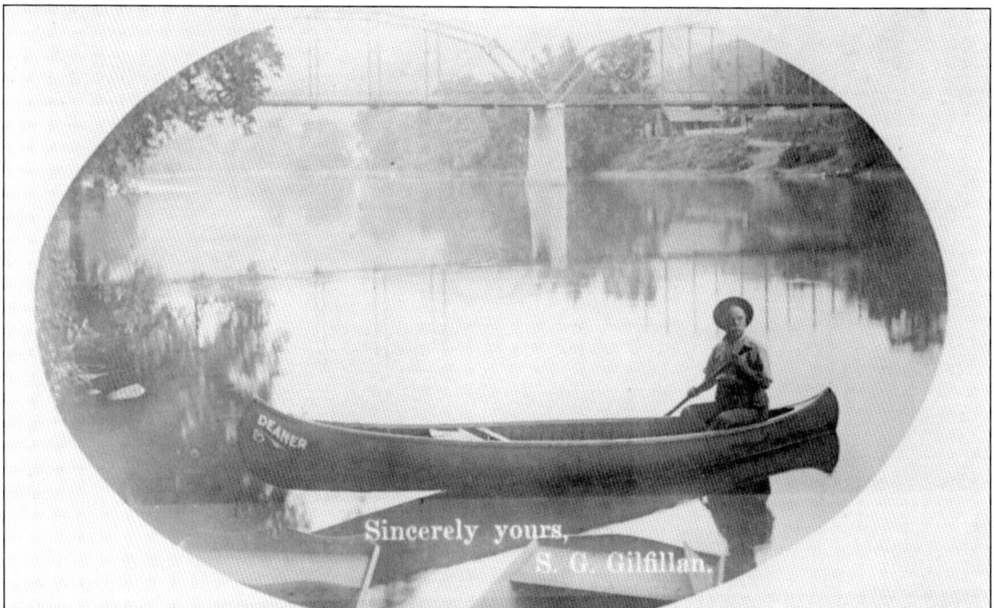

S. G. GILFILLAN, BOATING OFF HIS ISLAND. Note the bridge and the cabins in the distance. The oval format of this card was very popular. (Courtesy of Margaret Martin.)

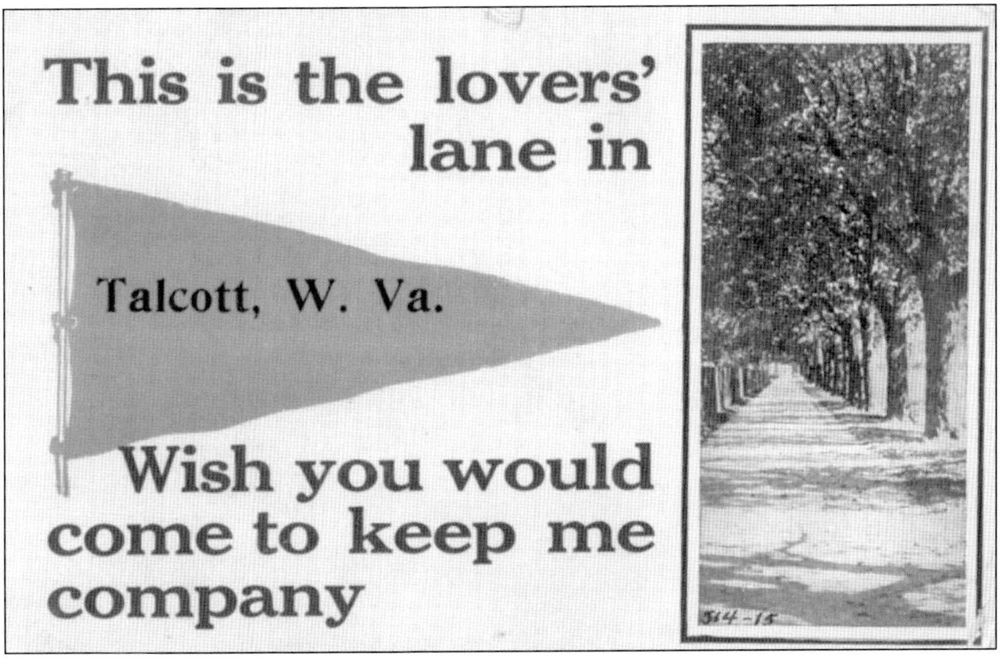

TALCOTT, WEST VIRGINIA—A FUN PLACE TO BE. Also the rage were generic postcards with sayings that would be funny anywhere. People used postcards to send pictures of their children to their relatives and to advertise products and/or businesses. (Courtesy of Margaret Martin.)

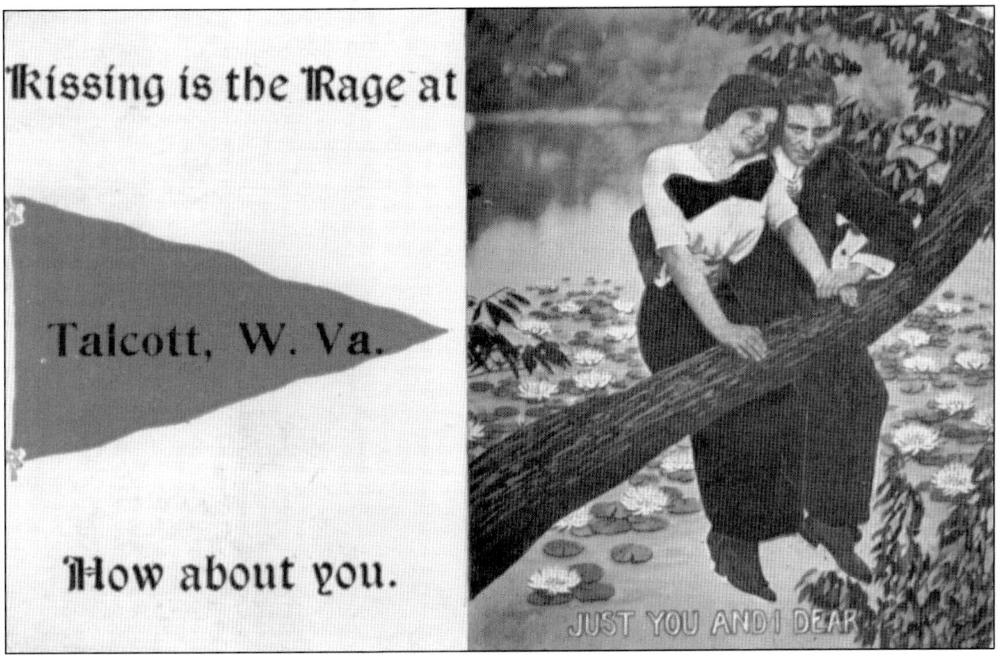

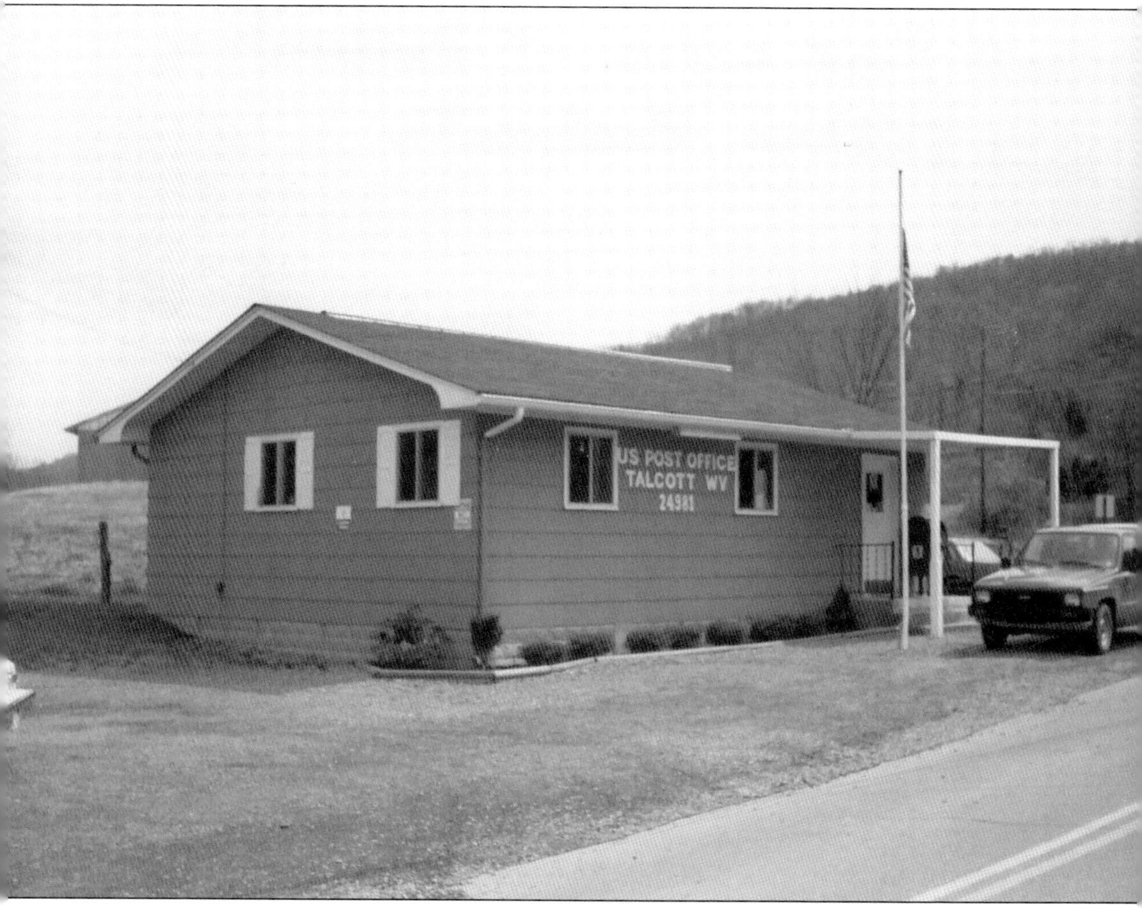

FORMER TALCOTT POST OFFICE IN ROLLINSBURG. This post office served the community during the years of 1973 to 1991. Bill Dillon was postmaster at the time this building went up. It was built on the site of the old W. W. Jones Store. It has since been torn down. (Courtesy of John Kesler.)

Three

C&O Railroad

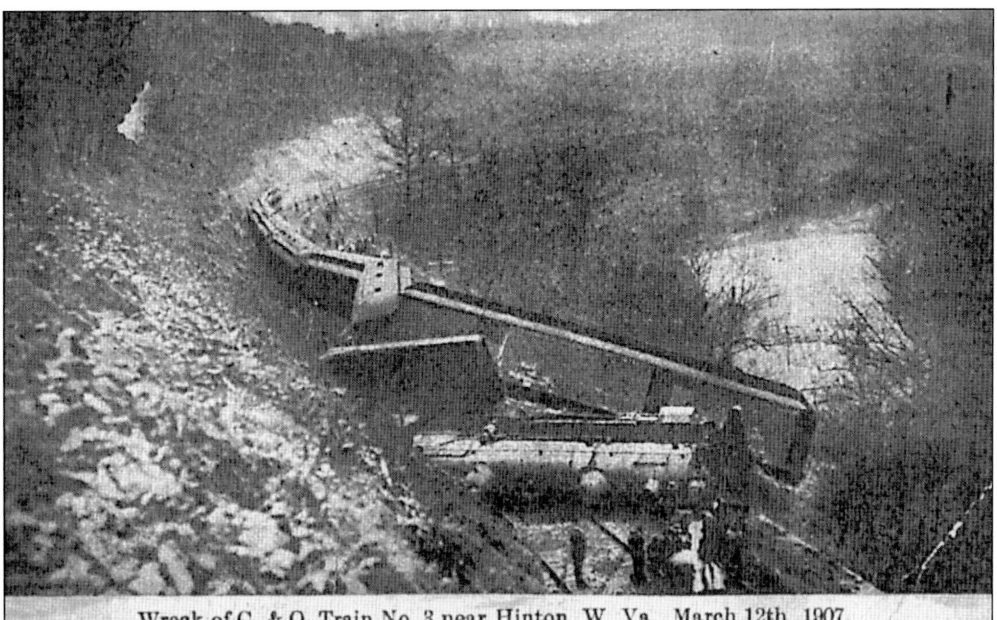

Wreck of C&O Train No. 8 at Hinton. One of the worst accidents to happen to the C&O Railroad in its history happened on March 12, 1907. (Courtesy of James Pettry and Betty Cooper.)

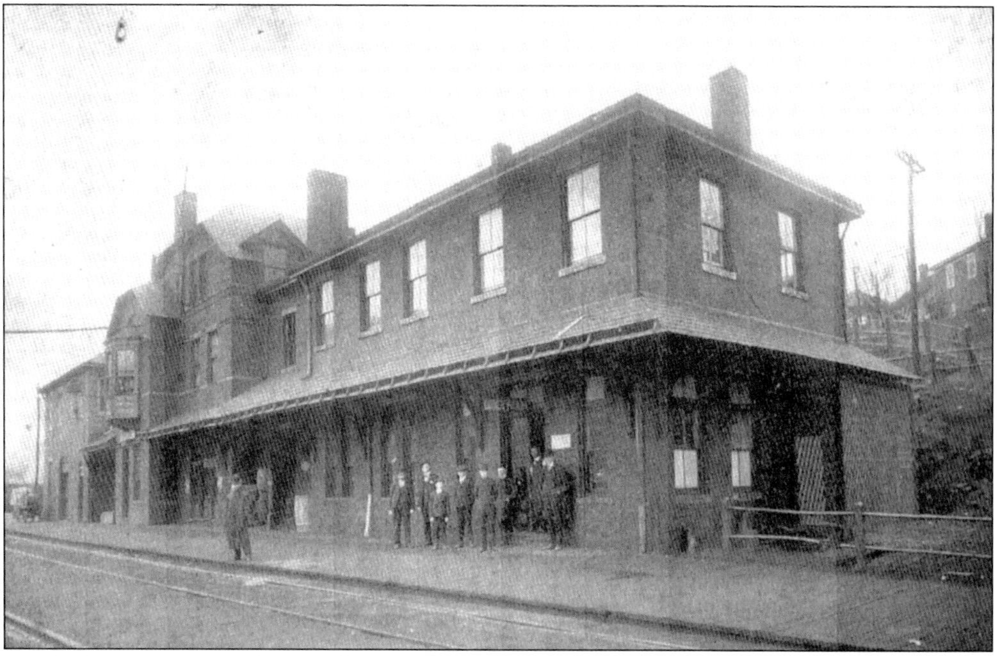

C&O Depot. Shown here is the C&O Railroad Depot in 1900 in Hinton, West Virginia. (Courtesy of Betty Cooper.)

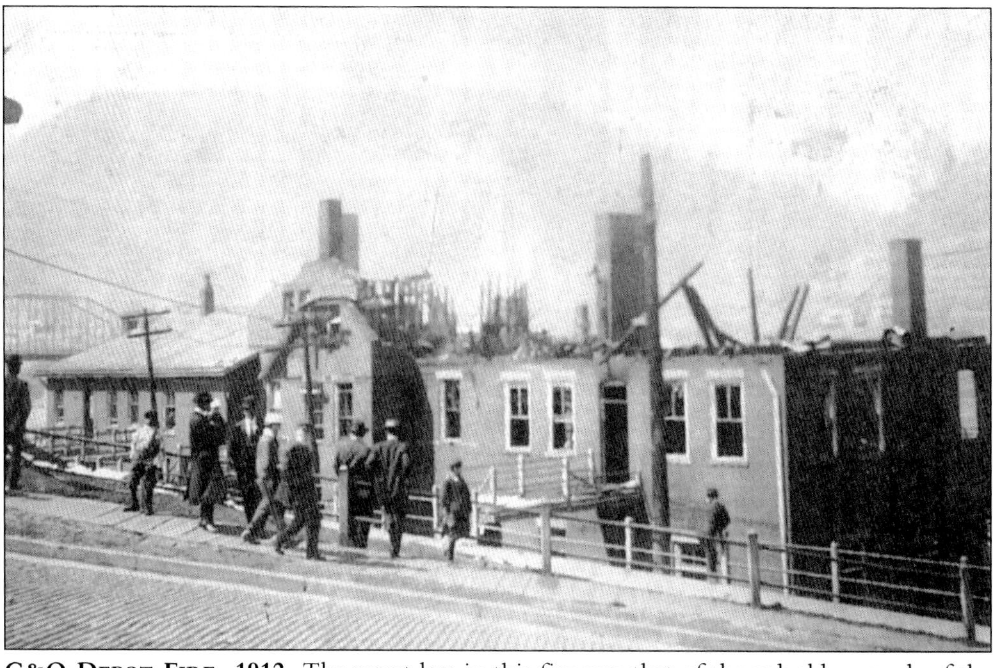

C&O Depot Fire, 1912. The worst loss in this fire was that of the valuable records of the C&O Railroad. The trainmaster's office and the baggage room were destroyed. (Courtesy of Betty Cooper.)

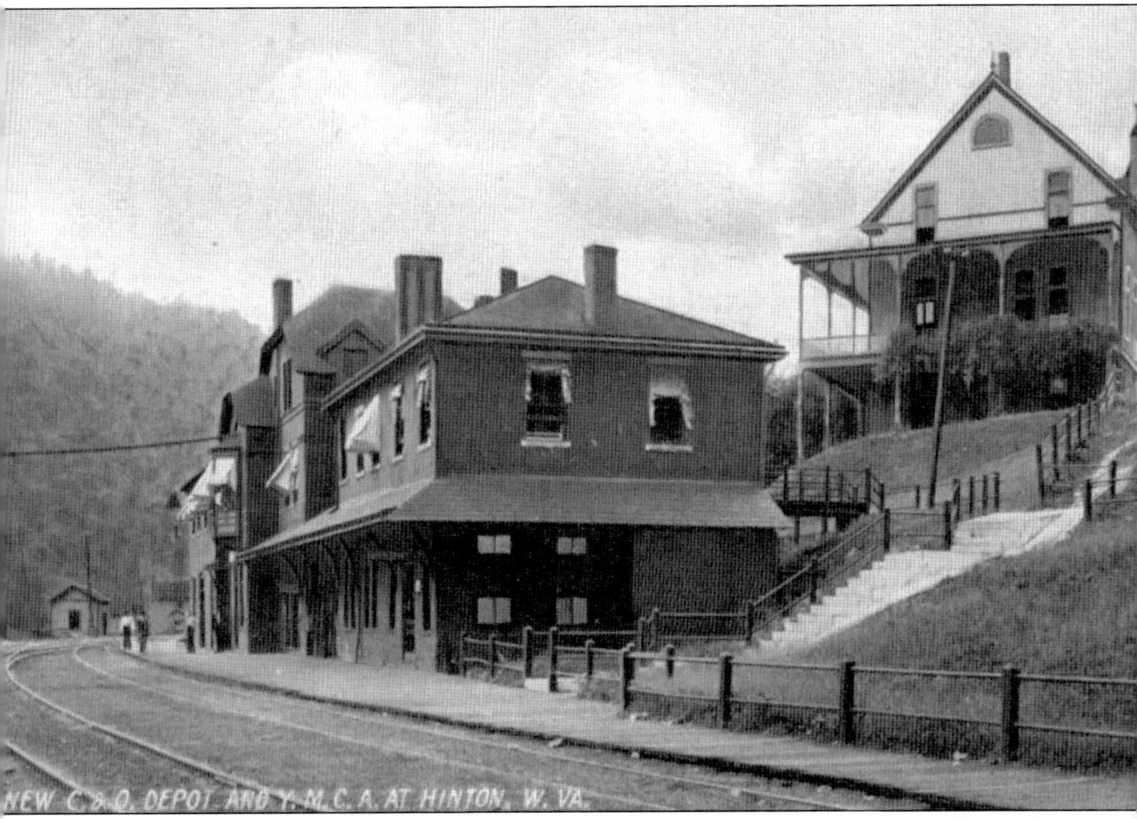

YMCA AND TRAIN STATION, C&O RAILROAD. The YMCA opened in 1891 and burned in 1911. This is the rebuilt building. This is still an active Amtrak passenger station. (Courtesy of James Pettry and Betty Cooper.)

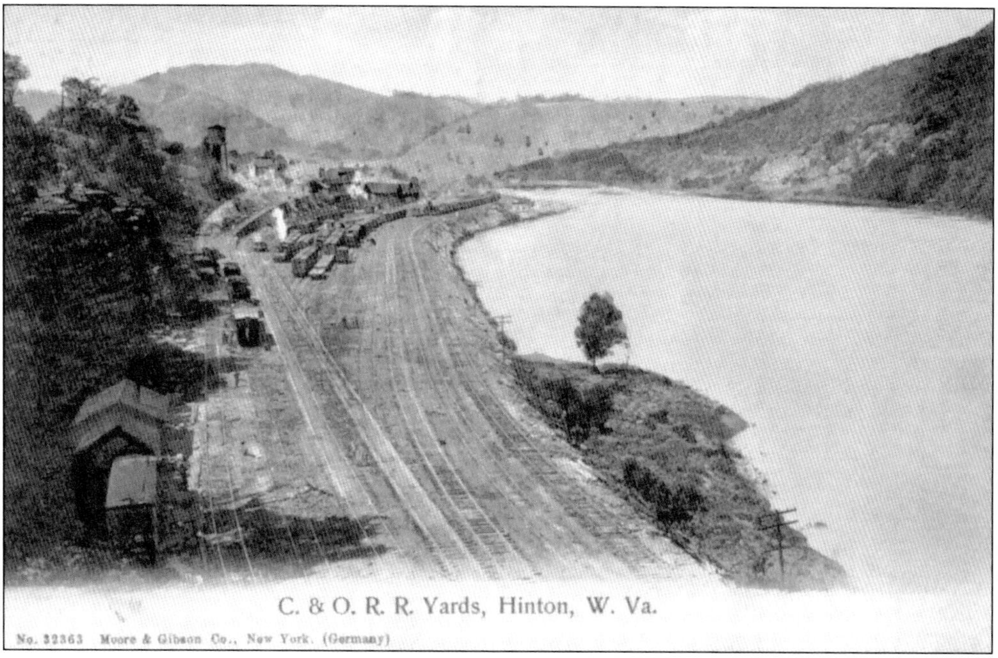

C&O RAILROAD YARDS, HINTON, WEST VIRGINIA. In March 1873, Hinton was selected as a division terminal and maintenance site. Hinton was a good location for the C&O, and the C&O was good for Hinton. The railroad was responsible for making Hinton the important railroad town it was. (Courtesy of Margaret Martin.)

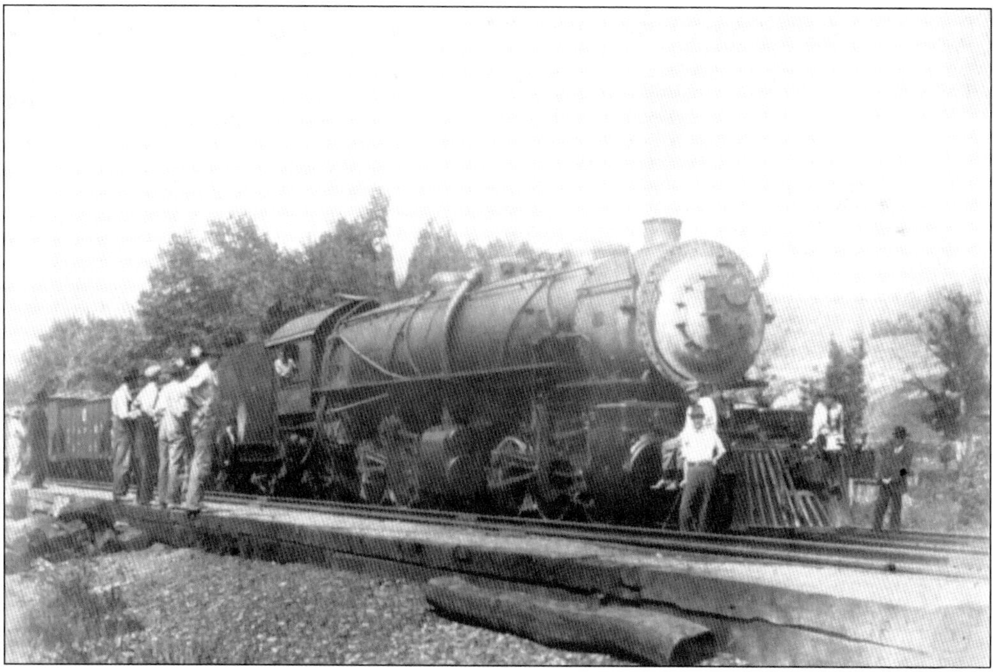

NEW ENGINE FOR THE C&O RAILROAD. This picture was taken at Talcott, West Virginia. Ben M. Marable was the engineer. (Courtesy of Margaret Martin.)

Four

Bluestone Dam

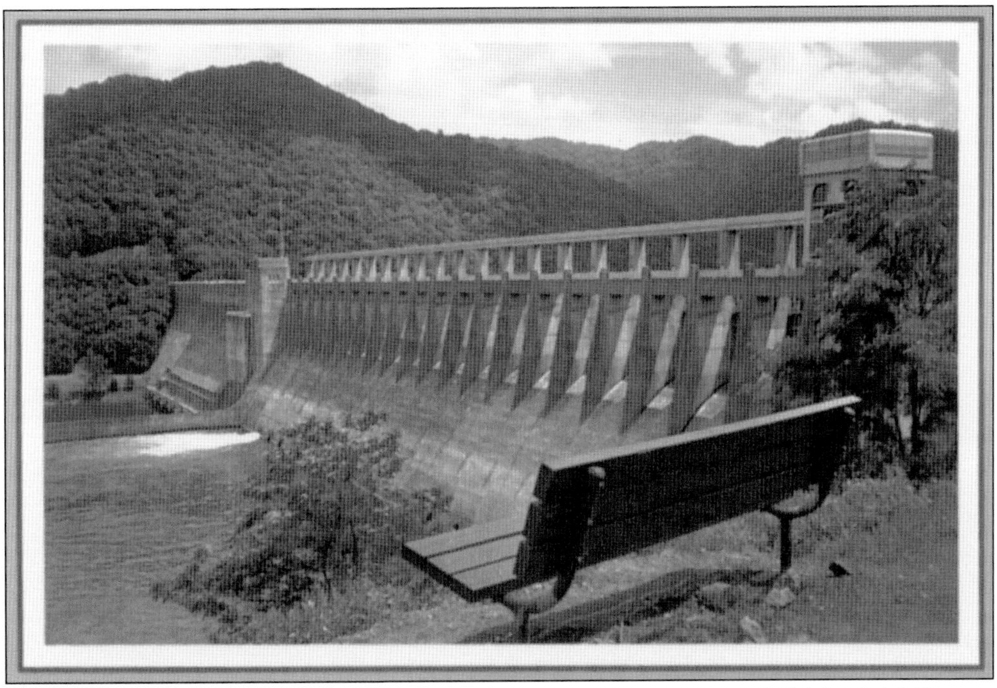

South of Hinton, West Virginia. On Route 20, Bluestone Dam holds back 1,860 acres of water. It rises 165 feet above the stream. (Published by Paige Creations, Morgantown, West Virginia; 1-304-599-0745.)

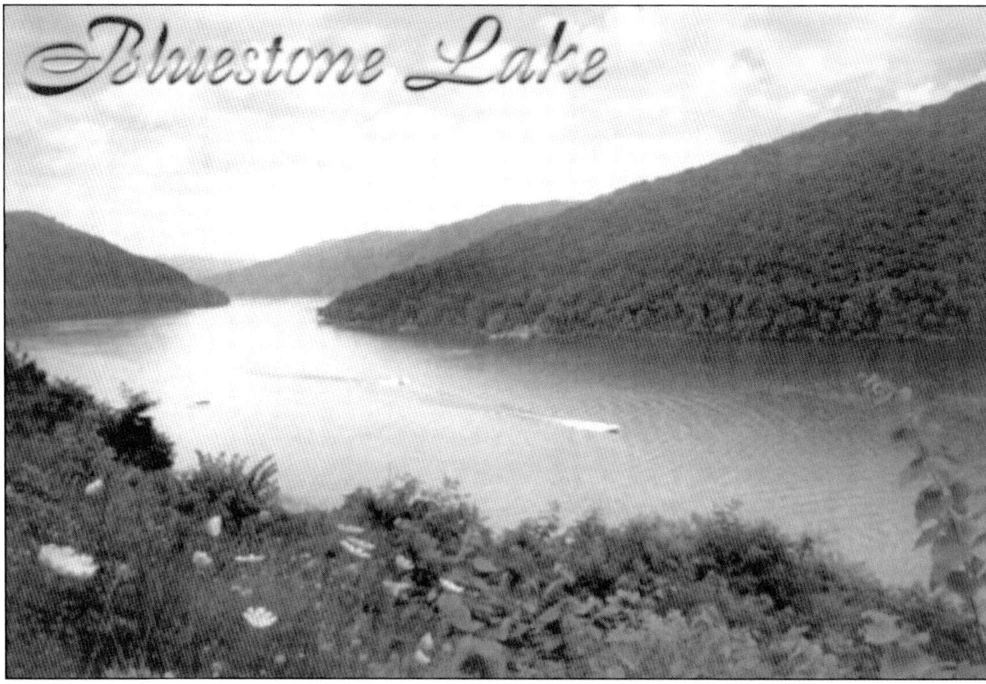

BLUESTONE LAKE. Located near Pipestem and Bluestone State Parks, Bluestone Lake is the third largest lake in West Virginia, covering 1,800 acres.(Published by Paige Creations.)

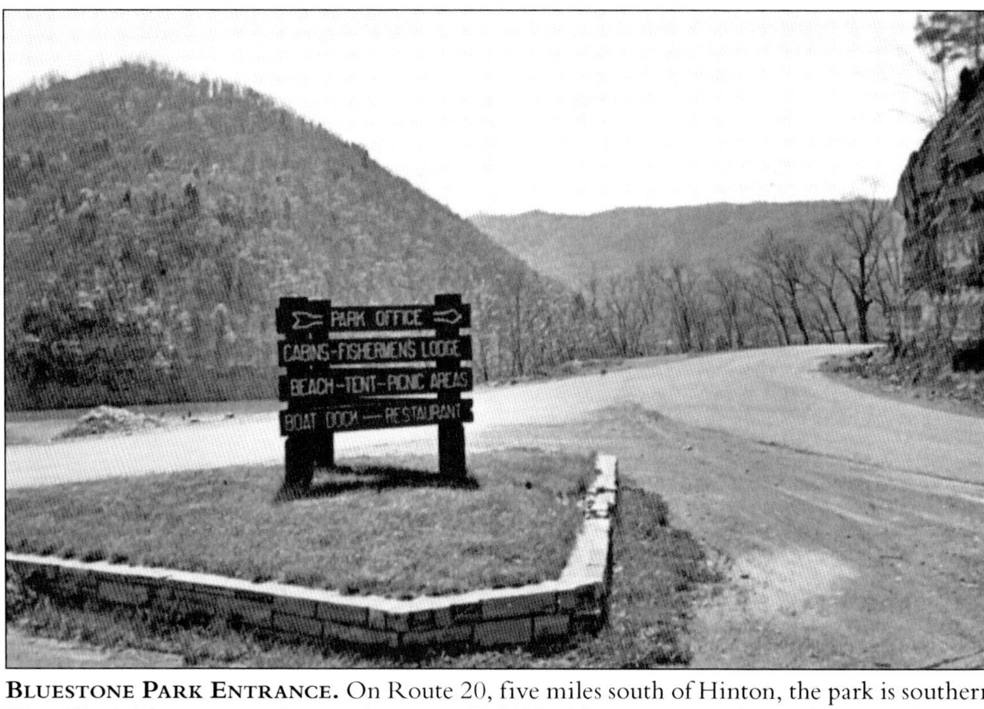

BLUESTONE PARK ENTRANCE. On Route 20, five miles south of Hinton, the park is southern West Virginia's most popular vacation area. (Published by Monroe and Creed, Hinton.)

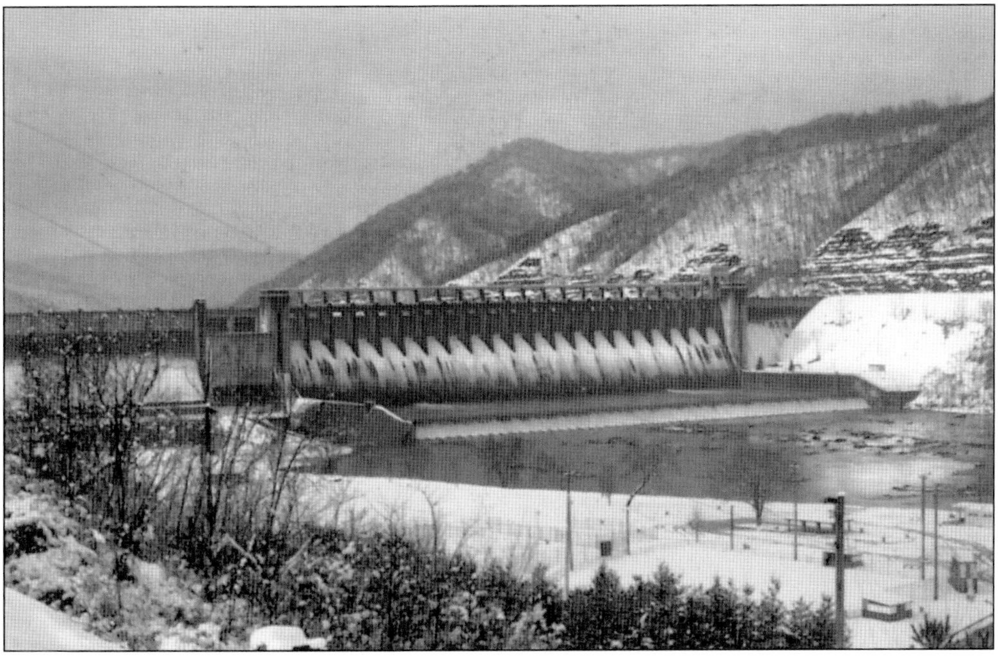

Bluestone Dam. Bluestone Dam was built and went into operation in 1952. It offers flood control for the Kanawha River Basin. (Courtesy of Curt Messer.)

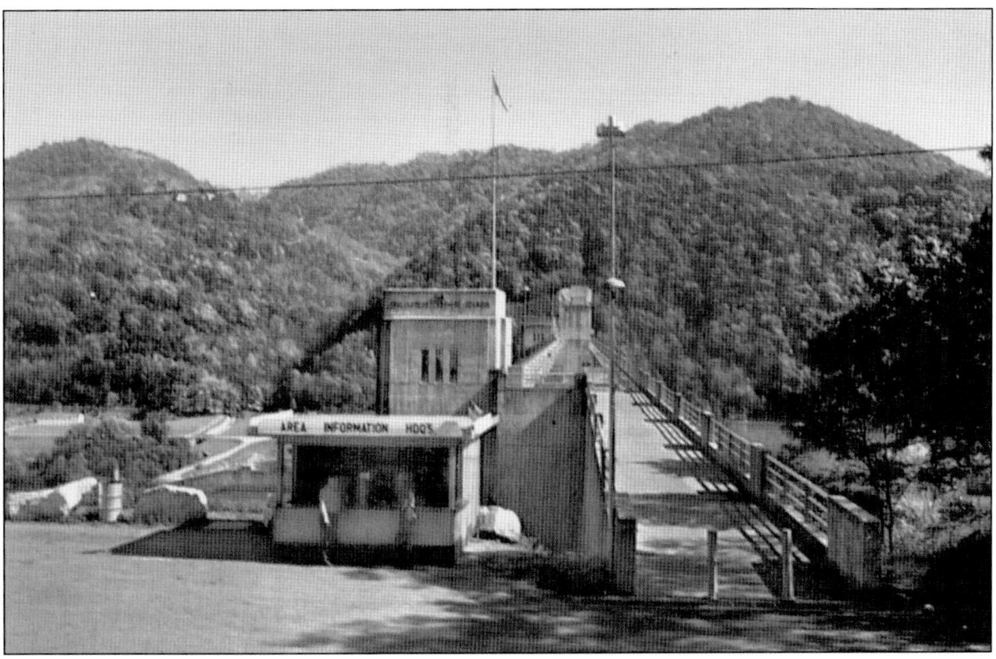

Entrance to Walkway, Bluestone Dam. Built for flood control below the junction of the New and Bluestone Rivers, the dam is 180 feet high. This image was published by the Beckley Magazine Agency. (Courtesy of Billy Joe Edwards.)

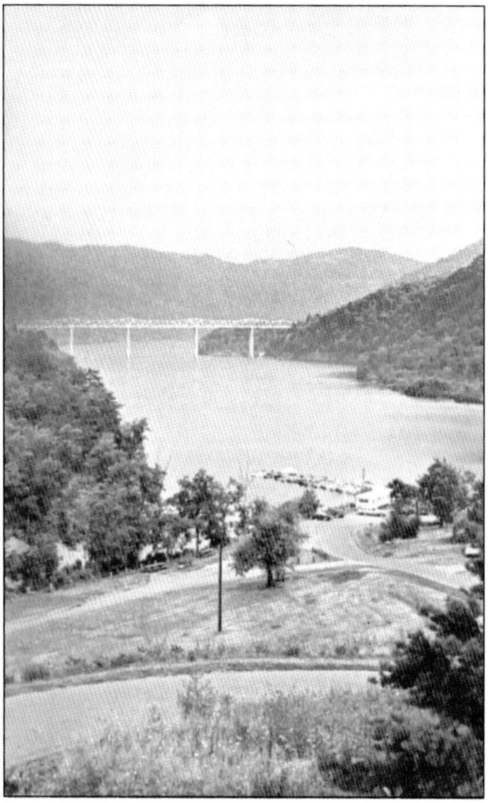

BLUESTONE DAM AND RESERVOIR. A part of the state park system, the dam and reservoir offer boating, swimming, and fishing. (Published by the West Virginia Department of Commerce; courtesy of Amy Parker.)

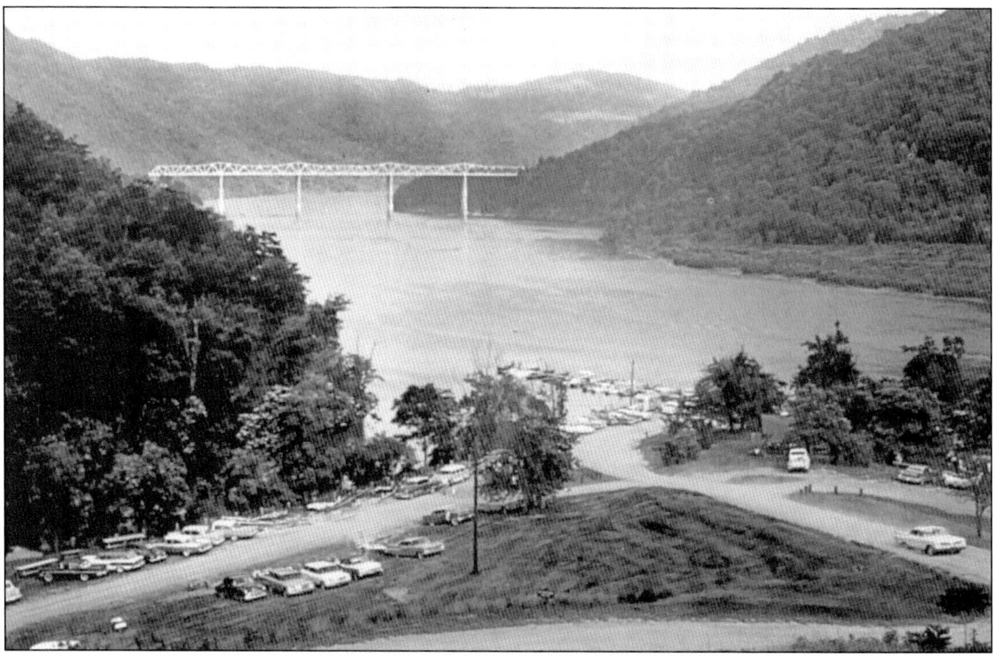

BLUESTONE STATE PARK. This image, taken from the park headquarters, shows the reservoir and the highway bridge in the distance. (Published by the West Virginia Department of Commerce; courtesy of Amy Parker.)

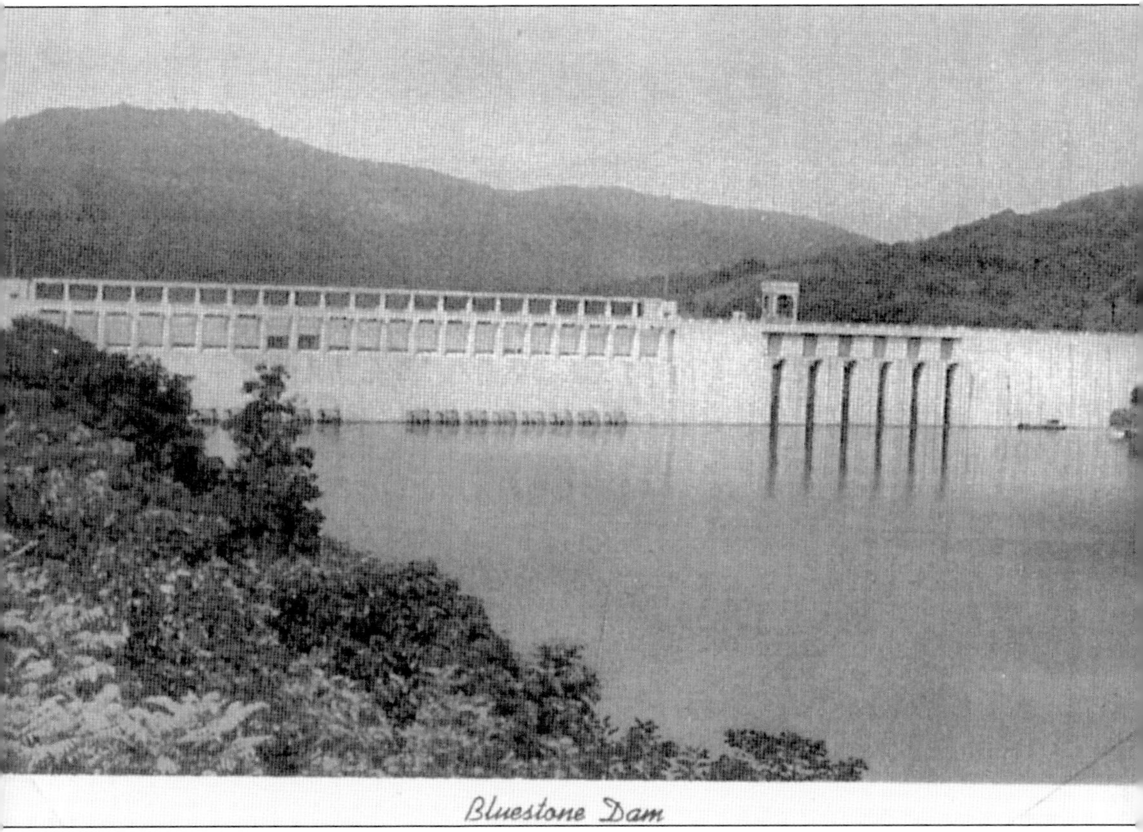

BLUESTONE DAM. The Dravo Corporation was awarded the contract for building the $22 million New River flood control and hydroelectric project. After the United States entered World War II, work on the dam was halted between the years 1943 and 1946. Dravo finished its work in 1948. (Courtesy of Betty Cooper.)

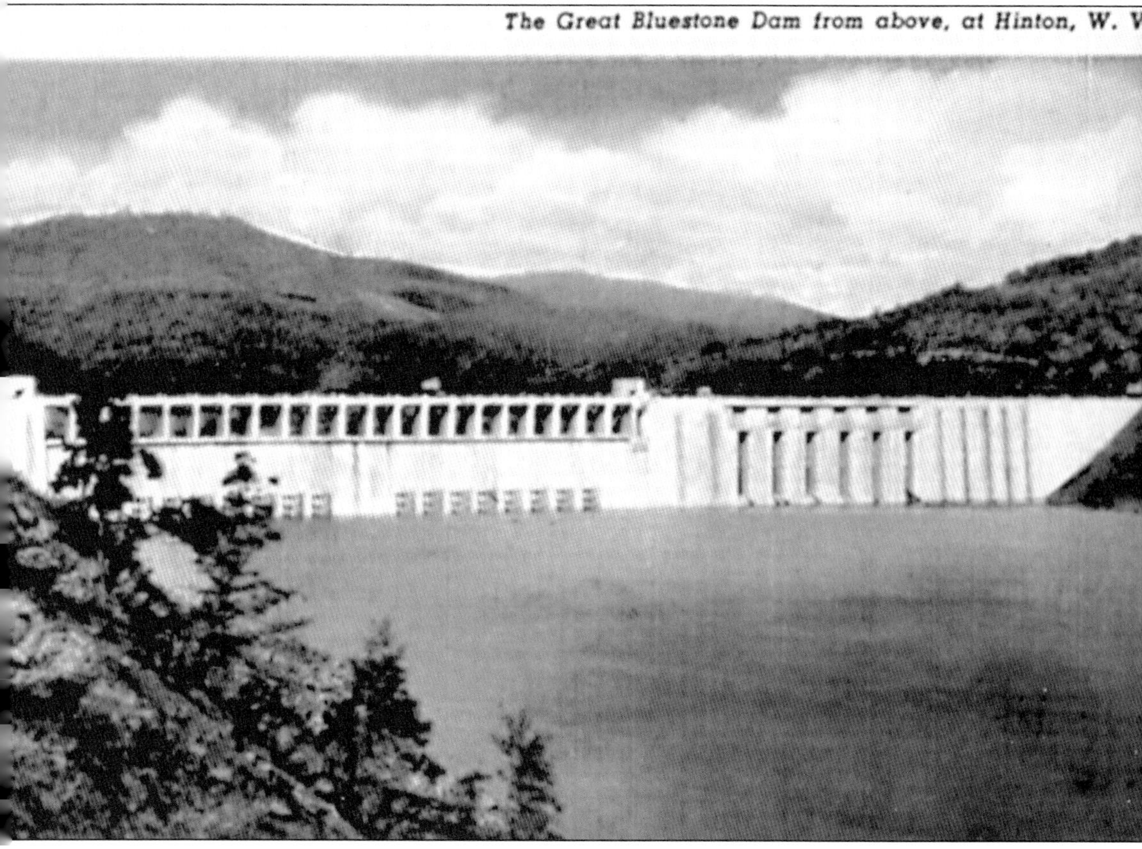

BLUESTONE DAM. The dam has functioned well. The project has prevented an estimated $520 million in flood damage since 1952. (Courtesy of Thomas N. Clark).

Five

Pipestem State Park

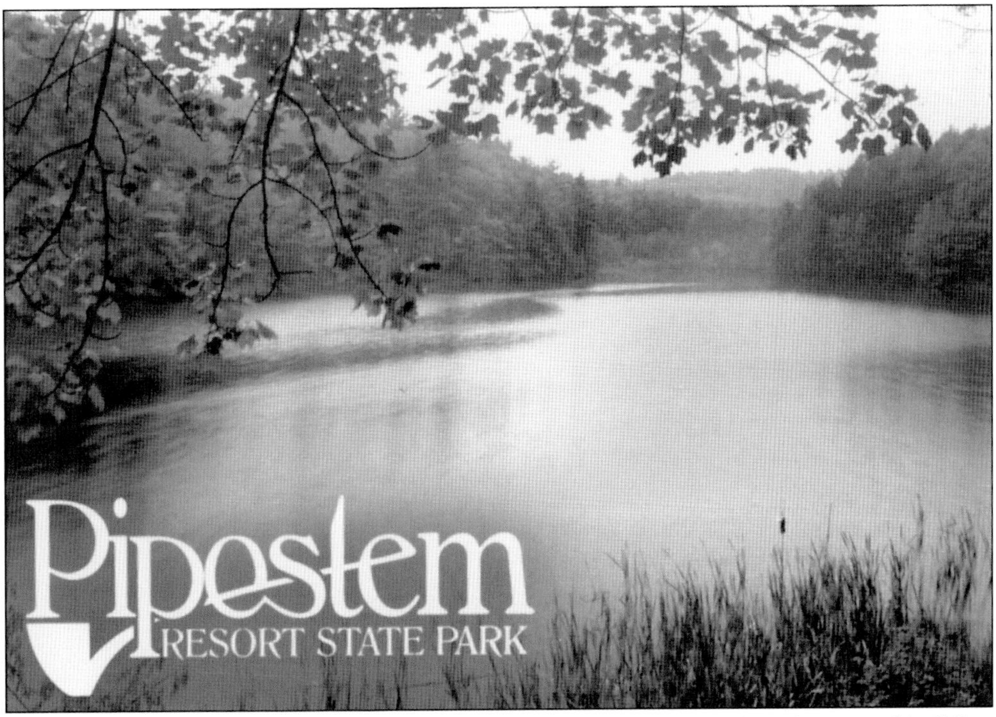

Pipestem State Park. This card shows morning at Long Branch Lake. The general building contract for Pipestem began April 1968 and was awarded to Baltimore Contractors of Maryland. The 16-acre lake and 11 park structures, except the tramway, were included. (Published by Vista Landscapes; photograph by Frank Ceravalo.)

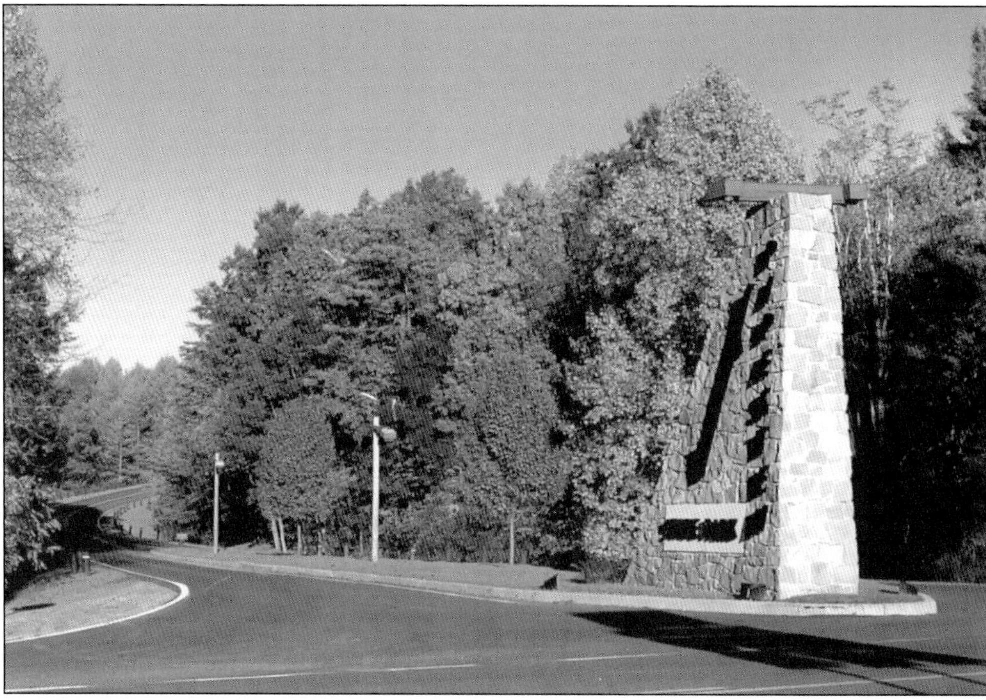

ENTRANCE TO PIPESTEM STATE PARK, ROUTE 20. The Mountain Creek Lodge opens the first weekend in May and books to capacity its 113 rooms until the end of October each year. (Courtesy of David Bair.)

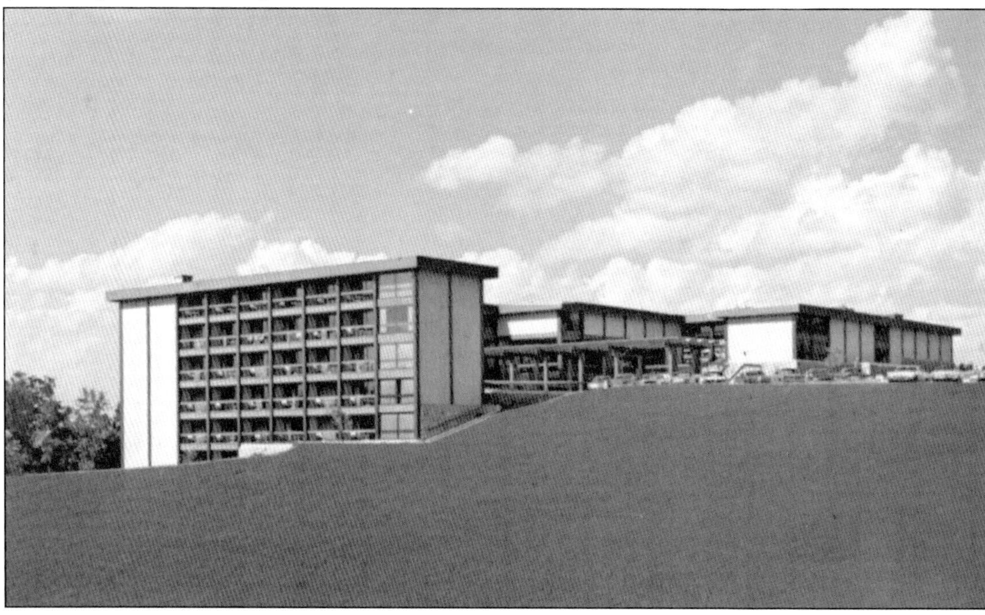

MAIN LODGE OF PIPESTEM STATE PARK, ROUTE 20, PIPESTEM, WEST VIRGINIA. When John F. Kennedy was president of the United States, he made a trip through West Virginia and visited with John Falcouner, editor of the *Hinton News*. The president heard what a great park this land would make. Now millions of people visit Pipestem and its activities every year. (Courtesy of Curt Messer.)

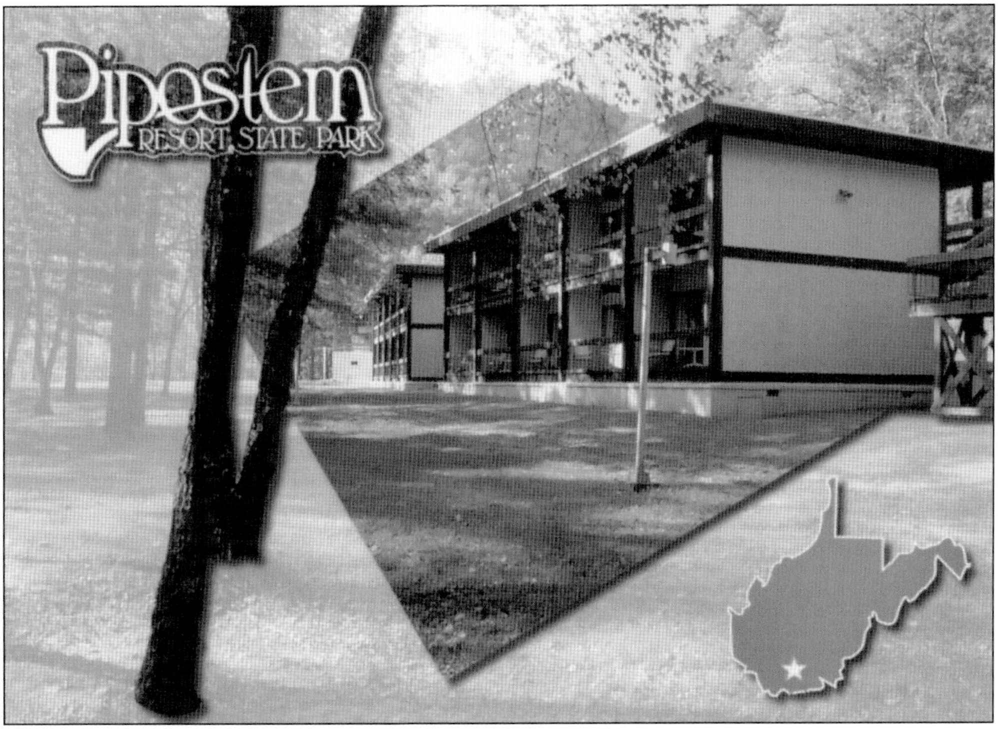

BLUESTONE RESORT STATE PARK. An aerial tramway descends to the bottom of Bluestone Gorge and the rustic Mountain Creek Lodge. (Courtesy of David Crown Enterprises, P.O. Box 1934, Charleston, West Virginia.)

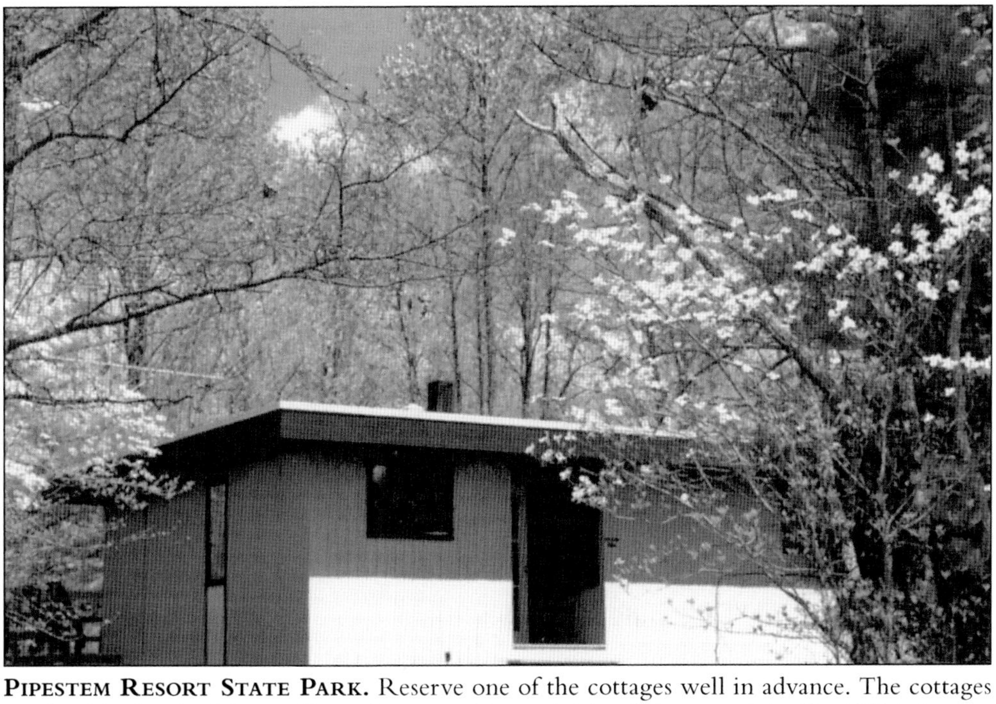

PIPESTEM RESORT STATE PARK. Reserve one of the cottages well in advance. The cottages are furnished and within walking distance of the activities. (Photograph by David Bair.)

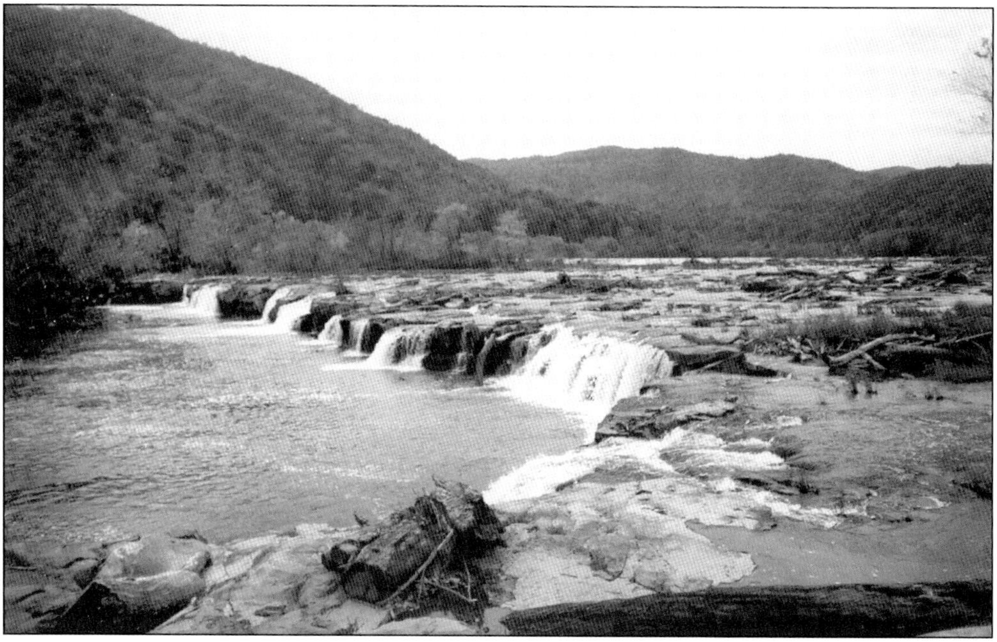

SANDSTONE FALLS. Pictured here are the falls after recent high water and flooding. Sandstone is located on New River on the western end of Summers County. At one time, it rivaled Hinton as a center of commerce, and there was a move to establish the county seat there. Notice the trash. (Courtesy of Dot Turman.)

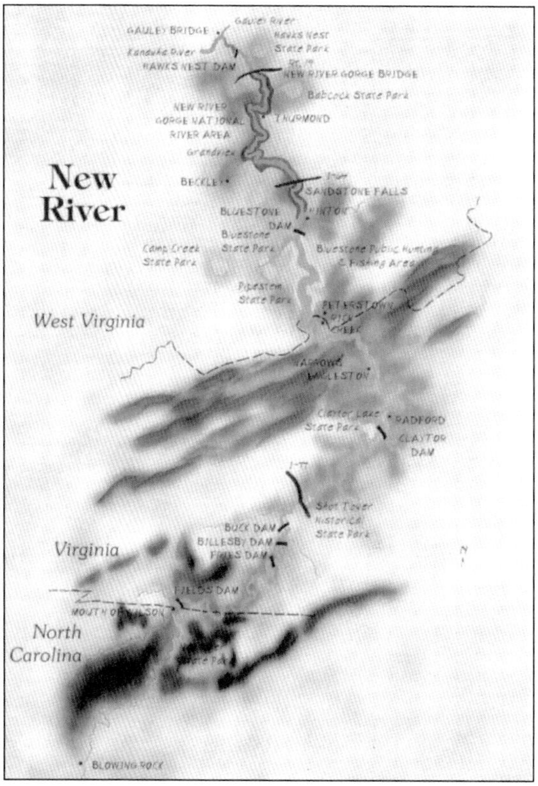

MAP FOLLOWING THE NEW RIVER. This map traces the river from Blowing Rock, North Carolina, to the Gauley Bridge. (The map is available at David Crown Enterprises of Charleston, West Virginia, and is reprinted from *New River: A Photographic Essay*. (Courtesy of Virginia Gadd.)

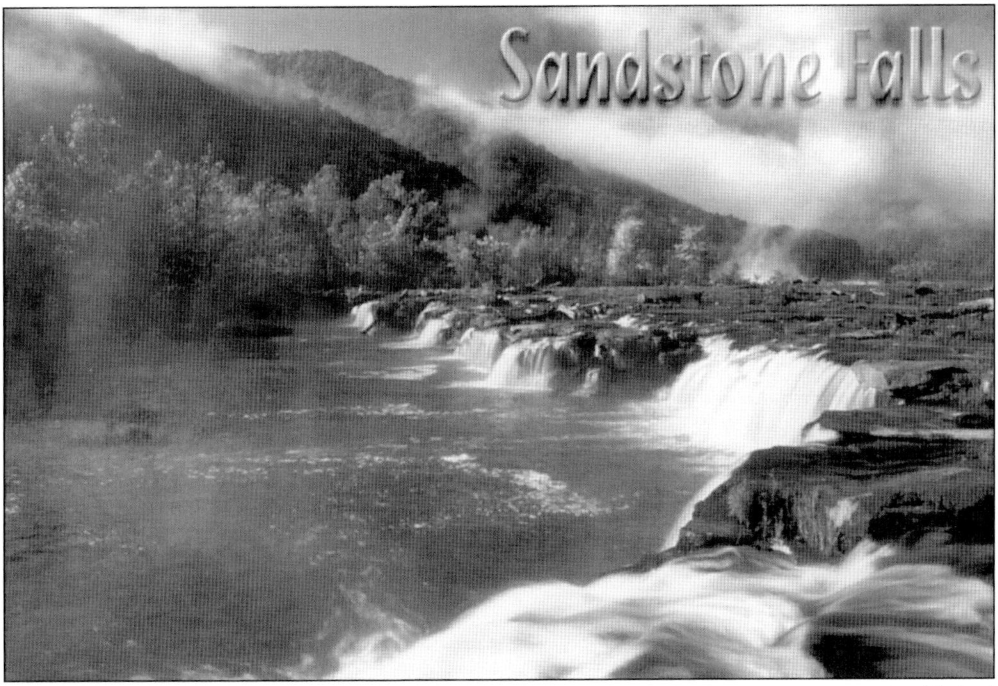

SANDSTONE FALLS. These falls cross the entire 1,500-foot width of the New River. (Published by Vista Landscapes; photograph by Frank Ceravalo.)

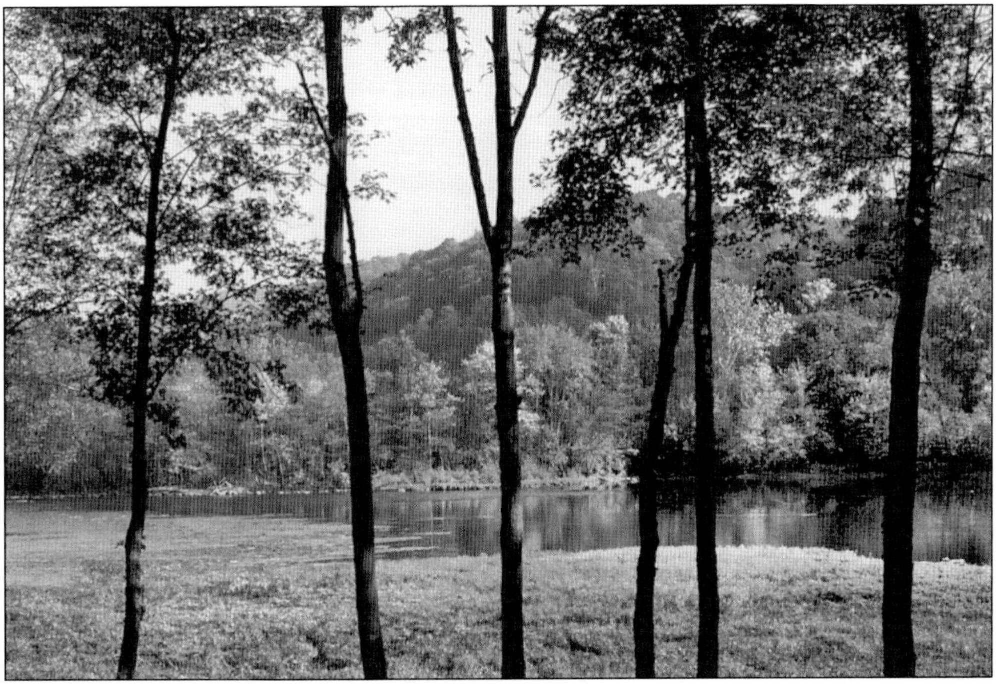

ACCESSING THE NEW RIVER FROM RIVER ROAD. The river is wide and lazy here, and fishing and canoeing are popular. (Photograph by David Bair.)

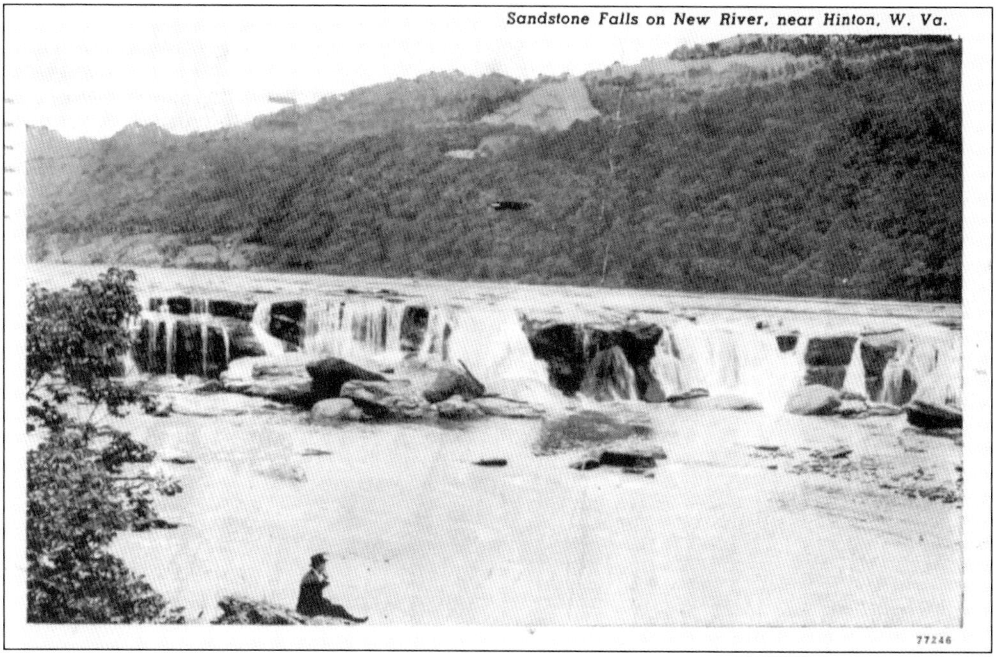

SANDSTONE FALLS. These are the largest falls on the New River and are located nine miles north of the historic railroading town of Hinton. (Courtesy of Larry and Dolores Moorman and Thomas N. Clark.)

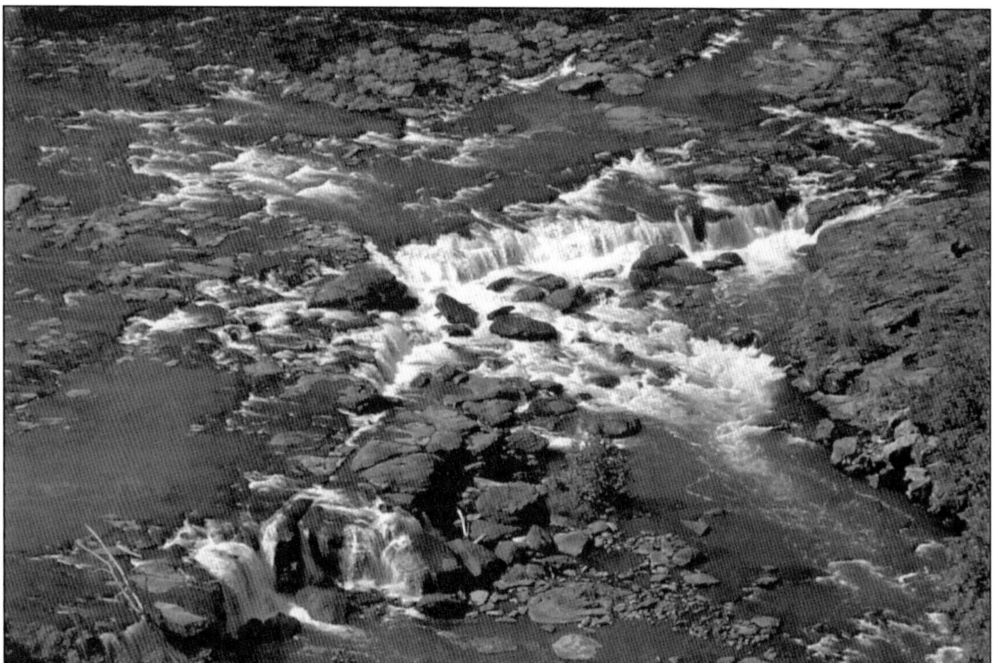

SANDSTONE FALLS. The main falls, on the east side of the river, are 800 feet wide and drop 25 feet. The lower falls are 425 feet wide and drop 10 feet. The falls can be accessed by a boardwalk. (Courtesy of David Bair.)

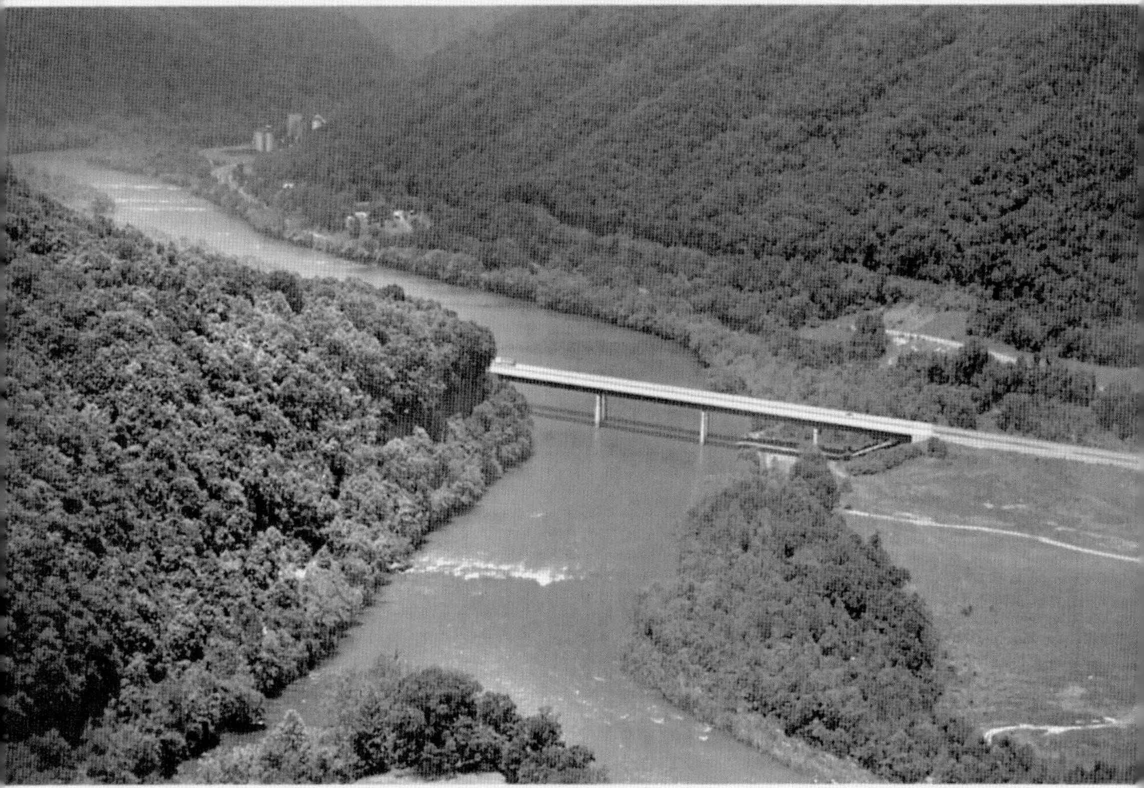

I-64 NEAR SANDSTONE, CROSSING NEW RIVER GORGE NATIONAL RIVER AT SANDSTONE. The name Sandstone comes from the rock quarry of that native stone. It is hoped that I-64 will make Sandstone a tourist destination and resort community. (Published by Paige Creations.)

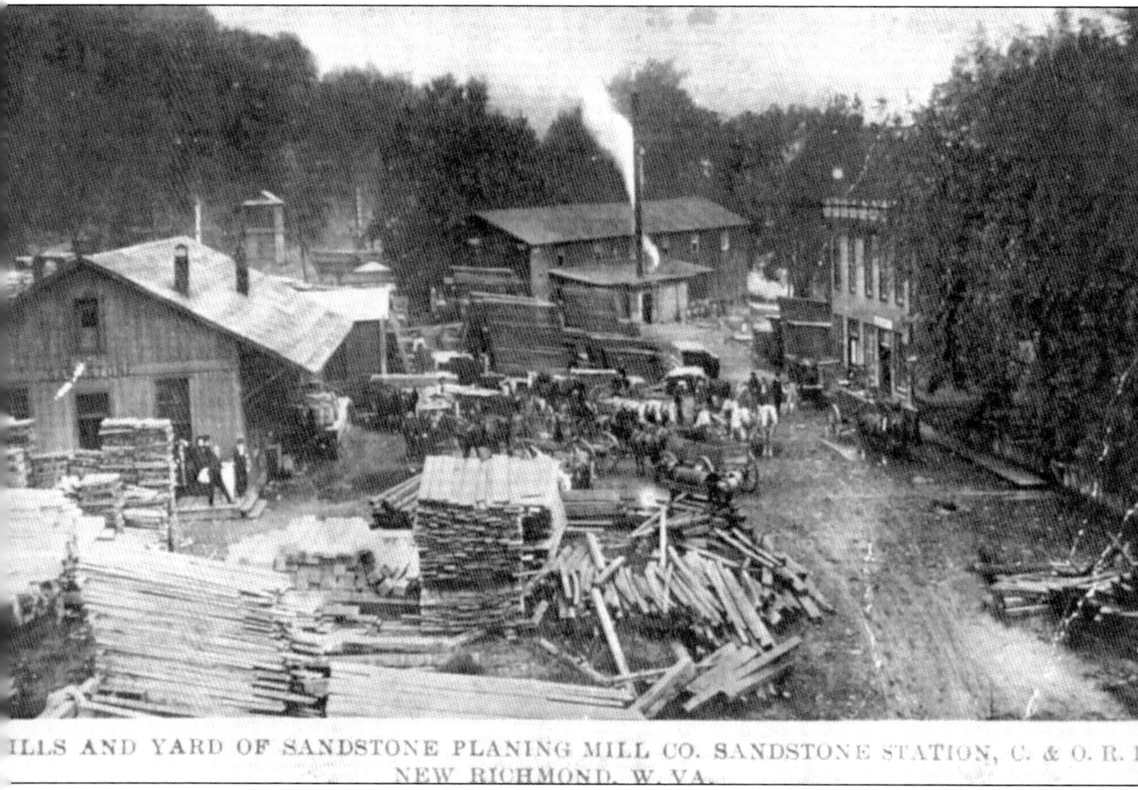

MILLS AND YARD OF SANDSTONE PLANING MILL CO. In addition to this sawmill, at Sandstone Station of the C&O Railroad in New Richmond, West Virginia, there was another lumber business in Sandstone, started by John Graham and O. T. Honaker in 1907. (Courtesy of Conrad Graham.)

Six

Pence Springs Hotels

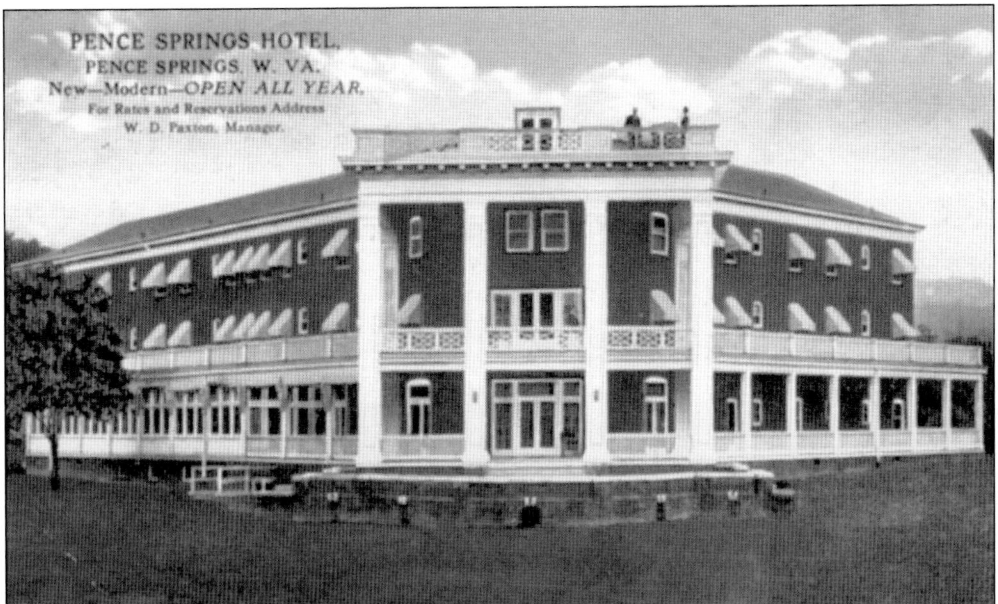

Pence Springs Hotel. Postmarked August 29, 1919, this ad announces that the "new and modern" Pence Springs Hotel is now open all year. (Courtesy of Margaret Martin.)

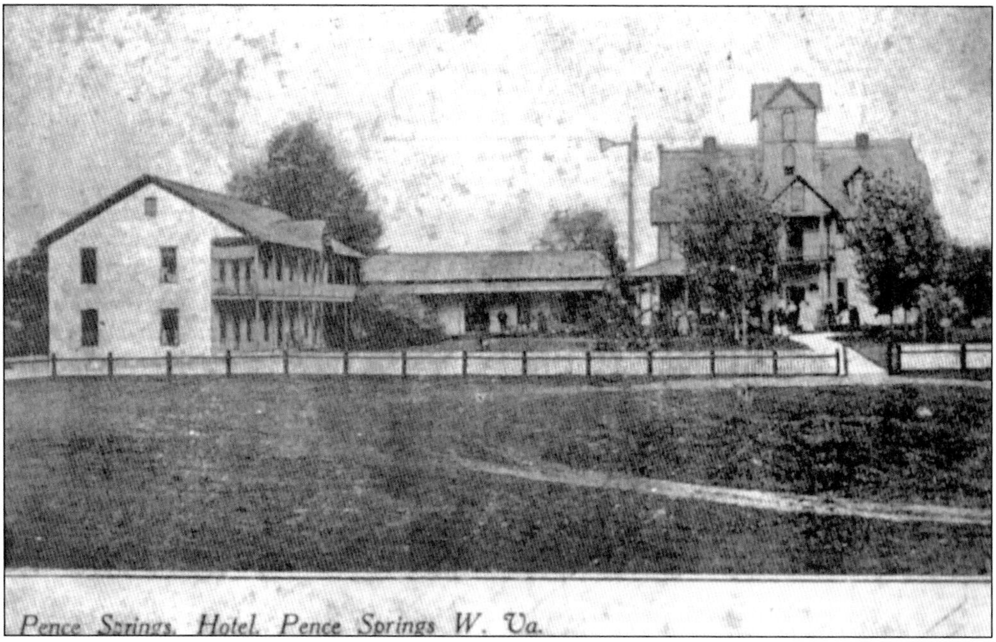

Two Views of the Original Pence Springs Hotel. The hotel was a gray, two-and-a-half-story building. It had a two-story observation tower on the front roof. The building was completed in 1897. (Courtesy of Fred Long and Steve Trail.)

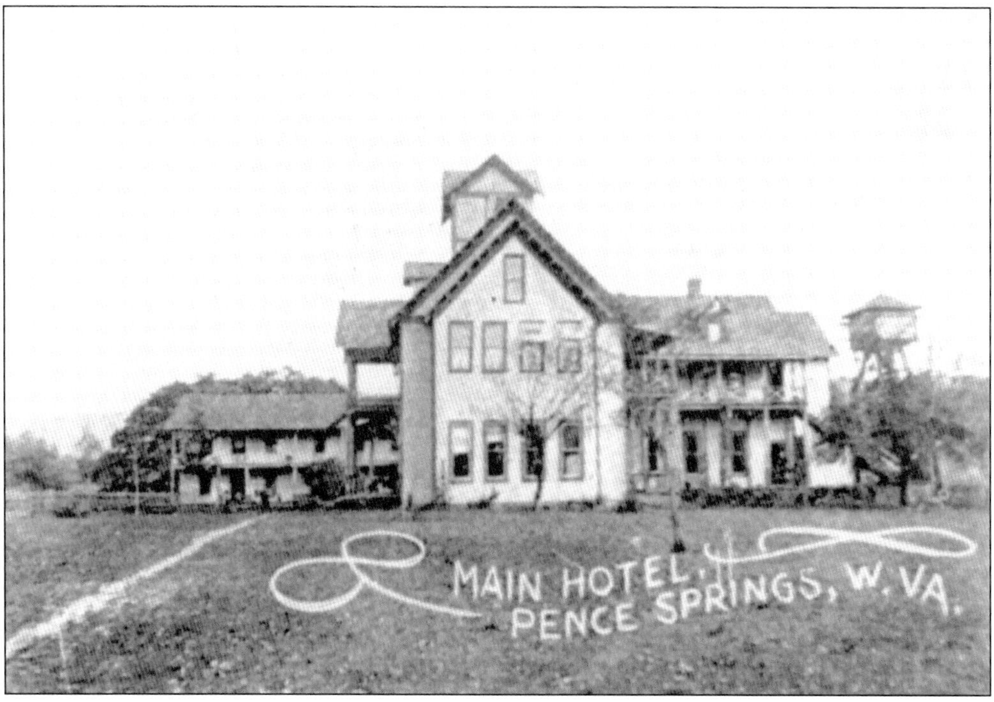

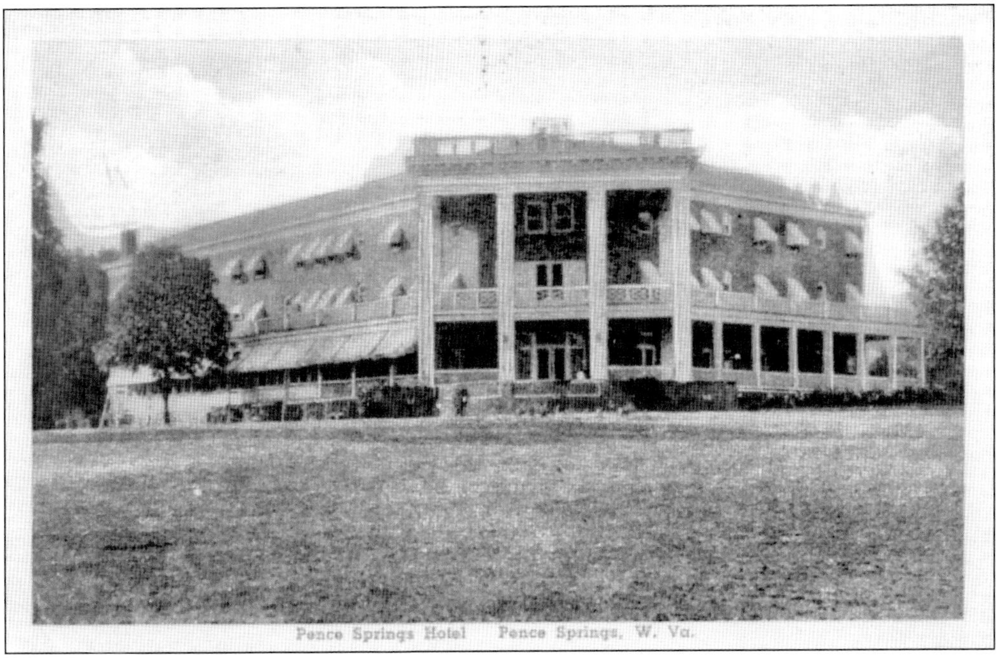

PENCE SPRINGS RESORT HOTEL. The hotel opened in June 1918 and in August of that year, more than 125 guests were staying at the hotel daily. They came from all over the United States. (Courtesy of John Kesler; photograph by W. Richard Ford.)

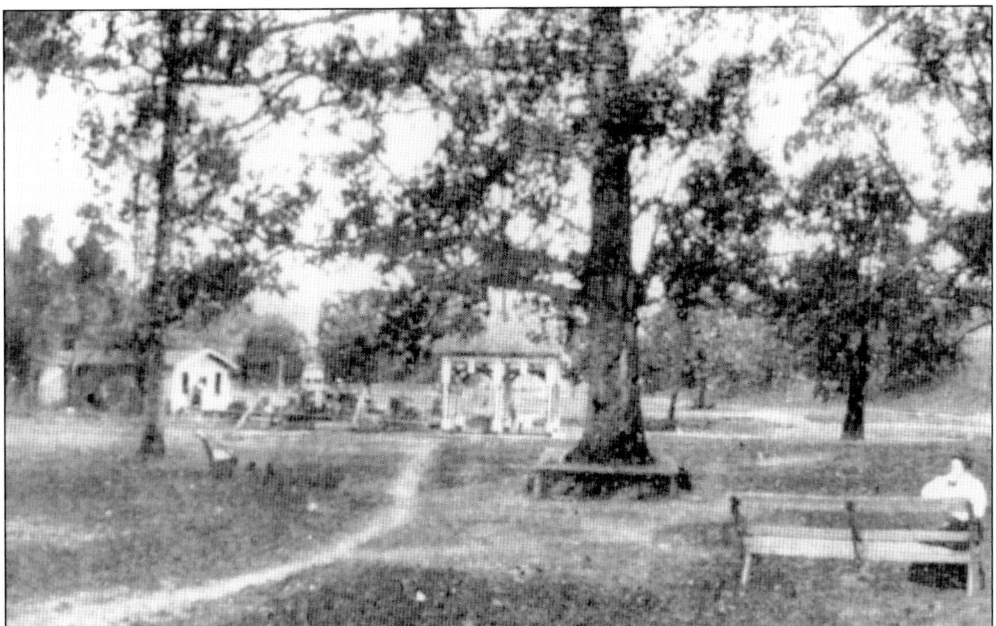

THE LAWN AT PENCE SPRINGS HOTEL. This image from an old postcard shows the spring property under development, especially the bottling house under construction. (Courtesy of Fred Long and Steve Trail.)

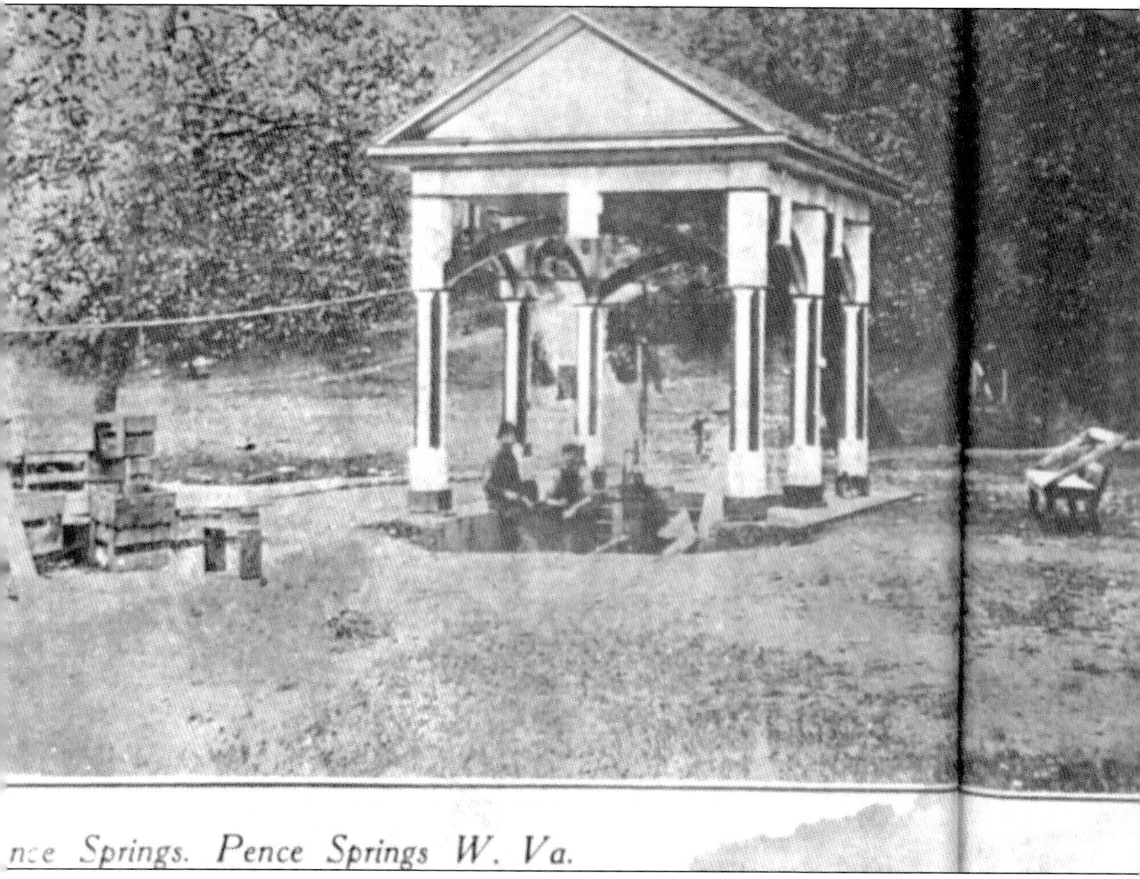

SPRING HOUSE AT THE SULPHUR SPRING. This image shows the equipment used in bottling the water, which was being sold at $2 a case. (Courtesy of Fred Long and Steve Trail.)

SULPHUR SPRING AT PENCE SPRINGS RESORT. This is an early view of the spring house, built under the direction of the spring's owner, Andrew Pence. Pence hired workers to dig up the area around the spring to find the exact source and to better control the water flow. He then confined the stream with cement and tiling. (Courtesy of Fred Long and Steve Trail.)

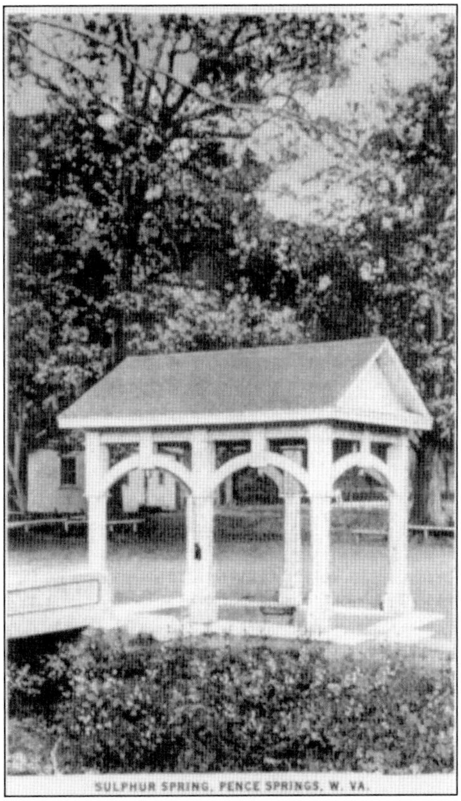

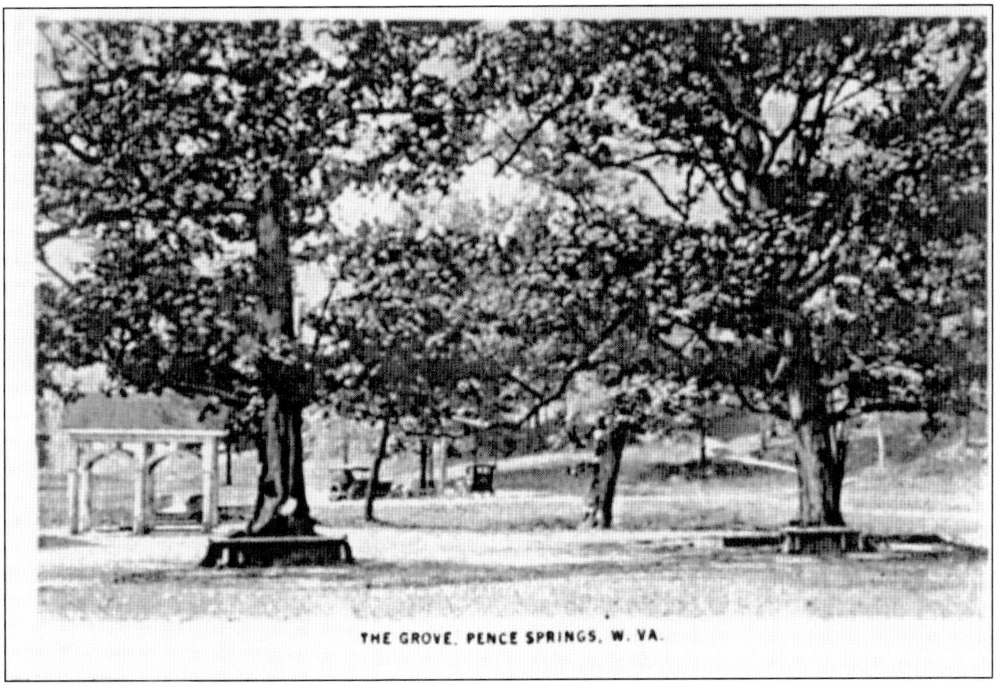

THE GROVE AT PENCE SPRINGS HOTEL. The spring house is visible in this postcard. (Courtesy of Fred Long and Steve Trail.)

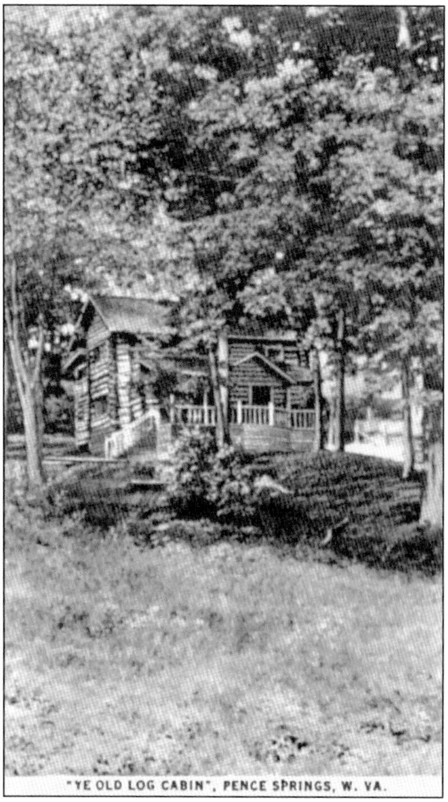

"YE OLD LOG CABIN," PENCE SPRINGS. The Thayers from Charleston, West Virginia, lived in this cottage above the Pence Springs. The cottage later burned. (Courtesy of Fred Long and Steve Trail.)

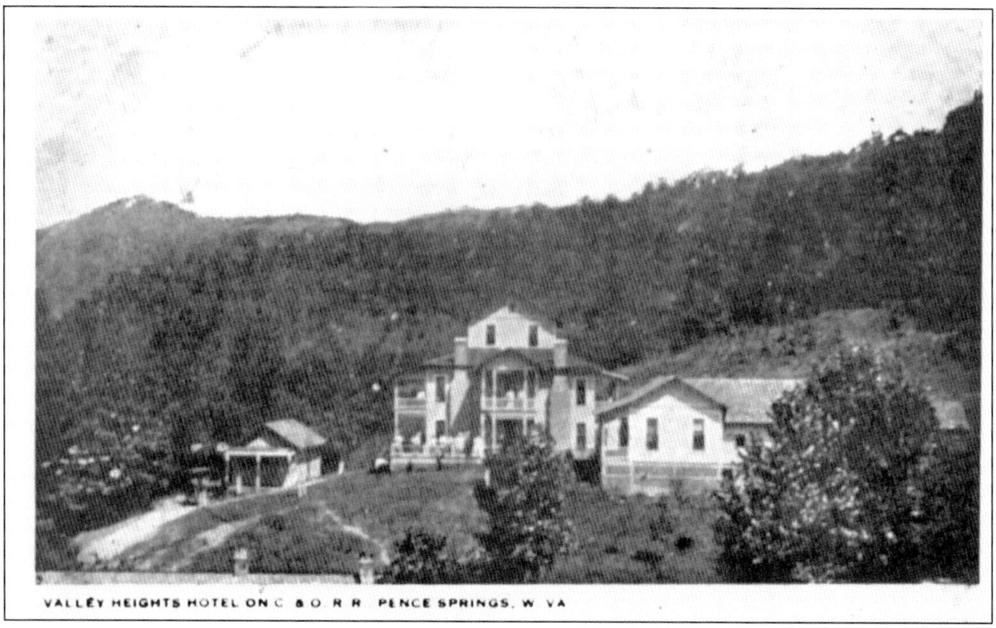

VALLEY HEIGHTS HOTEL AT PENCE SPRINGS. Valley Heights was another hotel, owned by Stan Bowden, that competed with Andrew Pence's Pence Springs Hotel for the sulphur water. Both owners were using steam pumps, and neither could obtain a satisfactory flow because of the other. (Courtesy of Fred Long and Steve Trail.)

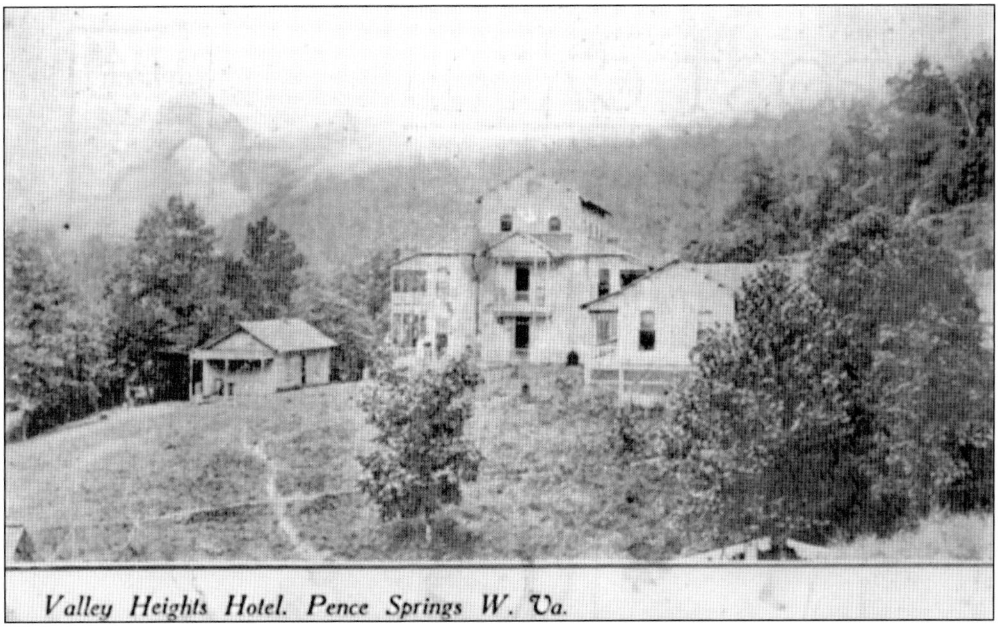

VALLEY HEIGHTS HOTEL. Erected in 1905, the building was Victorian in style and frame and featured two large, brick chimneys. It burned in 1910. The Pence Springs Hotel burned in 1912, but it was rebuilt and now, in its present life, is again a resort. (Courtesy of Fred Long and Steve Trail.)

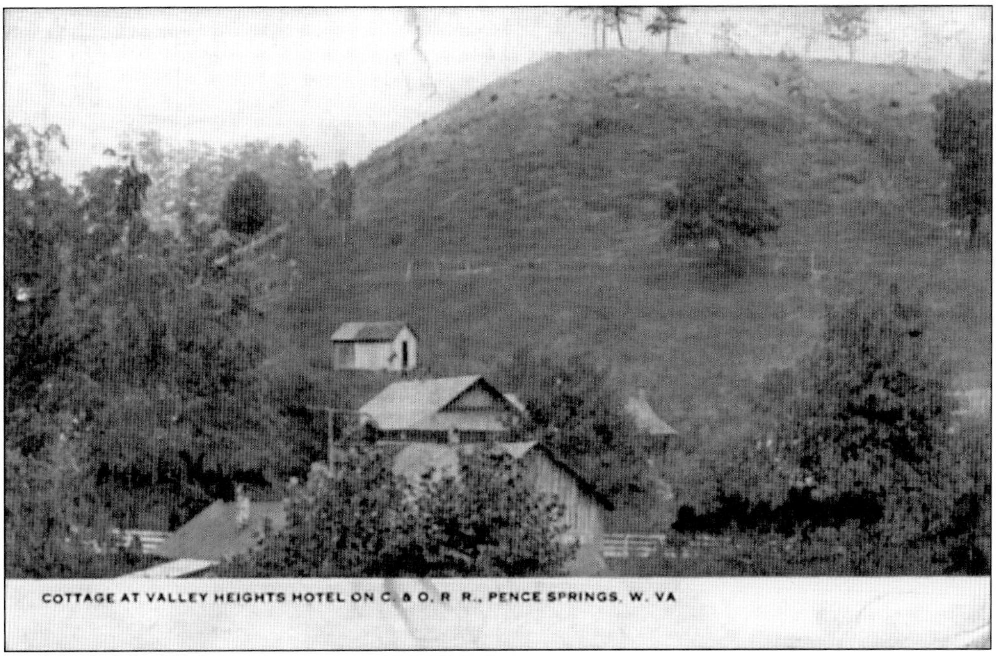

COTTAGE AT VALLEY HEIGHTS HOTEL, ON THE C&O RAILROAD, PENCE SPRINGS, WEST VIRGINIA. Guests sometimes preferred to stay in rustic cottages instead of the hotel proper. Some of the guests included governors, senators, and Elias Hatfield of the Hatfield-McCoy Feud fame. (Courtesy of Tim Halloran.)

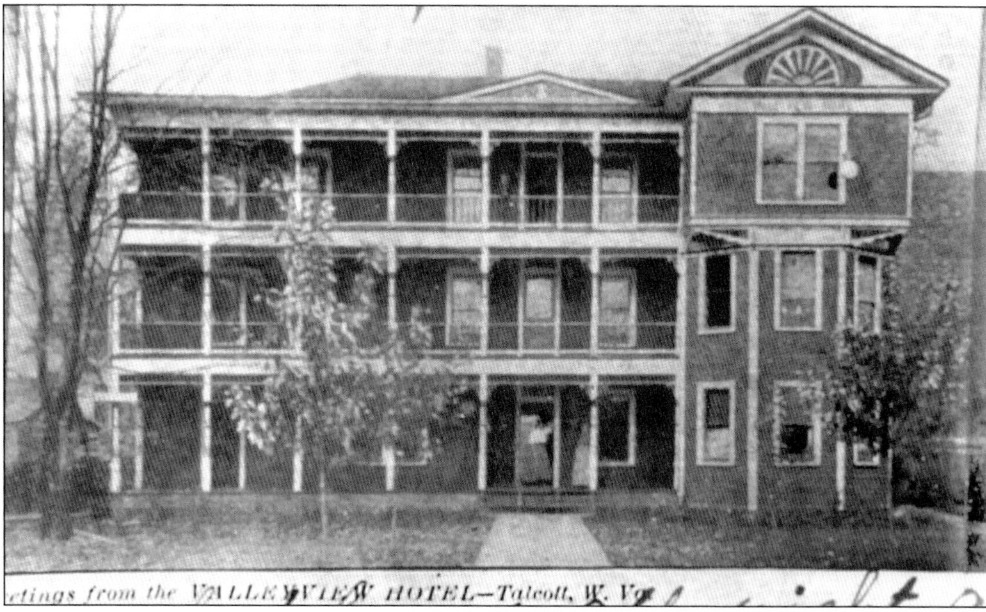

Valley View Hotel. Owned by John W. Willey and George Dunn, the hotel was destroyed by fire *c.* 1907, before the existence of a fire department. (Courtesy of Margaret Martin.)

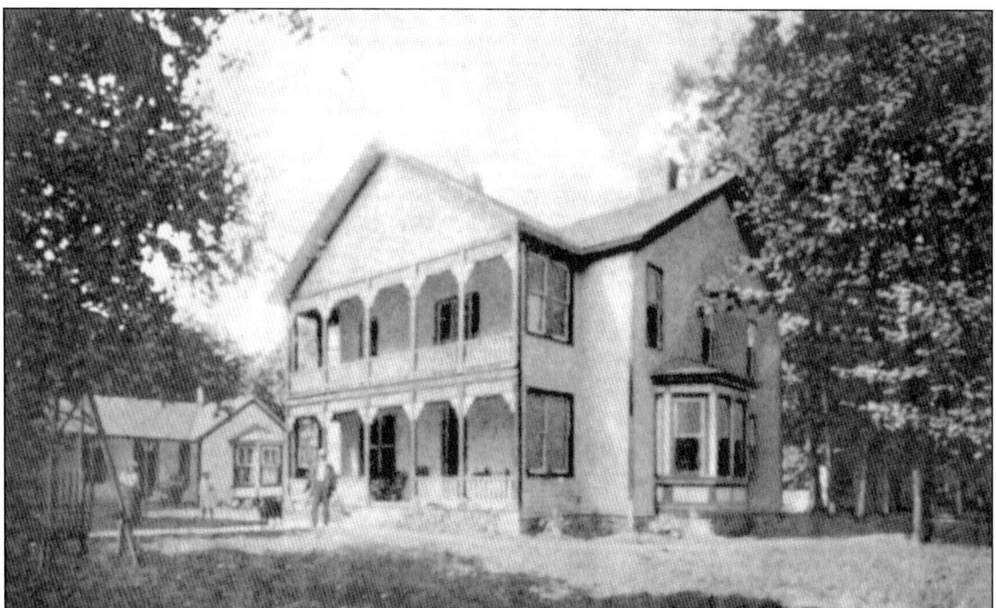

Lahey's Boarding House in Pence Springs. Places like this took care of the overflow of guests from the Pence Springs Hotel. Another boarding house was Coiner's. (Courtesy of Fred Long and Steve Trail.)

Seven

Jumping Branch

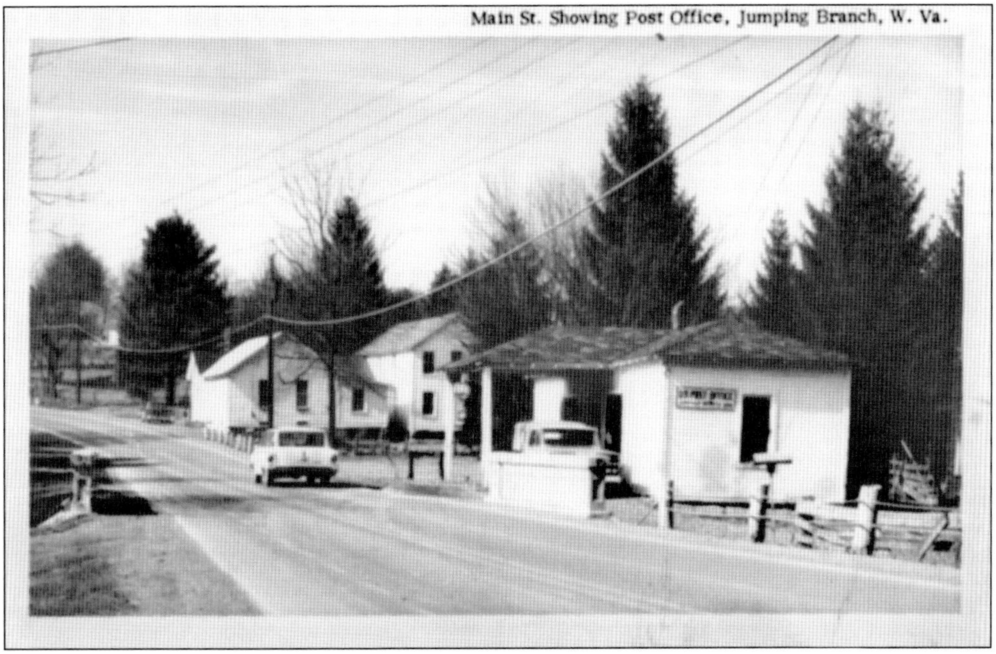

Jumping Branch, Main Street, Showing the Post Office. The *c.* 1966 pickup was used by Moody Vest, who carried the mail from Hinton to Shady Spring. His father, Luther Vest, carried the mail in a buggy. The postmistress at the time this picture was taken was Iva Dodd. The post office building was once a restaurant. Barely showing in the right of the picture is the grist mill owned by Frank Dodd, unused at this time. In the background are two white store buildings, which were for many years the general store of J. A. Walker. (Courtesy of Ben Vest.)

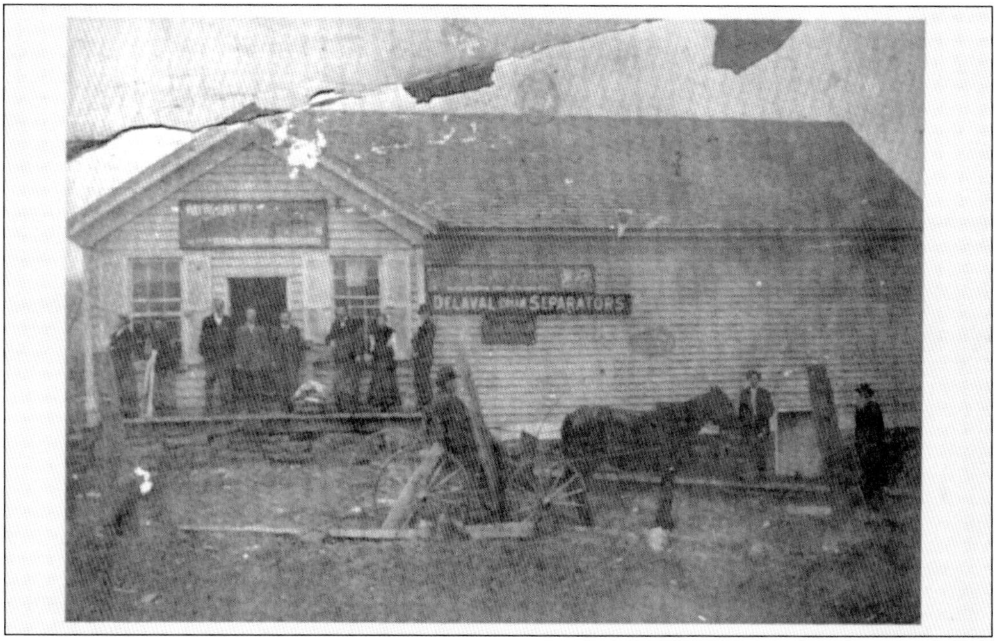

General Store, Jumping Branch, *c.* 1890. Notice the advertisement for cream separators on the wall. No information has been found as to who owned the store. Old records show that Jumping Branch was sometimes referred to as Jumping Creek or Jumping Branches. (Courtesy of Margaret Martin.)

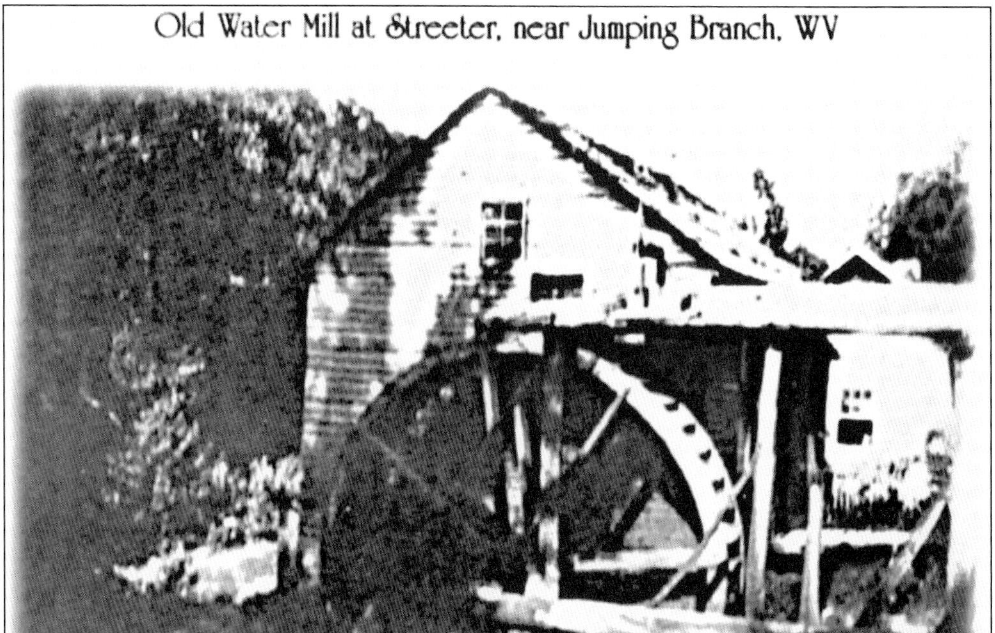

Old Water Mill near Jumping Branch, *c.* 1890. The mill was built by John Pack around 1845. It passed from him to his son, Samuel, then to his grandson, William Alexander Pack. The mill stopped running in 1935. (Information courtesy of Jack Pack; card courtesy of Margaret Martin.)

Eight

Novelties

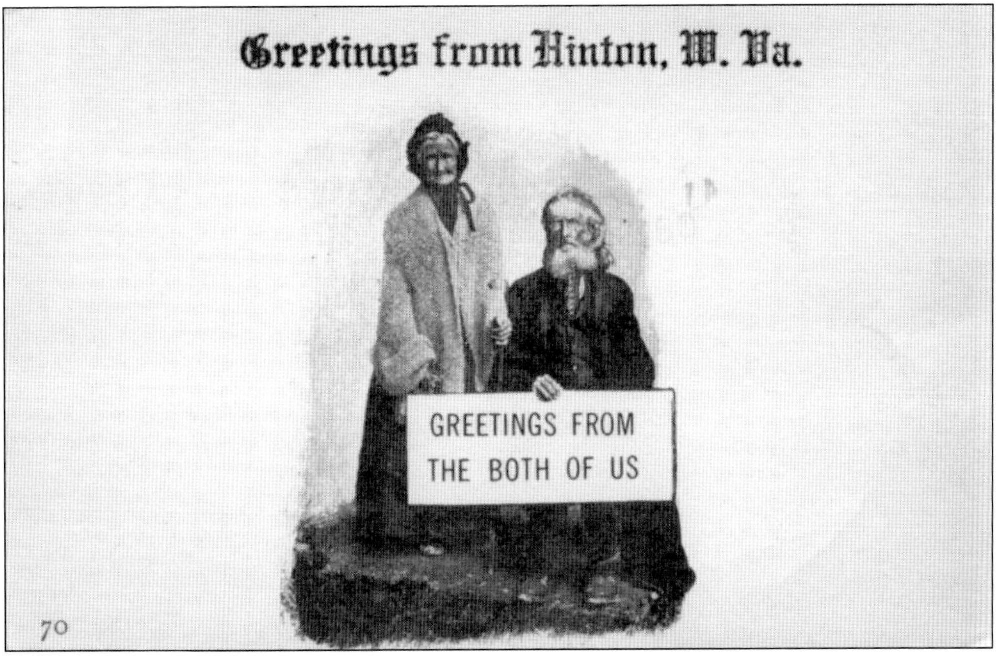

Greetings From Both of Us From Hinton. The card reads, "One of a series of serious postcards by a serious publisher in serious trouble." (Courtesy of Amy Parker.)

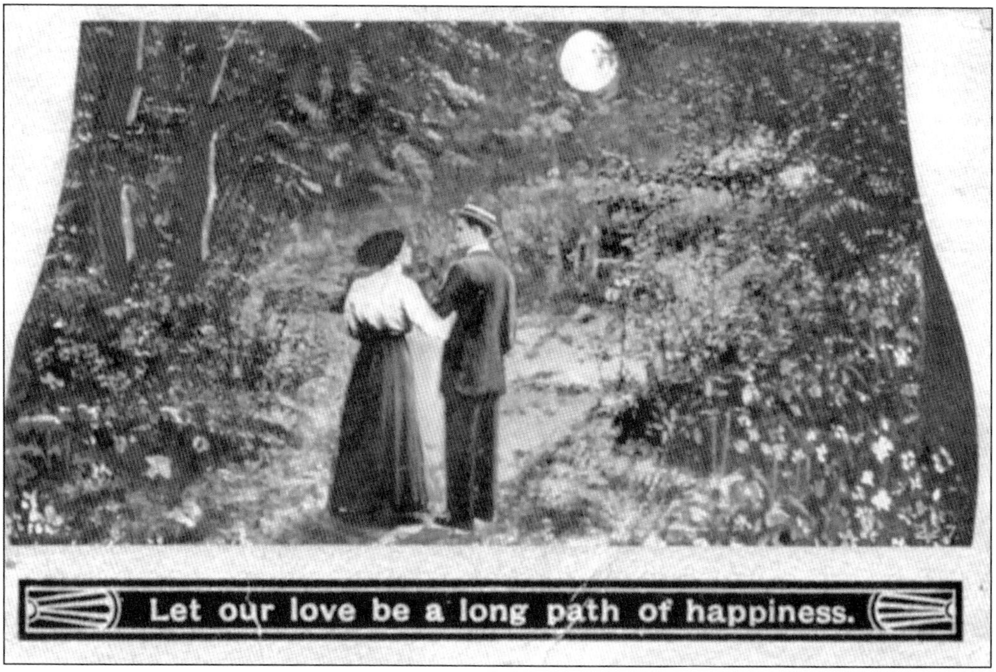

Let Our Love be a Long Path of Happiness and Get a Girl and an Automobile. The business of love and romance in the moonlight seems remote when viewed from our vantage point of 2005. The card below shows how our society became more mobile and affected even courting. (Courtesy of John Kesler.)

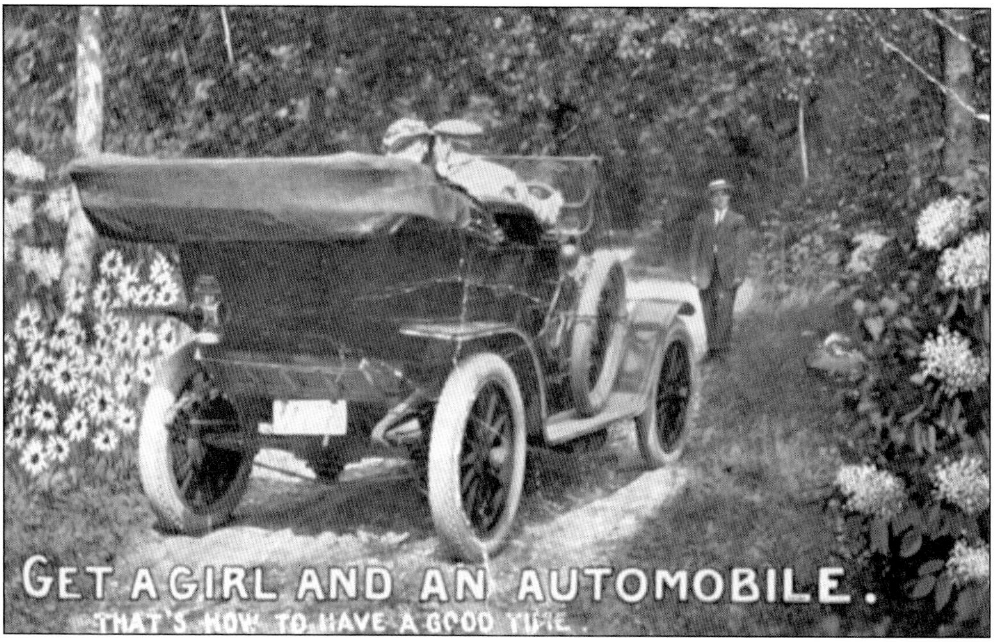

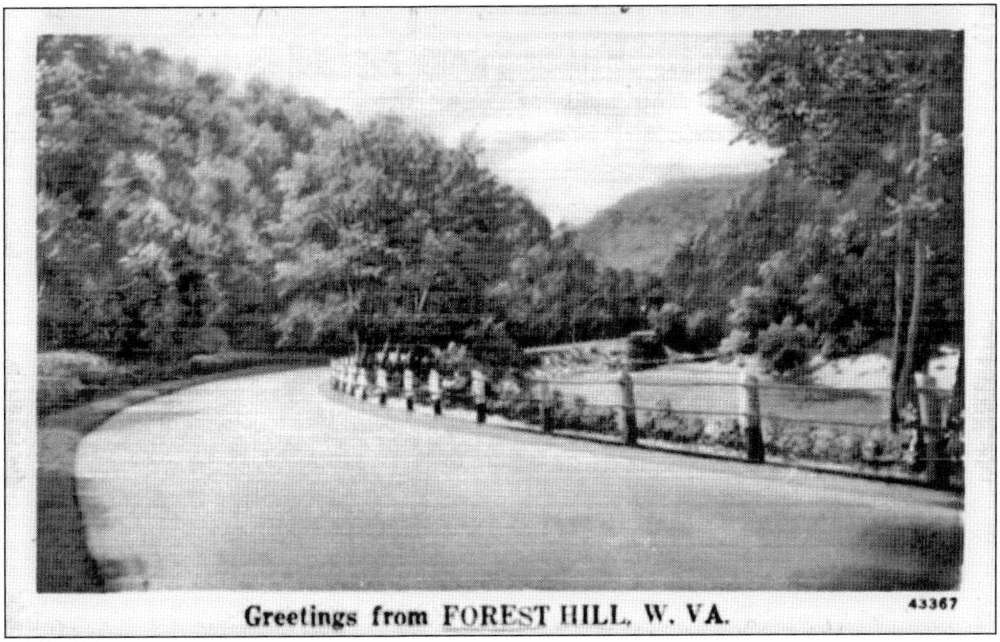

GREETINGS FROM FOREST HILL. This postcard paints a picture of a lovely life in Forest Hill, but the card below pictures a life that is more lively than lovely. (Courtesy of Pearl Lowry.)

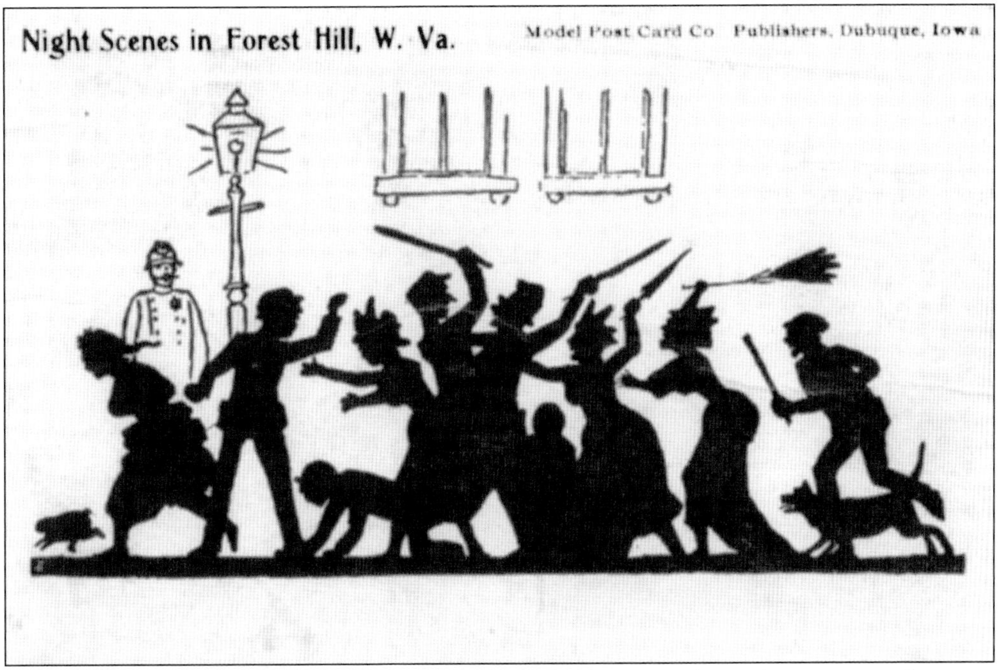

NIGHT SCENES IN FOREST HILL, WEST VIRGINIA. Forest Hill is located on Route 12 between Hinton and Peterstown, West Virginia. It is a charming country village. Some pioneer names of Forest Hill are Bolton, Hutchinson, Cottle, Woodrum, and Saunders. (Courtesy of Larry and Dolores Moorman.)

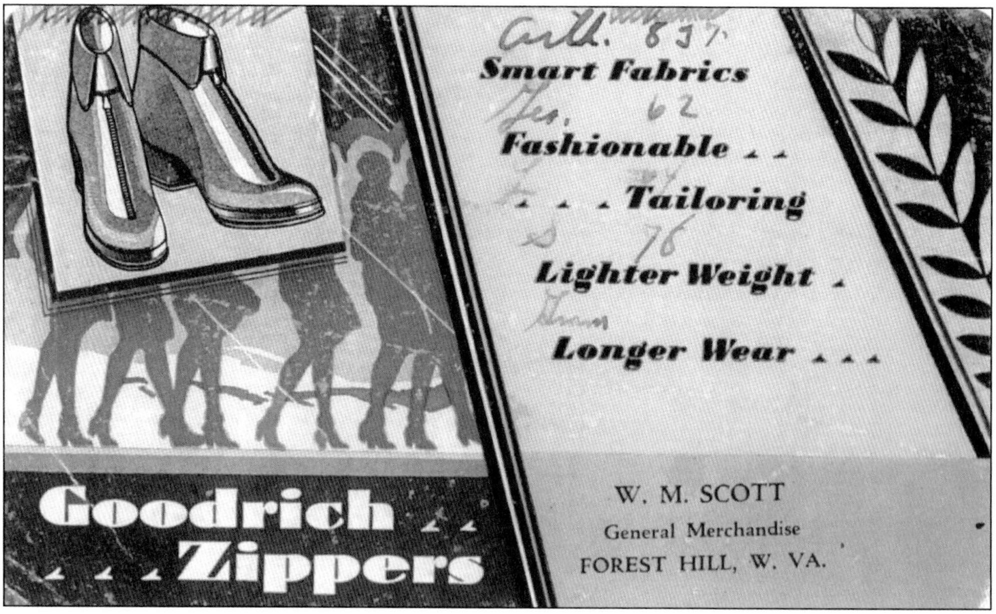

GETTING THE WORD OUT. Postcards had a lot of uses. These two were used to advertise everything from boots to banks. (Courtesy of Larry and Dolores Moorman.)

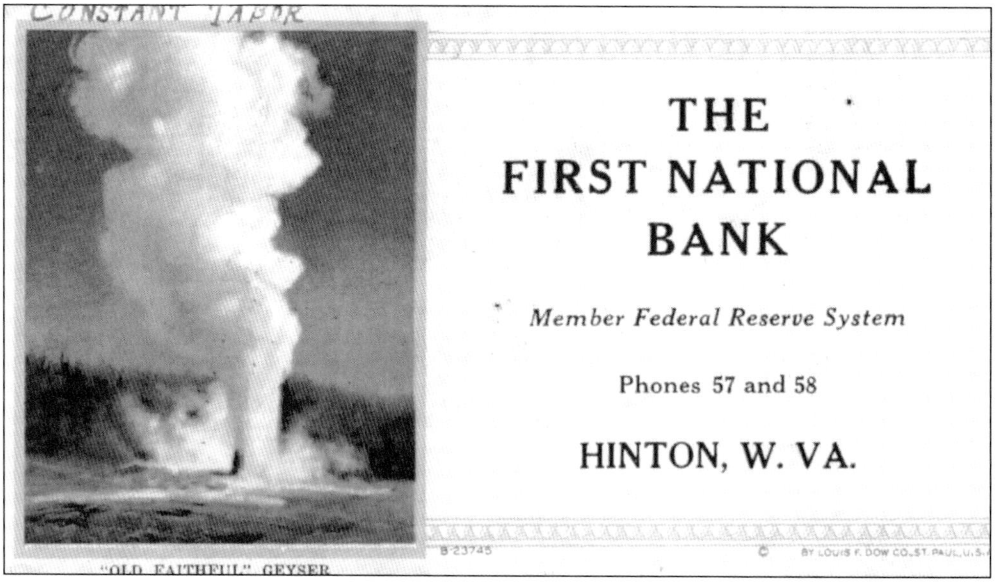

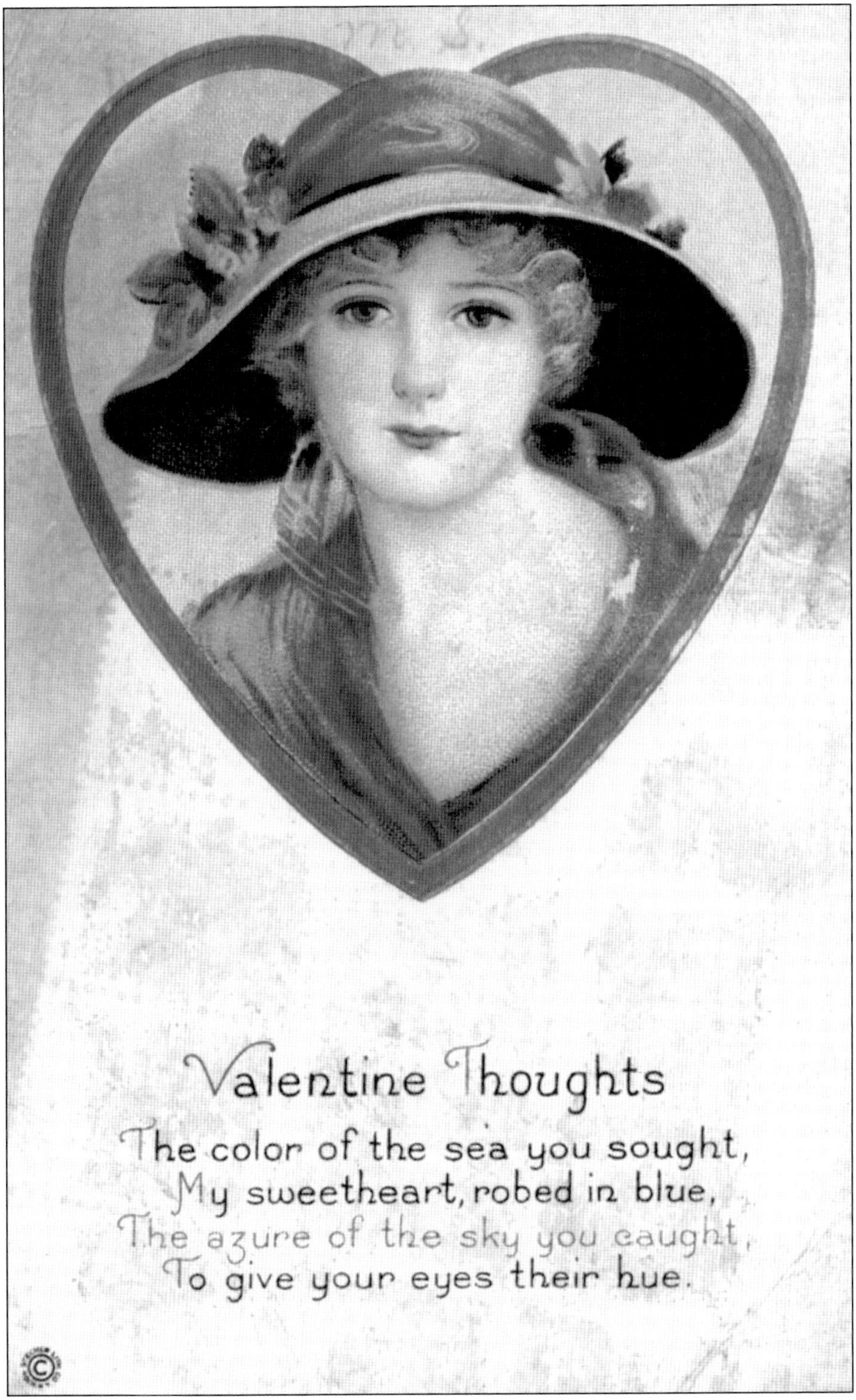

THE LADY OF MY LIFE. The custom of Valentine's Day can be traced back to the 1400s. Supposedly, birds began to pair off on that day. (Courtesy of John Kesler.)

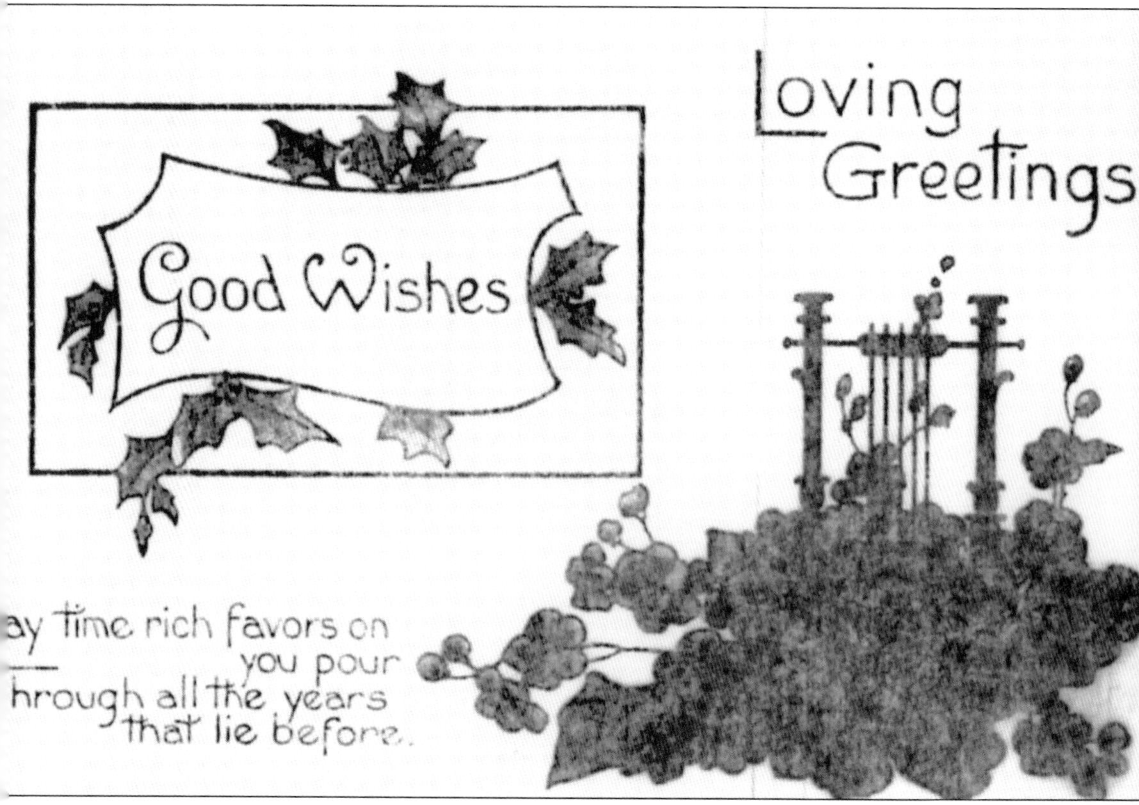

VALENTINE GREETINGS. This Valentine card was sent to Mr. S. T. Lowry by his future wife, Sallie Turner. She was teaching school and boarding in the town of Wiggins. (Courtesy of Dot Turman.)

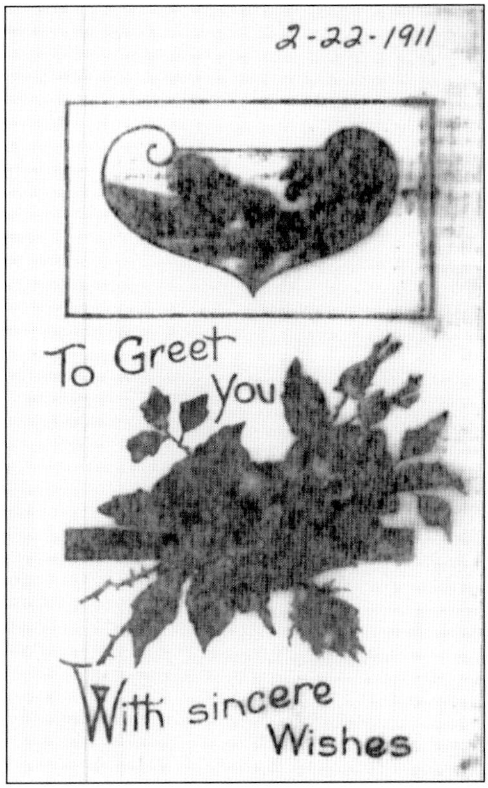

PRECIOUS MEMORIES. These Valentine and loving greeting cards sent to and from S. T. Lowry and Sallie Turner must have worked. They were married the same year the cards were sent—1911. (Courtesy of Dot Turman.)

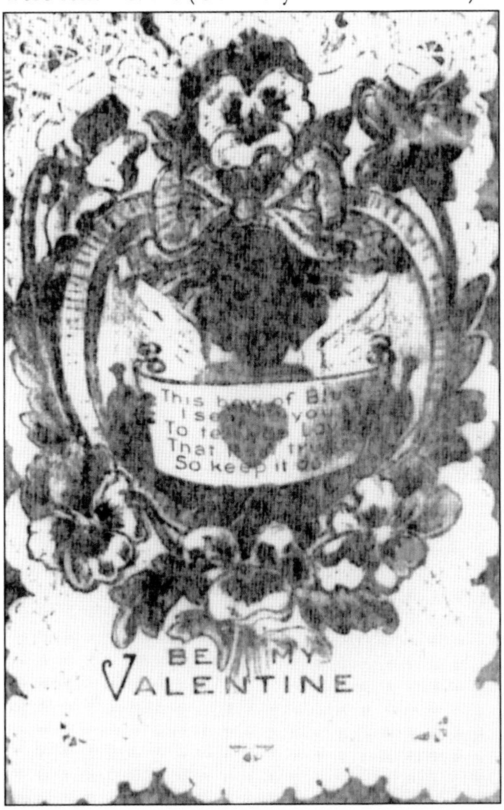

CHRISTMAS CARD FROM THE PAST. This Christmas card from Sallie Turner to S. T. Lowry asks about his 1910 holiday. (Courtesy of Dot Turman.)

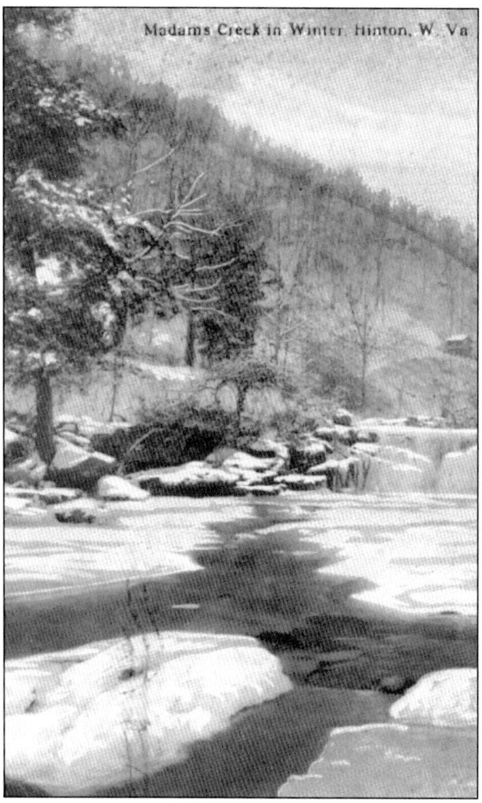

MADAM'S CREEK IN WINTER. This generic postcard, featuring Madam's Creek in winter, was sent to a postmistress from a gentleman asking to have his mail forwarded to Hinton. (Courtesy of Margaret Martin.)

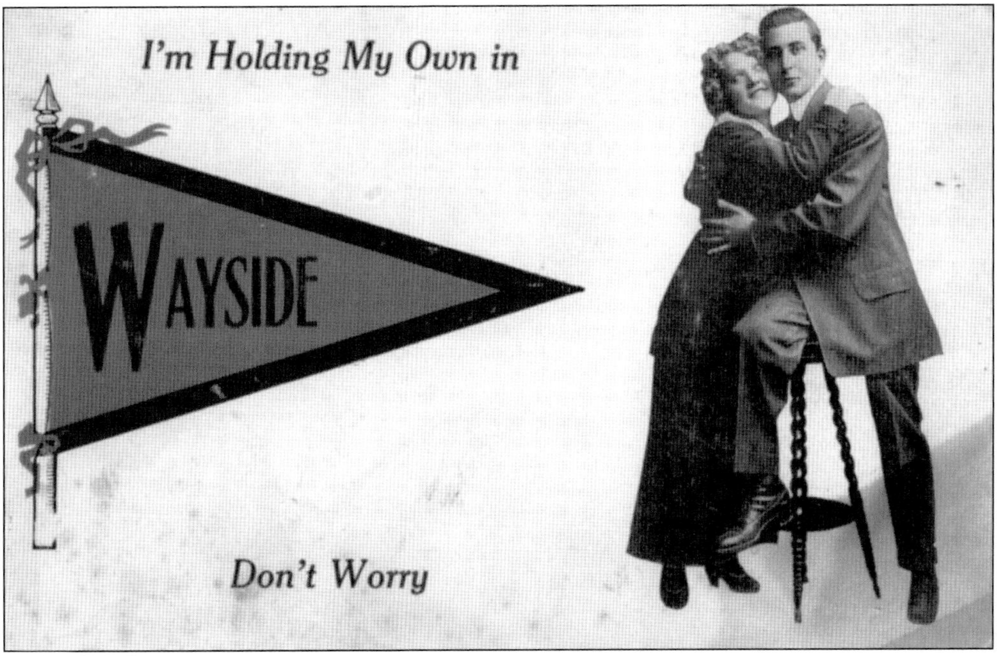

DON'T WORRY. This postcard, postmarked 1912, was sent to a Mr. Allen, scolding him for missing the pie supper. A pie supper was a fund-raising event in which girls baked pies and placed them in decorated boxes, and boys bid on the pies and for the privilege of eating with the girls. (Courtesy of John Kesler.)

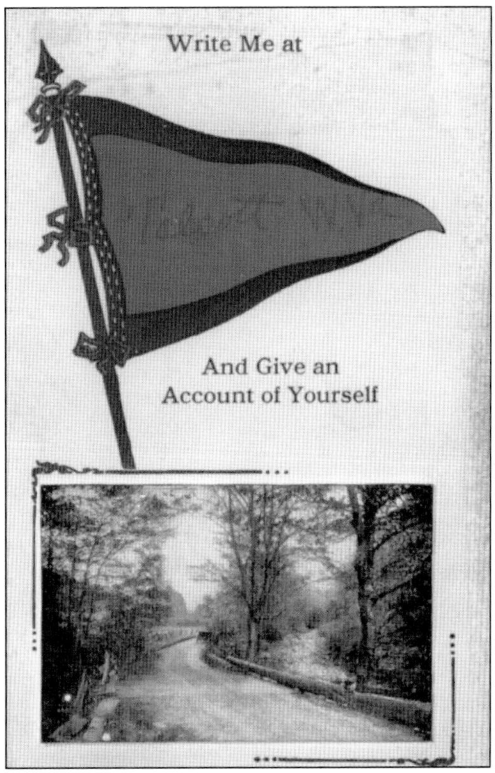

HOW ARE YOU? This postcard sends a humorous command to someone to write to Talcott, West Virginia, and give an account of himself or herself, tell how he is doing and how the family is faring. (Courtesy of Margaret Martin.)

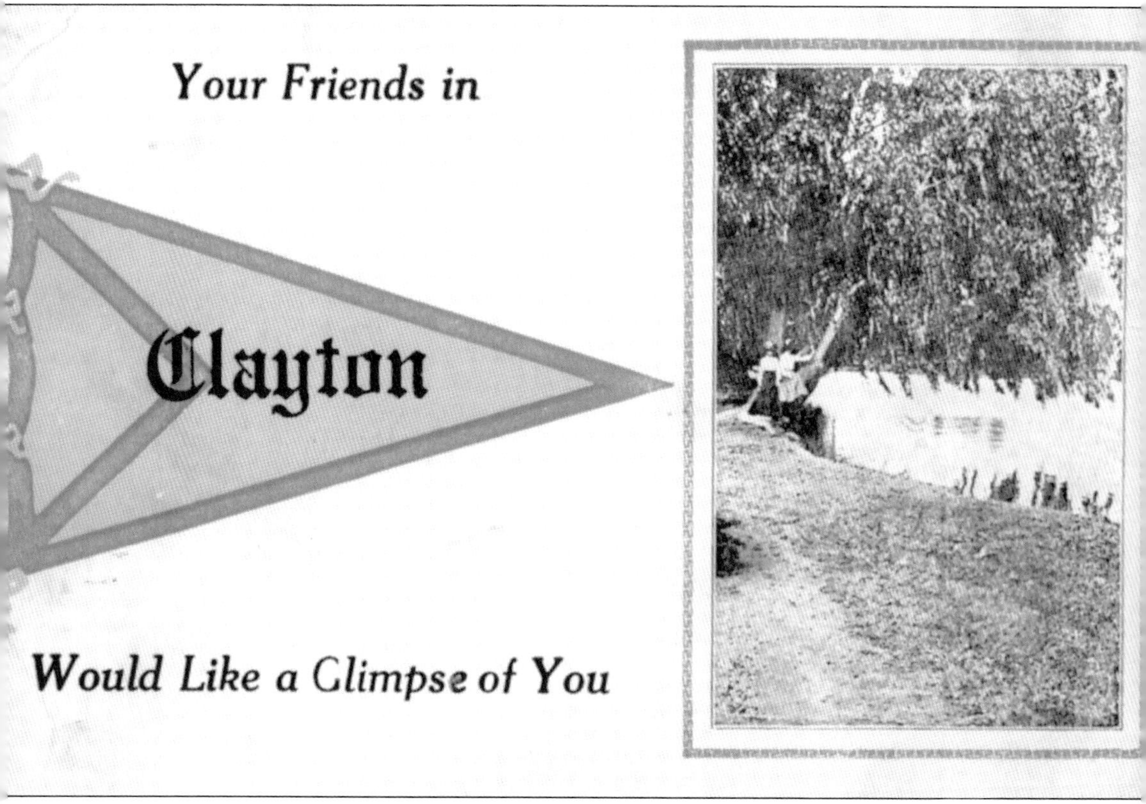

CLAYTON. This Clayton postcard is postmarked 1913. In 1835, Richard Clayton left Cincinnati in a balloon, and nine-and-a-half hours later, he landed on Keeney's Mountain. In 1879, it was decided that a post office would be located where the balloonist had landed. It would be called "Clayton" for the "man from the sky." (Courtesy of Tim Halloran.)

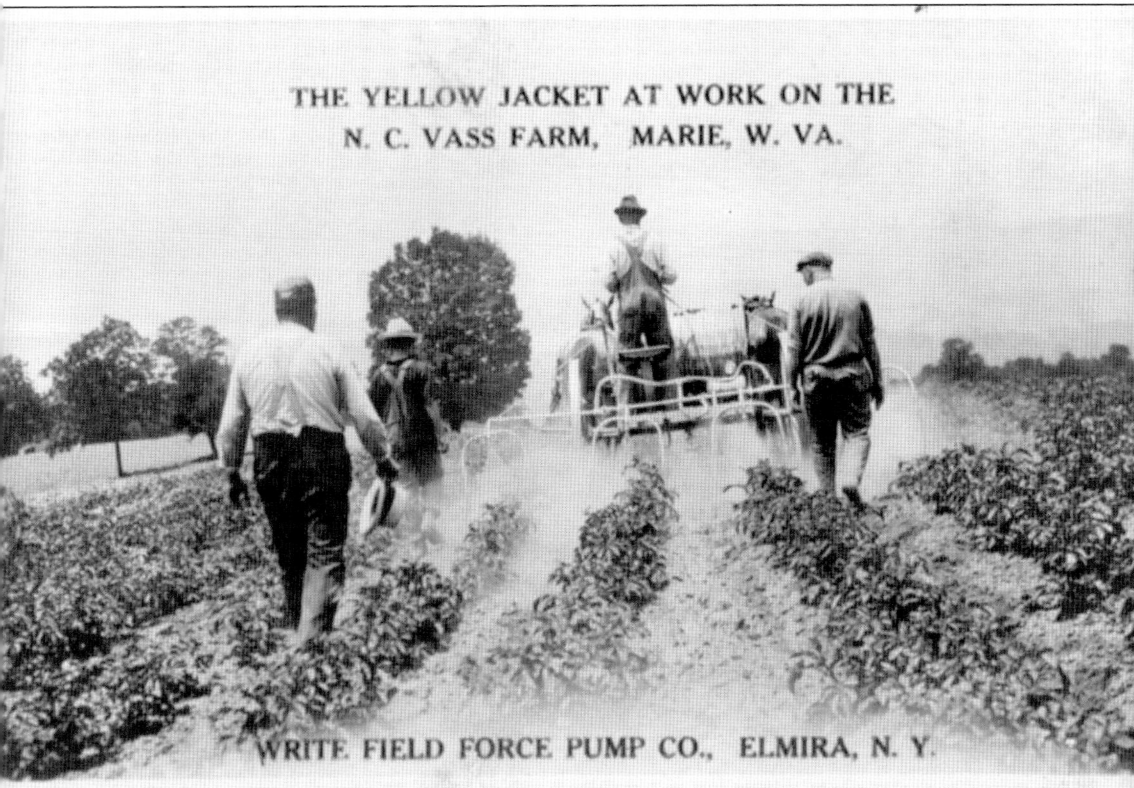

THE YELLOW JACKET. A cultivator called the "Yellow Jacket" is shown at work on the farm of N. C. Vass at Marie, West Virginia. The workers are unidentified, but it can be imagined how hot and tired they are. (Courtesy of Billy Joe Edwards.)

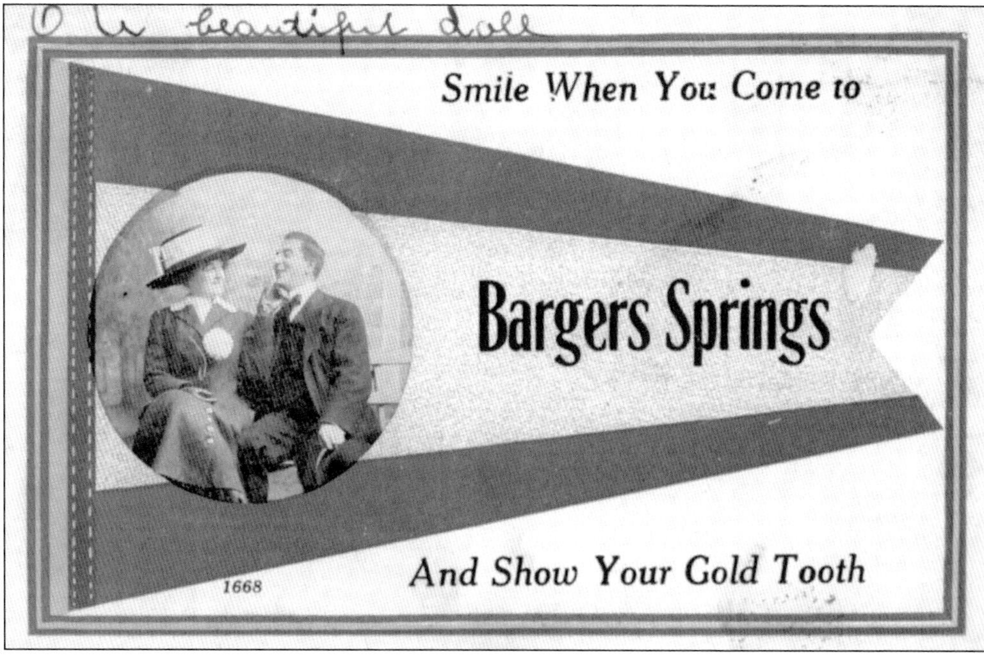

Bargers Springs. In 1924, a camp for Summers County 4-H members was held at Bargers Springs. The girls slept in the Bargers Springs Hotel building and the boys slept in tents in the field. (Courtesy of John Kesler.)

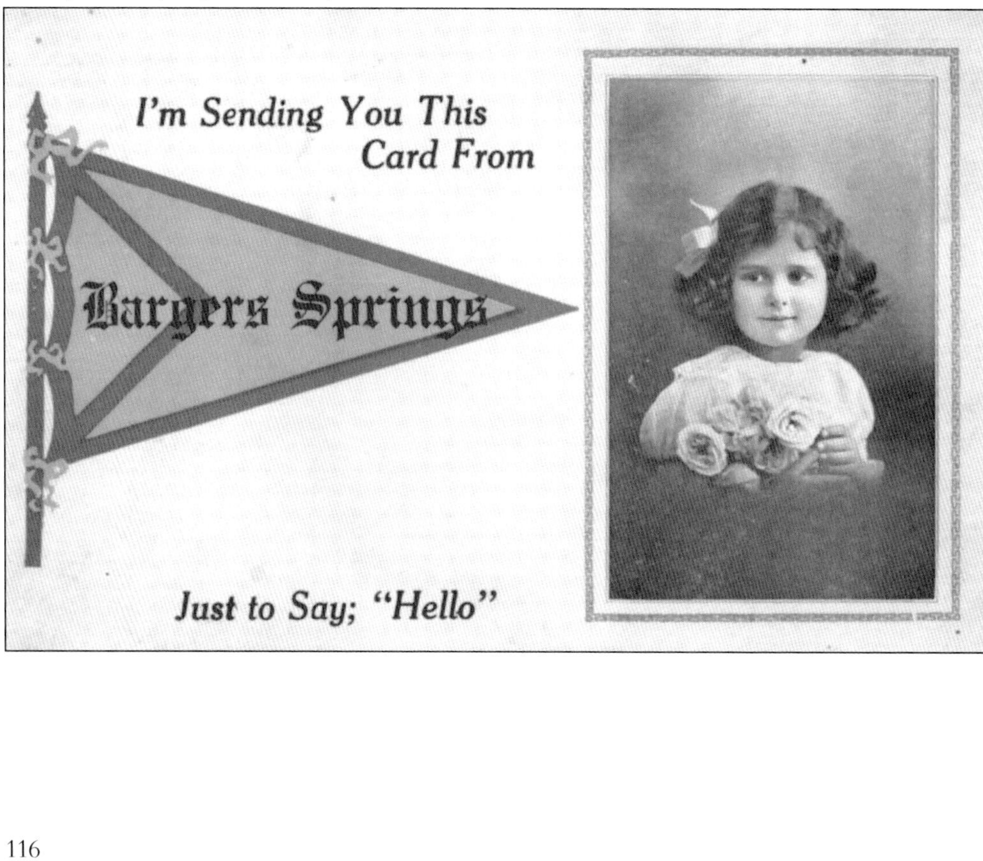

Nine

MISCELLANEOUS IMAGES

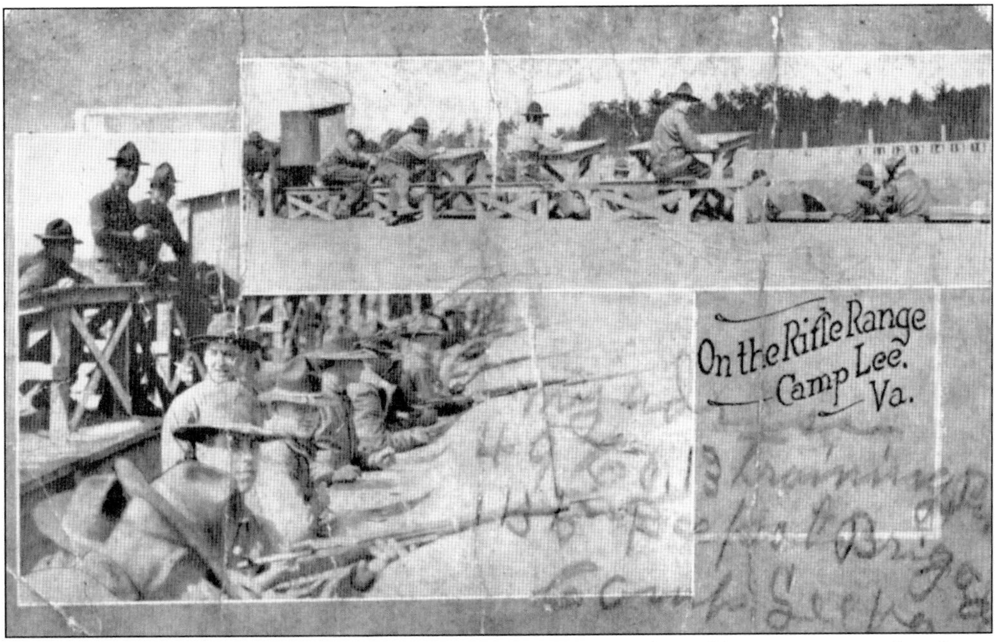

A LONELY SUMMERS COUNTY WORLD WAR I SOLDIER. This soldier was stationed at Camp Lee, Virginia, and was writing home to his family. The image was published by Thompson Illustragraph Company, Camp Photographers, at Camp Lee, Virginia in 1918. (Courtesy of Billy Joe Edwards.).

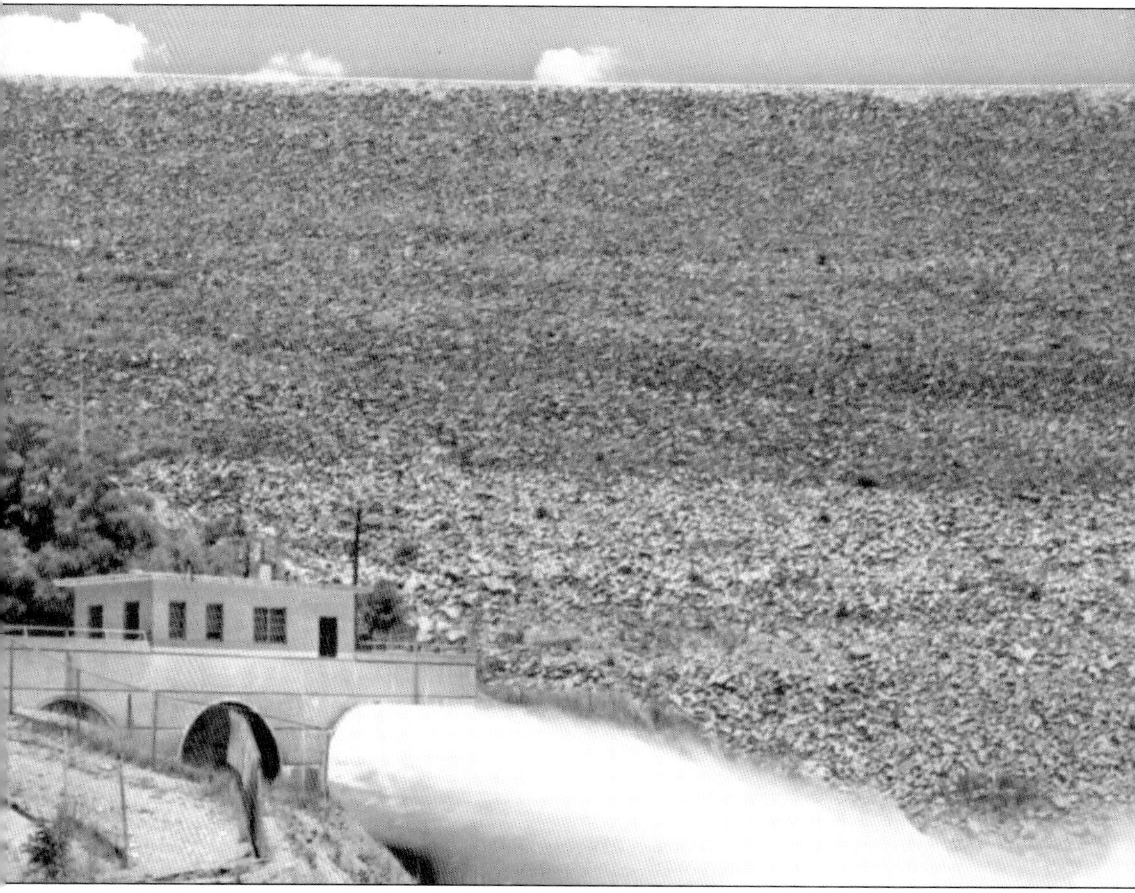

SUMMERSVILLE DAM, ROUTE 129, MOUNT NEBO. Built by the U.S. Army Corps of Engineers, this dam is the largest earth-filled dam in the East, and it controls the Gauley River. (Courtesy of David Crown Enterprises.)

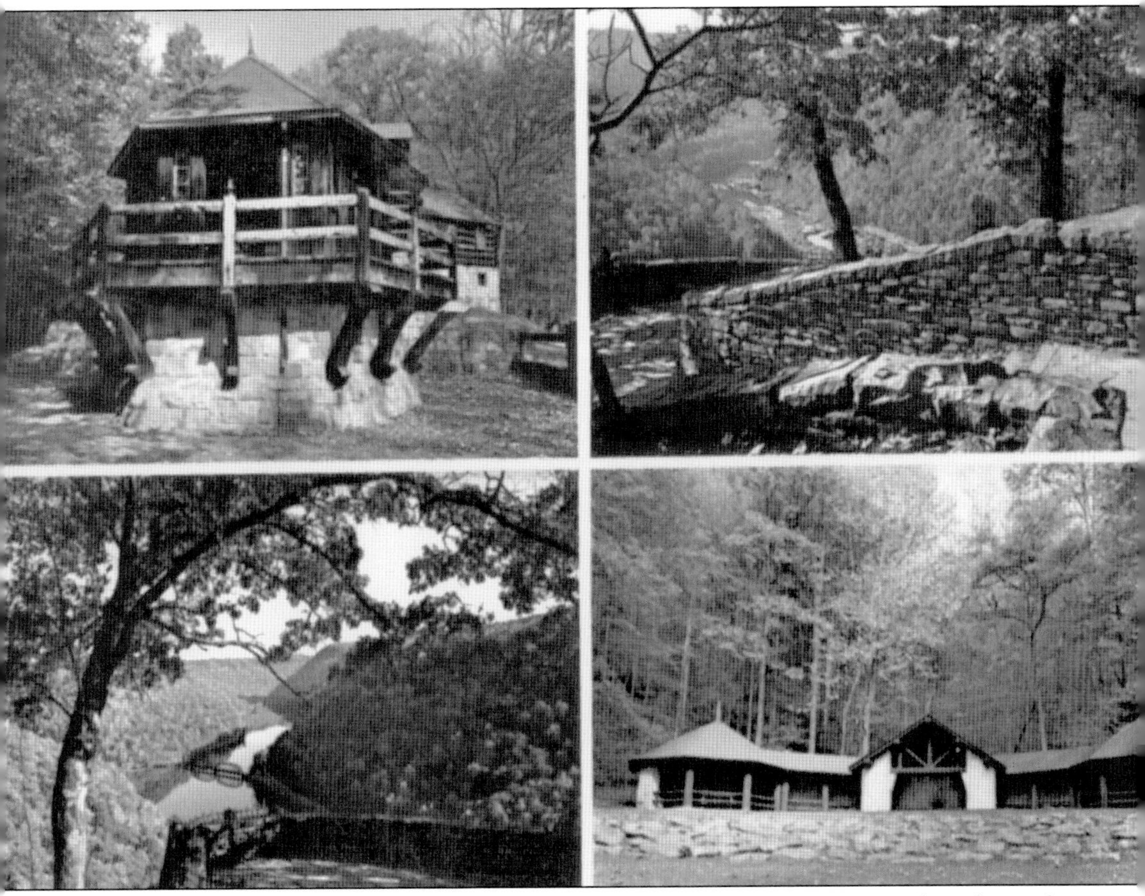

HAWK'S NEST STATE PARK. This postcard features four pictures on one card. It shows the museum, a view of New River, the entry to a cliffside overlook offering views of New River and Hawk's Nest Dam, and the picnic area.

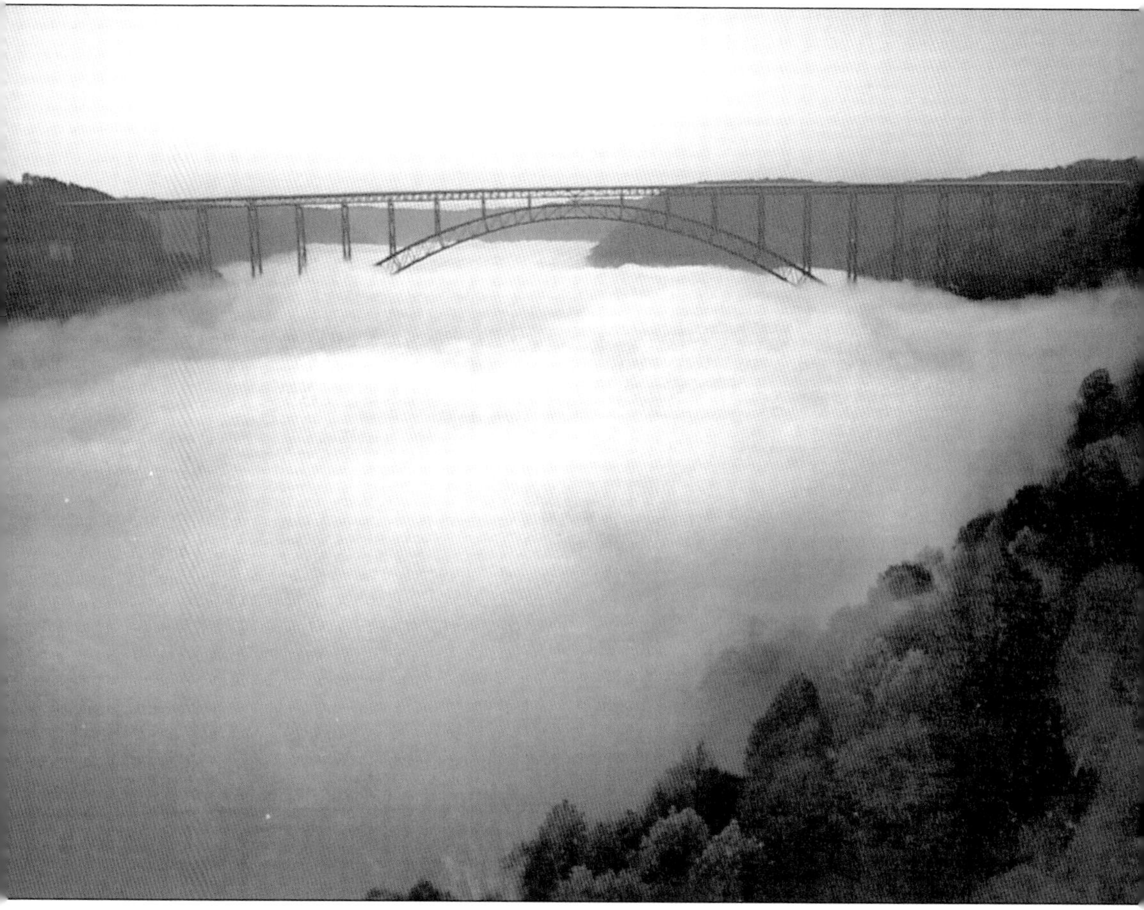

NEW RIVER GORGE BRIDGE. The New River has carved the gorge north of Hinton and formed the natural pathway that in 1872 was to become the main line of the C&O Railroad. The bridge opened on October 22, 1977, and is a part of the West Virginia highway system. It is the second highest bridge in the nation. (Published by Coastal Exposures, Maine; photograph by Don Kodak.)

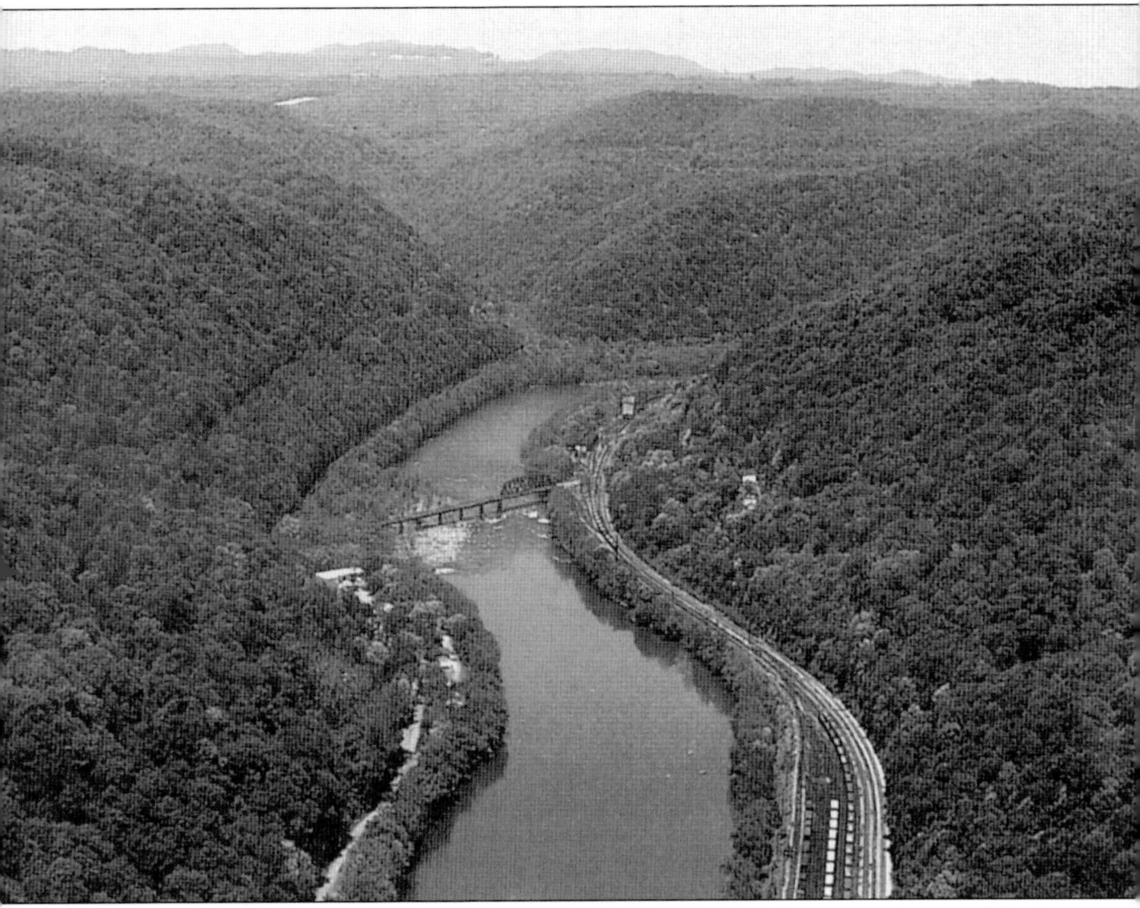

New River Gorge National River. Thurmond was a railroad town serving as a shipping point for coal. The Thurmond Depot has been restored and is used for a visitor center. (Courtesy of David Crown Enterprises.)

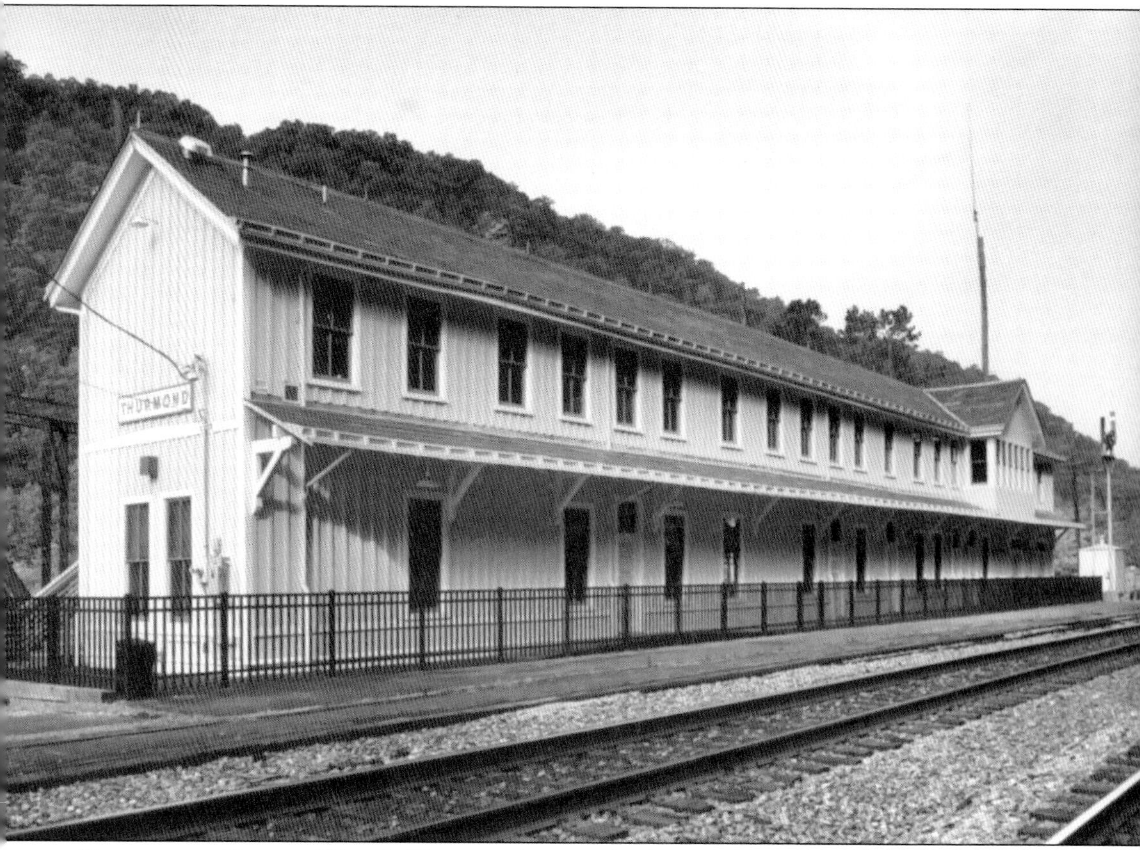

THURMOND DEPOT. Historic Thurmond Depot, built in 1904, served the C&O Railroad in the New River Coal Field. It was purchased by the National Park Service in 1991 and restored. (Published by Ideas, Inc., Summersville, West Virginia; photograph by Jurgen Lorenzen.)

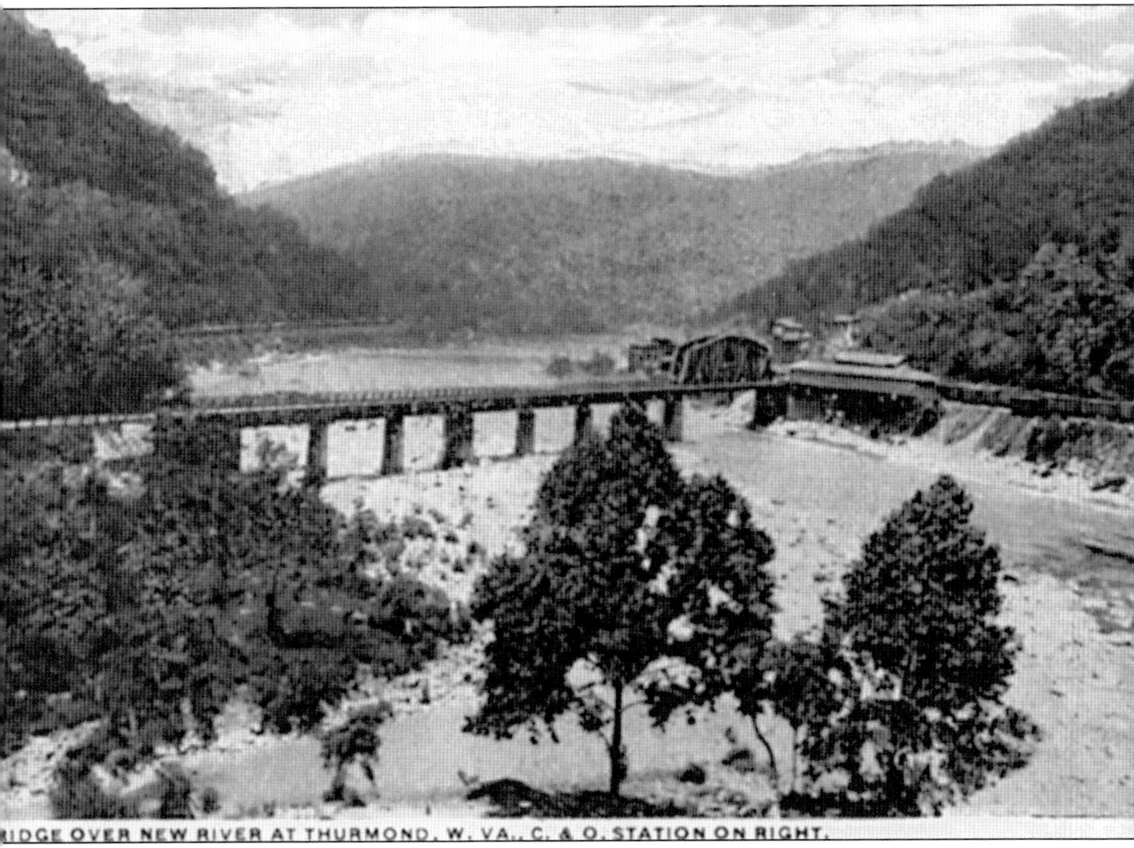

BRIDGE OVER NEW RIVER IN THURMOND. In 1889, a post office was established in Thurmond in the store of the Jones brothers and C. T. Thurmond. (Courtesy of Thomas N. Clark.)

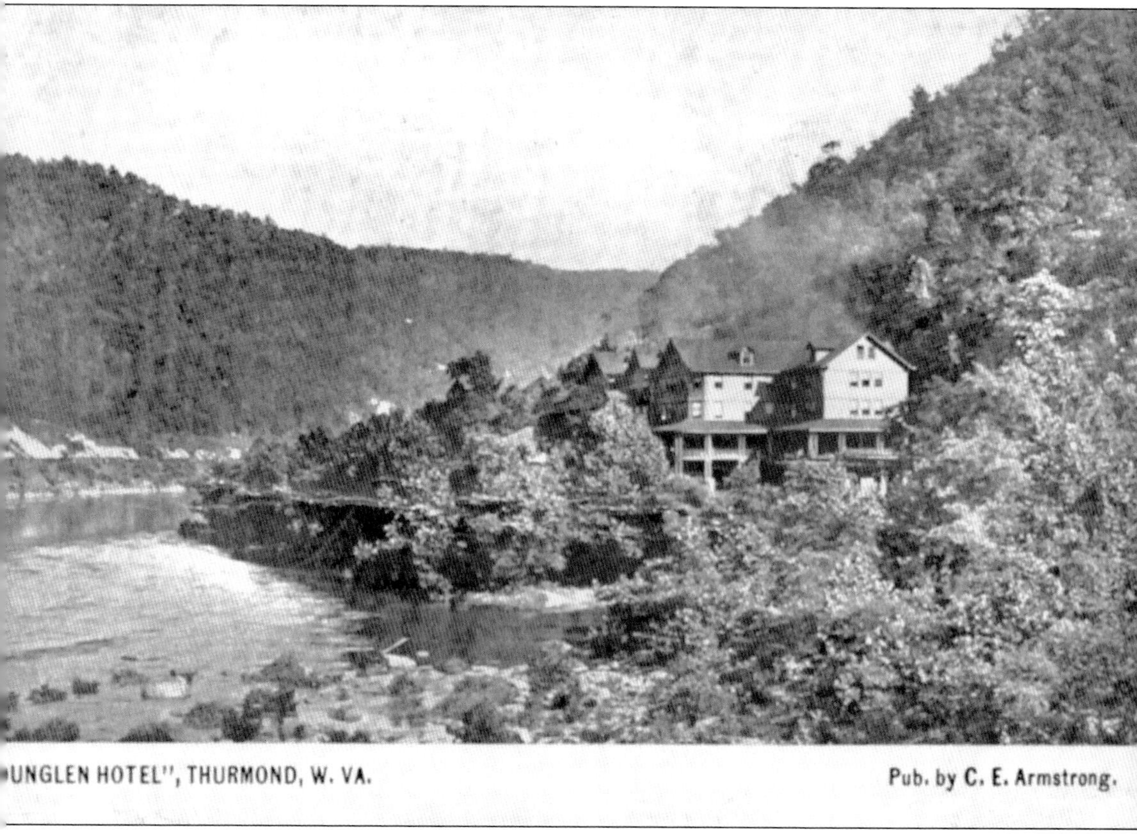

INFAMOUS DUNGLEN HOTEL IN THURMOND. In 1930, Thurmond had begun to decline. That year, the Dunglen was destroyed by fire. (Courtesy of Margaret Martin.)

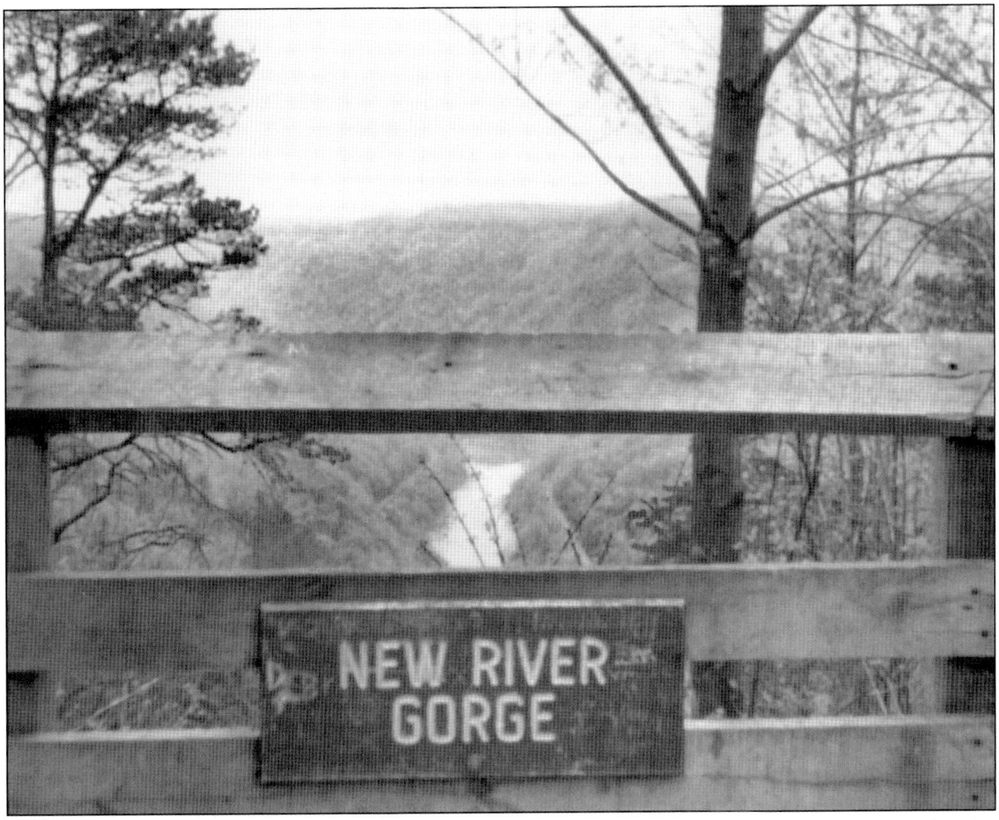

LOOKING DOWN INTO THE NEW RIVER GORGE. This stretch of the gorge was once the site of many industrial towns by the river. As many as 1,000 plant species grow here now. This area of the New River is known for white-water rafting. (Courtesy of Dot Turman.)

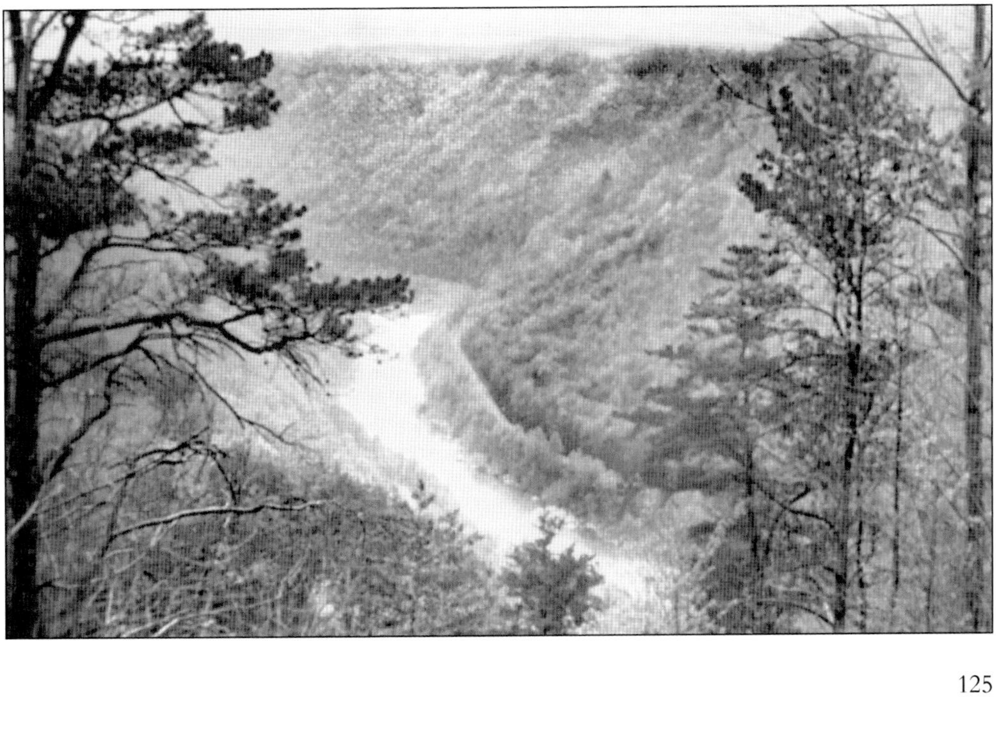

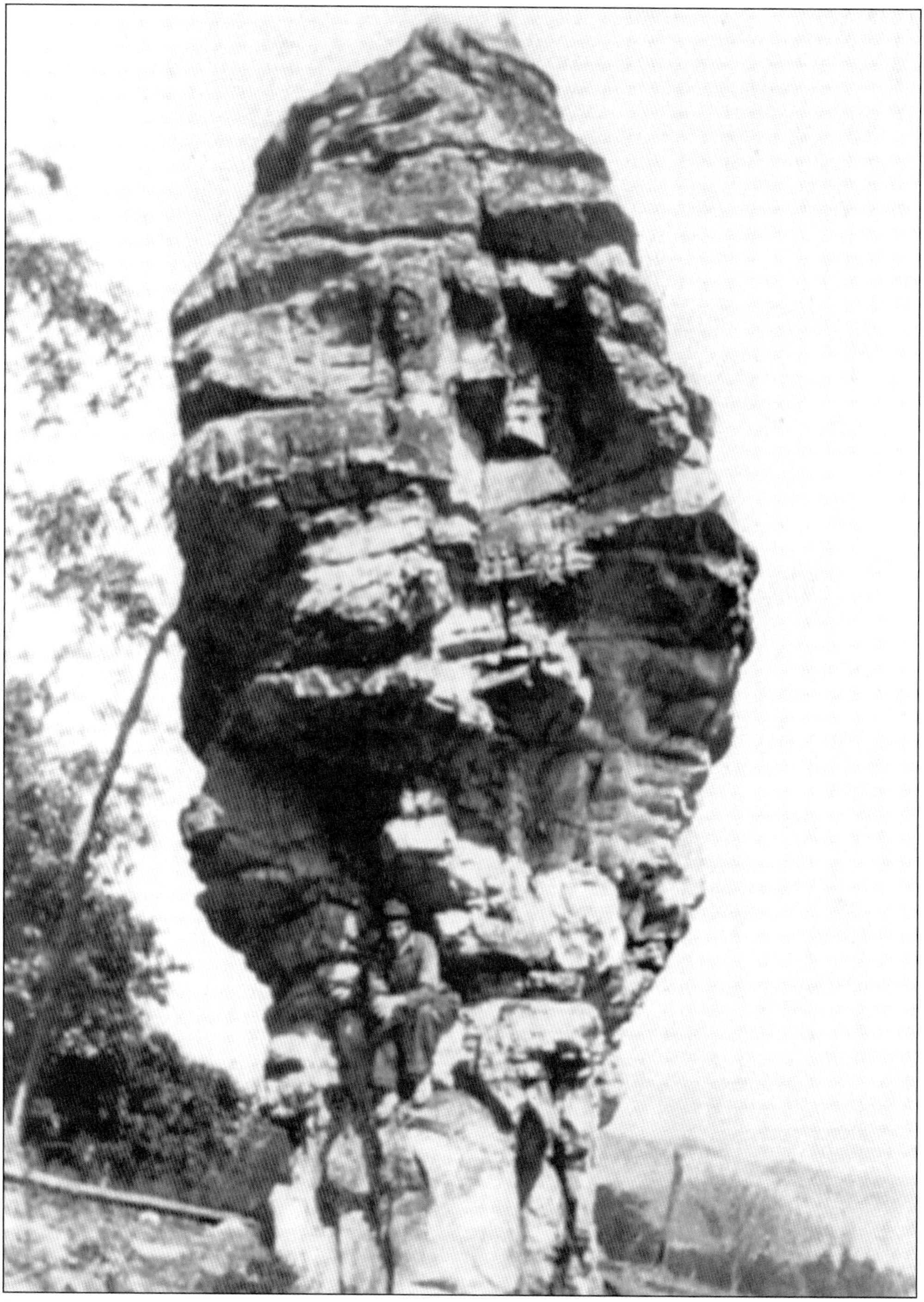

Seven Wonders. One of the natural wonders of Summers County is located in Forest Hill District, one-and-a-half miles off the Seminole Road, on the farm of the late Bertha and Charlie Foster. It is an immense rock in the shape of an inverted pyramid. The rock is covered with carved names and dates, some of them more than 125 years old. (From the collection of the late Verona Canterberry.)

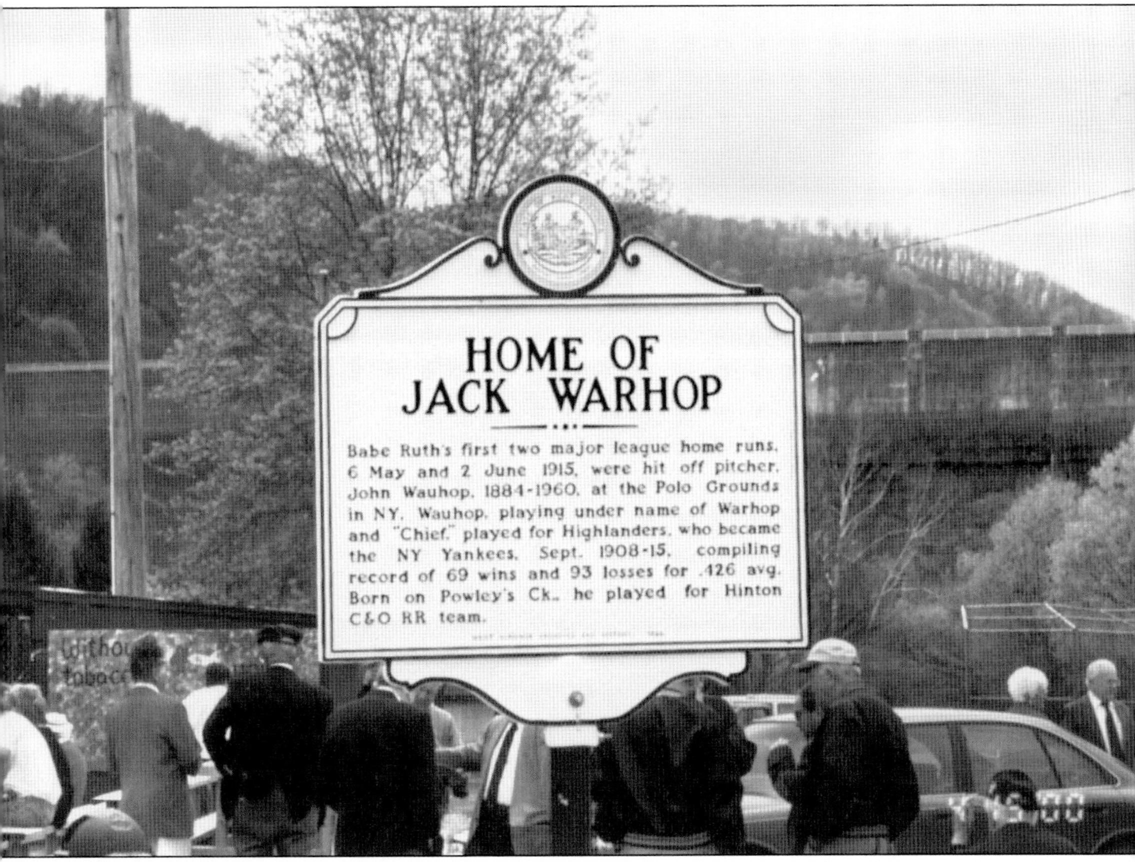

HONORING A HOMETOWN BOY. Jack Warhop had a 3.12 ERA during his eight years in major-league baseball. He was very competitive and had good control. (Information from Images of America: *Summers County*, by Ed Robinson; photograph courtesy of John Kesler.)

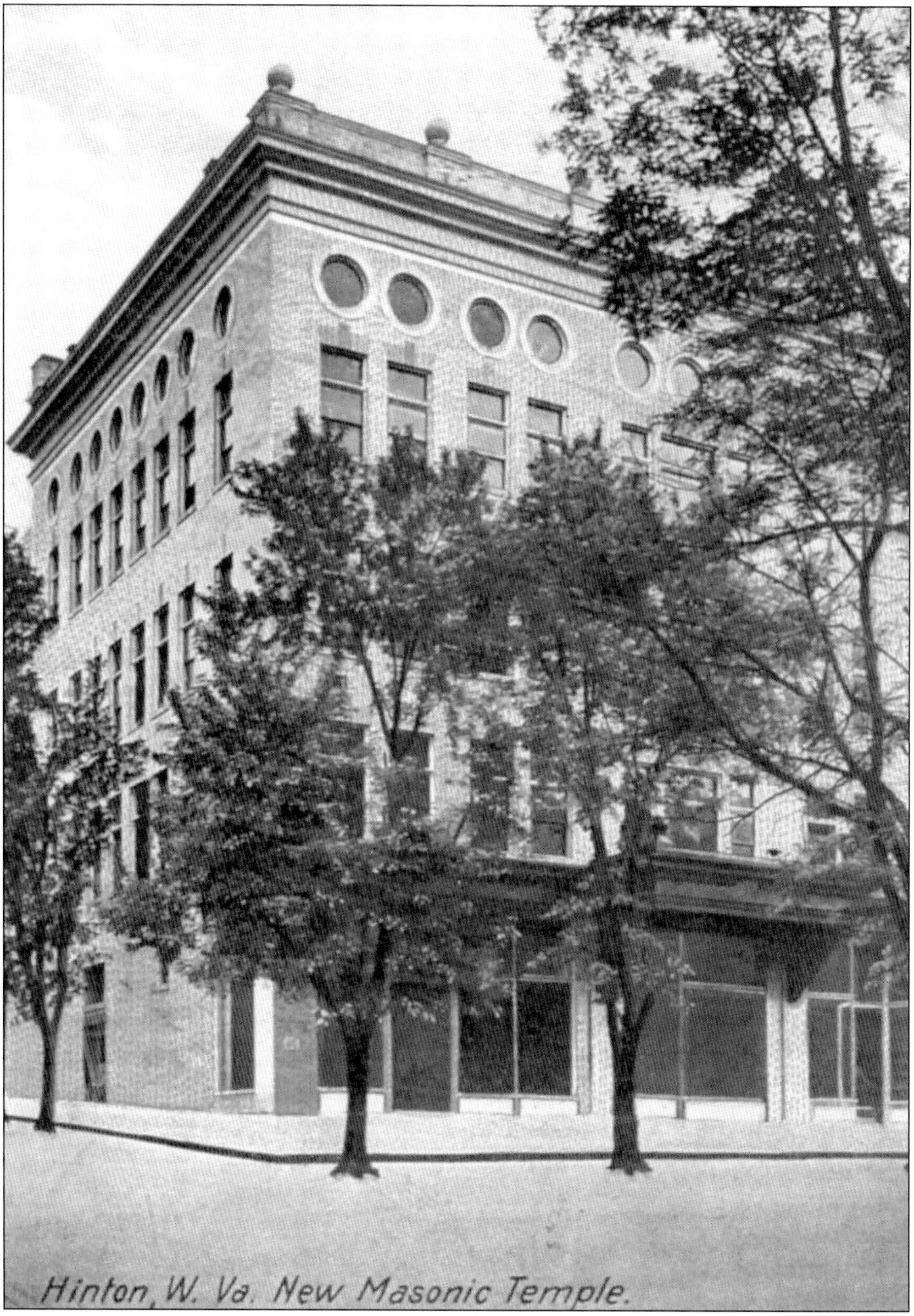

MASONIC TEMPLE, HINTON, WEST VIRGINIA. Construction began on this building on April 23, 1907. The architect was Frank P. Milburn. The final cost of the edifice was $75,000. On September 9, 1908, *Under Southern Skies* by Lottie Parker was the first play given in the new Masonic building. (Courtesy of the DiStefanos.)